Thinking through primary practice

The Open University Postgraduate Certificate of Education

The readers in the PGCE series are:

Thinking Through Primary Practice
Teaching and Learning in the Primary School
Teaching and Learning in the Secondary School
Teaching English
Teaching Mathematics
Teaching Science
Teaching Technology
Teaching Modern Languages
Teaching History

All of these readers are part of an integrated teaching system; the selection is therefore related to other material available to students and is designed to evoke critical understanding. Opinions expressed are not necessarily those of the course team or of the University.

If you would like to study this course and receive a PGCE prospectus and other information about programmes of professional developments in education, please write to the Central Enquiry Service, PO Box 200, The Open University, Walton Hall, Milton Keynes, MK7 6YZ. A copy of *Studying with the Open University* is available from the same address.

Thinking through primary practice

Edited by Jill Bourne
at The Open University

London and New York
in association with
The Open University

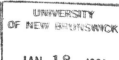

First published 1994
by Routledge
11 New Fetter Lane, London EC4P 4EE

Simultaneously published in the USA and Canada
by Routledge
29 West 35th Street, New York, NY 10001

Selection and editorial matter: © 1994 The Open University

Typeset in Garamond by Florencetype Ltd, Kewstoke, Avon
Printed and bound in Great Britain by
Biddles Ltd, Guildford and King's Lynn

British Library Cataloguing in Publication Data
A catalogue record for this book is available from the British Library.

Library of Congress Cataloging in Publication Data
Thinking through primary practice/edited by Jill Bourne.
  p.   cm.
  Includes bibliographical references and index.
  1. Education, Elementary – Great Britain. I. Bourne, Jill, 1947– .
LA633.T45   1994
372.941–dc20   93–19473
                                                                 CIP

ISBN 0–415–10257–X

Contents

Foreword

The form of teacher education is one of the most debated educational issues of the day. How is the curriculum of teacher education, particularly initial, pre-service education to be defined? What is the appropriate balance between practical school experience and the academic study to support such practice? What skills and competence can be expected of a newly qualified teacher? How are these skills formulated and assessed and in what ways are they integrated into an ongoing programme of professional development?

These issues have been at the heart of the development and planning of the Open University's programme of initial teacher training and education – the Postgraduate Certificate of Education (PGCE). Each course within the programme uses a combination of technologies, some of which are well tried and tested while others, on information technology for example, may represent new and innovatory approaches to teaching. All, however, contribute in an integrated way towards fulfilling the aims and purposes of the course and programme.

All of the PGCE courses have readers which bring together a range of articles, extracts from books, and reports that discuss key ideas and issues, including specially commissioned chapters. The readers also provide a resource that can be used to support a range of teaching and learning in other types and structures of course.

This series from Routledge, in supporting the Open University PGCE programme, provides a contemporary view of developments in primary and secondary education and across a range of specialist subject areas. Its primary aim is to provide insights and analysis for those participating in initial education and training. Much of its content, however, will also be relevant to ongoing programmes of personal and institutional professional development. Each book is designed to provide an integral part of that basis of knowledge that we would expect of both new and experienced teachers.

Bob Moon
Professor of Education, The Open University

Introduction

Jill Bourne

Everyone has been to primary school, and so everyone is, in some sense, an expert on primary practice. Most people have opinions on what should be taking place in schools: politicians, the media, parents, young people themselves, as well as teachers. Such opinions, some well informed, some less informed or even mis-informed, are woven into our daily lives in a background tapestry of television news programmes, phone-ins and newspaper articles.

For new teachers, coming to an understanding of what is really going on in classrooms, and sorting out the relevant from the irrelevant, considered judgement from prejudice, is not a merely theoretical business. Learning to teach means learning to make decisions about how to act at every moment of the day in order to enable and enhance children's learning. It is with developing a principled basis for those decisions that this book is concerned. It provides an introductory experience of contemporary research as a basis for teacher decision-making.

CLASSROOM RESEARCH

What research tells us about classrooms is the accumulation of the experiences of many teachers and pupils, recorded and written down by researchers, who have usually also been teachers, in order to share these experiences with others in the present and in the future. It opens up classroom practice and makes it accountable to a wider group than those immediately involved. It can therefore put new teachers in touch with many more classrooms and many more strategies for teaching children and organising classrooms than the direct experience offered in any form of initial teacher training. It therefore complements school-based experience.

However, reading classroom research can also *add* to school-based experience, by offering the new teacher a range of possible methods and strategies for finding out about classrooms, and for thinking about primary practice. Its interest, therefore, is at least twofold: its empirical findings about how classrooms work widen experience and set particular experiences in context;

and it supports the classroom-based research which all new teachers need to do to understand the particular situation they find themselves in.

The findings of educational research indicate more of a consensus on the problems of primary practice and on promising directions for improvement than the public 'Great Debate' scenario in the media would suggest. This consensus will be clarified and illustrated over the chapters in this collection. What seems to be now in no doubt is that different professional practices do affect the quality of children's learning. Children's achievements are not fixed and their potential is not necessarily predictable. What is also clear is that, while the National Curriculum has introduced significant changes in practice, particularly in the emphasis on testing and assessment, there has been no sharp break in a continuing tradition of classroom-based research and curriculum development in which teachers have been centrally involved.

However, while researchers press for teaching to become more consciously 'research-based', it is important to remember that research is itself a social practice, with its own procedures, its own community, its own journals, conferences and meeting places. Teachers therefore need to read research critically, to see how far the questions proposed seem to be of importance to their classroom practice, and, most crucially, to children's learning; and to examine the assumptions – for example, about childhood, about cultural backgrounds, about teacher/pupil relationships, about the extent of teacher autonomy in bringing about changes – that underlie researchers' presentation of their findings about primary practice. Teachers might also question where the data were collected, and the implications of the absence, for example, of data on particular regions of the country, or type of school. Researchers are not privileged with 'the knowledge' about practice; they have simply been afforded the opportunity to amass some evidence, and have then interpreted it critically and in accordance with some framework of existing concepts, beliefs and values. Both this interpretation and the methods by which they gathered their data are open to scrutiny and question.

Studies of primary practice take three main forms: there are studies which help to clarify the ideas which shape classroom practice (conceptual and historical studies); there are those studies which collect, collate, present and interpret empirical data across a variety of classroom situations ('quantitative' research studies); and there are small-scale, focused studies, sometimes of just one classroom, and usually including a narrative element, which aim to illuminate our understanding of the processes of teaching and learning ('qualitative' or 'ethnographic' studies). This book includes examples of all three of these types of research.

CURRICULUM STUDIES

However, classroom practice is not 'content free'; there is always something which is taught and learnt. Research also needs to focus on the curriculum, on what is taught in schools. It is crucial for the new teacher to understand that, although there are long-established traditions of what should be taught in the primary school, there is no 'natural' primary curriculum; the curriculum has always involved a choice of what should be taught, and to whom. The curriculum has in the past always been a matter for public debate but, in primary schools, most often left to the individual class-teacher to decide. More recently, the curriculum has become a matter for parliamentary statute in the 1988 Education Act.

The 'Three Wise Men' (Alexander *et al.* 1992) inquiry into primary practice gave new emphasis to a reappraisal of what the different 'subjects' in the National Curriculum might mean, defining the 'subject' as 'public knowledge embodied in our cultural traditions' (para. 64), and arguing that the teacher's responsibility is to mediate each child's encounters with this knowledge and its own particular practices: 'Pupils must be able to grasp the particular principles and procedures of each subject' (para. 66). In this context, the importance of examining carefully the underlying principles, goals and practices of different subject disciplines seems a major task, if we are to be able to see in which ways disciplines might be integrated to mutual enhancement, and in which ways they might require different and special approaches. I have included a core section of papers focusing on the curriculum in this collection, in order to provide readers with the opportunity to begin to explore this issue.

THE STRUCTURE OF THIS BOOK

The texts collected in this book are intended to be used in a number of different ways. They can provide a source for reference on what is known about classrooms, some models of different approaches to classroom observation and analysis, resources for practice in the critical reading of research, and a source for the identification of particular issues which new teachers themselves would like to study in their own classrooms, related to their own teaching.

I have organised the volume in the following way. Part I provides the context for the chapters which follow. It begins with a chapter by Brian Simon, which places current primary practice in historical perspective. This is followed by an extract from a book by Robin Alexander, which offers a conceptual framework for analysing primary practice. The third chapter is a wide-ranging empirical review of classroom research by Caroline Gipps, who raises a set of questions relating to what is 'effective' primary practice.

The chapters that follow are arranged into five parts. Part II includes three papers that analyse ways of managing the curriculum and of managing learning, each based on the findings of large-scale empirical research. Part III focuses on the curriculum itself. It contains a collection of new and previously published papers that attempt to 'think through' different areas of the curriculum in the context of what is now known about learning and about the possibilities of classroom practice. Most of these papers were selected by those preparing curriculum materials for the Open University Primary PGCE course as key discussion texts alongside other materials in the Primary PGCE Resource Box. However, Part III also includes papers on language in learning across the curriculum, and moves from the discussion of issues specific to certain subject areas towards cross-curricular themes, ending with a study of those 'critical events' which can extend the National Curriculum in the classroom.

Assessment is a fundamental part of the teacher's role, but it remains very problematic, and Part IV considers a number of issues relating to the assessment of learning. Continuing this theme, Part V contains a set of classroom-based studies which illustrate the ways in which 'achievement' is constructed in the practices of the classroom. Finally, Part VI introduces pupils' own perceptions: how they think of themselves as learners, and their views of teachers' management. It is arguable that unless we get to know how pupils respond to teaching, our attempts to find more 'effective' practices will stand little chance of succeeding. The final chapter in the book pulls together pupils' perceptions and classroom management. It illustrates how teachers respond pragmatically to pupils' perceptions of classroom life, and how they reconcile this need to respond with the professional demands made upon them.

REFERENCE

Alexander, R., Rose, J. and Woodhead, C. (1992) *Curriculum Organisation and Classroom Practice in Primary Schools: a Discussion Paper*, London: DES.

Part I

Setting the context

Chapter 1

Primary practice in historical context

Brian Simon

This first chapter sets the scene for the rest of the book. In it, Brian Simon summarises the history of compulsory primary education. He introduces the complexities of developments in primary practice, as it responded to wider societal changes and outside influences from the 1860s to the early 1990s, and, directly addressing teachers, marks out a direction for the future in line with the lessons of the past.

The nature of primary teaching has become a highly charged political issue over the last few years. This has been marked by a strong, indeed almost unceasing, attack on 'modern' (sometimes called 'progressive') methods in the primary school by powerful sections of the media (especially the tabloid press), supported, on occasion, by government spokespeople (for instance, Kenneth Clarke, when Secretary of State for Education and Science, 1991–92). These have focused on a call for the return to streaming, whole-class teaching, and of course for more 'rigorous' assessment and testing. There has also been a call for a return to subject teaching (language, maths, science, technology, history, geography, and so on), fuelled by the imposition of the National Curriculum (defined on a subject basis) in place of topic and project work involving integrated (or cross-curricular) approaches. The report of the so-called 'Three Wise Men', commissioned by the government and published early in 1992, raised all these, and other related issues (Alexander *et al*. 1992). A widespread discussion is taking place about the nature and purpose of primary education among teachers and more widely among the public as a whole.

There is a tendency, in this discussion, to present 'traditional' and 'progressive' approaches as stark alternatives, and to see the issue as one of struggle between these, as if each was, in practice, the opposite of the other, and as if all schools fell into one or other of these categories. But, as I hope to show, this is not an accurate representation of the position. The situation, both in the schools themselves and in thinking about primary education, is a great deal more complex than this reduction to a struggle between opposites appears to indicate. In order to understand something of this complexity, it is worth looking briefly at the way primary education has developed historically, and tease out some of the influences which have formed its procedures both in terms of school organisation and classroom teaching.

The first thing to get clear is that primary schooling has a long history, and that it came into being in specific circumstances that determined its nature – in the early days at least. Elementary education for Britain's then enormous working class was imposed as compulsory during the 1870s, but was first established, in its 'modern' form, earlier – at the beginning of the nineteenth century. That the workers should be educated (or schooled, rather), was very widely seen as a *political* (and economic) necessity by about 1870. This perception was closely related to the extension of the franchise (in 1867) and to a growing awareness of the strength of foreign competition fuelled by more advanced systems of education on the Continent. But, in the closing decades of the nineteenth and early twentieth centuries, the determination to educate the workers led to overcrowded schools with huge classes (between 50 and 100 was common), while fully trained teachers formed only a small minority of those coping with them. In order to get by, the strictest discipline was imposed; very precise classroom procedures were devised while the teaching itself was (indeed, had to be) exclusively didactic, involving drill methods, much class repetition, and so on.

There was very little scope for creativity in these schools – informal relations between pupils and teachers were impossible. Considerable reliance was placed on corporal and other forms of punishment. The system of 'payment by results', brought in during the 1860s and remaining in force until the late 1890s, linked the individual teacher's salary with the number of passes pupils achieved in annual exams in 'the basics' conducted by HMIs. As a direct result of all these influences a highly mechanised system of teaching was fastened on the schools, their teachers and pupils, and it was this system that flourished up to and beyond World War I and that provided the soil from which present practices grew. Of course this system was outwardly successful – in the sense that the imposition of schooling in this form did result in the production of a literate population both in terms of language (reading and writing), and of numeracy (facility with the manipulation of figures in simple sums). The system also, of course, brought the entire child population within the area of organised and institutionalised schooling and so, in a sense, promoted their disciplining as 'citizens'.

However, while this huge system was being built up (with extraordinary rapidity), certain developments were taking place which began to call such procedures into question. Quite outside the now publicly provided system (under the control of the School Boards, as they were called), new, and certainly more liberal, approaches were being developed in the nurseries and 'kindergartens' being set up for middle-class children, especially in London and the North (particularly Manchester and Leeds, where German immigrants, often successful industrialists, were prominent). These took their inspiration from the work of the German (Prussian) educator Friedrich Froebel. Influenced by the innovative Swiss teacher and educator, Pestalozzi, Froebel's activities had, in the 1860s, come under a political ban in Prussia as a clear reaction to his liberal outlook.

Here, the approach to education and teaching took a very different route from that of the mass elementary schools just described. Classes were, of course, small, while Froebelian philosophy emphasised the child's inner development, and provided scope for, and encouraged, his or her spontaneous activity. Froebel held that each child was born with certain inner qualities, or propensities, and that it was the job of the educator, during the child's early years, to 'make the inner outer', as he put it. Didactic teaching, at this stage, was inappropriate, even deadly. What was needed was the provision of a rich environment giving scope for children's many-sided activity, the satisfaction of their curiosity, and so on. The teacher's job was primarily to facilitate this development – to provide the conditions for the child's growth.

This view of education, already making a considerable impact in the period 1860 to 1900, was reinforced by the influence of the American philosopher and educationist John Dewey, by that of the Italian Maria Montessori, and in England by the influence of another remarkable woman, Margaret McMillan, the real founder of the nursery school movement in Britain. Indeed, the whole issue exploded in 1911 when Edmond Holmes, the ex-Senior Chief Inspector of Schools (a very prestigious post), wrote, after retirement, a striking book entitled *What Is and What Might Be*. This contained a searing critique of the over-didactic and anti-humanist nature of mass elementary education, as well as a passionate description of an (actually existing) country school utilising modern methods, based on an amalgam of the teaching of the educationists just mentioned. Holmes in fact proposed that our entire system should be transformed along the 'progressive' lines implemented by his Egeria – the head of the (anonymous) school he described in his book. Coming from such a source, this book was widely influential; indeed, the whole movement favouring 'progressive' forms of education was soon to be institutionalised through the establishment of the New Education Fellowship in the early 1920s. Although centred on private schools, this movement (for the 'New Education') carried all before it from an ideological point of view during the 1920s and 1930s – greatly assisted by a shift in the general mood relating to education as a result of the horrifying experience of World War I. By 1939, a leading historian has concluded, a watered down progressivisim had become the 'intellectual orthodoxy' among most leading educationists (Selleck 1972: 156), even if practice in the elementary schools remained primarily didactic (classes remained large in those days, so the scope for informality and 'progressive' approaches was necessarily limited).

But there was one area where the new approaches could effect a significant entry to the heart of the state system: within the few nursery schools now brought into being and also, by extension, within the infant schools. These latter have a long history of enlightened practice, going right back to the early years of the nineteenth century when Robert Owen established his famous infant school (for children aged 2 and upwards) at his model factory at New Lanark. This tradition was fractured, but, almost by chance, the 1870 Act made school entry at the age of 5 compulsory – earlier than every other European country – while infant schools (or departments) for children aged 5 to 7 were established as separate entities within elementary schools. These achieved a certain independence, even in the late nineteenth century. It was here that Froebelian influences were concentrated, some School Boards, for instance, attempting to bring in somewhat mechanised versions of Froebelian methods and approaches. When, in the 1960s, there took place what some have called the 'break-out' in primary education, it was practice as developed independently in the infant schools which now spread upwards into the junior school range (7 to 11). This needs to be borne in mind.

As already mentioned, in spite of the hegemony (or primacy) of 'progress-ive' approaches intellectually (as it were) in the inter-war period, the actual conditions within the schools acted as a powerful force preventing any transformation of the system at that time. However, during this period, the seeds of change were planted through structural reorganisation, and this slowly began to create a new situation. These changes were signalled by three influential reports from the Consultative Committee to the Board of Education – an official advisory body which no longer exists. This consisted of educationists – teachers, administrators and others – but having consider-able prestige at that time, and given the responsibility of charting the way forward. The first of these, the Hadow Report of 1926, proposed what became finally the break at age 11 – and so the establishment of separate primary schools catering for children aged 5 or 7 to 11. Earlier these had been lumped in with older children in all-age elementary schools taking children from 5 to 14. The Hadow reorganisation on these lines was accepted as official government policy in 1928. By the outbreak of World War II, in 1939, roughly half the children aged 5 to 11 were in separate primary (or infant and junior) schools or departments, half remaining in the old-type 'all-age' elementary schools.

Now, for the first time, it was possible to consider the needs of children of primary school age as an entity, and in 1931 and 1933 the Consultative Committee produced two more important reports, one on the primary school (Hadow 1931), the other on infant and nursery schools (Hadow 1933). Both these reports, which also received official support, were highly influential in the development of thinking about primary education; both fundamentally accepted, and propagated, a 'progressive', 'child-centred' approach. Both included the same key phrase identifying the nature of a true education as the Committee saw it: 'The curriculum of the primary school', the reports affirmed, 'is to be thought of in terms of activity and experience, rather than of knowledge to be acquired and facts to be stored.' This emphasis on 'activity and experience' marked a fundamental change in thinking about the main thrust of education at the primary stage, and was to prove highly influential when conditions improved within primary schools in the late 1950s and 1960s.

Following World War II, the opportunity for any serious break-out from the didacticism of the past (inherited from the nineteenth century) was lost; primary education now went through a critical phase and, in a sense, one marked by increasing frustration which lasted some 20 years (1945 to 1965). The immediate cause of this had more to do with secondary than primary education. The 1944 Education Act, as is well known, introduced 'secondary education for all' – indeed, that was its great achievement. But although this Act did not lay down how this secondary education should be organised (it had to be provided to meet 'the different ages, abilities and aptitudes' of the children), in practice governments in the post-war period, both Labour (1945–51) and Conservative (1951–64), imposed the 'tripartite' system of parallel grammar, technical and modern schools. Of these the grammar schools monopolised the road to opportunity (professions, universities, and so on), so that competition to enter these escalated rapidly, the decision as to whether a particular child should gain entry being determined by performance at the 11-plus examination. By definition, only about 25 per cent, on average, were or could be successful; the rest were relegated to the modern school (technical schools only took about 3 per cent of the age group). To do the best by their pupils, all primary schools that were large enough now adopted the system of streaming, whereby the intake was divided into two, three or more streams according to the pupils' performance at the age of 7 (sometimes earlier) on a juvenile test, usually of 'intelligence'. This system had, in fact, been strongly recommended by the inter-war report on the primary school (Hadow 1931), on the advice of the leading educational psychologist at that time, Cyril Burt.

Two circumstances emerging at this time increased the pressure on primary schools to adopt this method of inner-school organisation. The first related to enhanced parental aspirations for their children which emerged as a significant factor following World War II. Only those selected for 'A' streams had any serious chance of passing the 11-plus, for which young children were now increasingly prepared while at school. Second, governments now gave priority to completing Hadow 'reorganisation' when building materials at last became available in the 1950s, so that the remaining 50 per cent of children in the old all-age schools were, over a period, now provided for in separate junior or primary schools. This was the condition making streaming possible and, as Brian Jackson (1964) put it, streaming spread 'with barely credible rapidity' throughout the country. Indeed, the late 1950s and early 1960s were the high point of this form of inner-school organisation.

One aspect of streaming is that it permitted the extension of inherited didactic teaching procedures, in theory at least. A streamed class was supposed to contain children of a similar level of 'ability' (or 'intelligence'). It was theoretically (or intellectually) respectable, therefore, to continue to rely on whole-class teaching as the main approach, and this also, of course, allowed a further lease of life to the didacticism which, as we have seen, was endemic within elementary (and so primary) education from the start. In other words, during these 20 post-war years, the situation became crystallised. Primary schools were bound into a rigid and precise structure through this form of organisation, legitimised both by the actual existence of the 11-plus exam, and by the theory and practice of 'intelligence' testing which, with its insistence on the inborn, fixed and unchangeable nature of 'intelligence', seemed to give educational credence to this form of organisation. As everything ground almost to a halt it was difficult to see by what means any serious transformation of the situation could be brought about.

However, just such a transformation was in view, and it came suddenly and with extraordinary rapidity in the late 1960s and early 1970s. Its fundamental causation must be found among the economic and social, and indeed scientific and technological, changes which characterised British society in the post-war period – particularly the growth of new, science-based occupations consequent upon the 'third industrial revolution'. All this certainly led to enhanced aspirations on the part of parents for their children and, with this, a strong shift of opinion against the divided and crystallised system which determined, at so early an age, children's opportunities and so their futures.

This movement of opinion expressed itself educationally in a very strong grass-roots movement, or swing, against the 11-plus and the then existing divided system of secondary education, and as a consequence, in favour of the comprehensive secondary school. Such views spread rapidly throughout the country from the late 1950s and early 1960s, culminating in the issue of Circular 10/65 by the Labour government in July 1965, requesting local authorities to submit plans for comprehensive education. It became a 'roller coaster', in Margaret Thatcher's words, in the early 1970s, so that, by the early 1990s, well over 90 per cent of secondary pupils (in the maintained system) were in comprehensive schools in England, over 95 per cent in Wales, and 100 per cent in Scotland.

At the same time, primary schools, liberated (if that is the right word) from the exigencies of preparing children for the 11-plus, now began to abandon streaming – a deliberate act undertaken by the teachers in individual schools, but one which developed with extraordinary rapidity during the mid to late 1960s and early 1970s. The Plowden Committee, which issued the last report of the Central Advisory Council for Education

(England) in 1967, itself proposed the abandonment of streaming, and there is no doubt that this recommendation had a profound effect.

This created a new situation. As schools unstreamed, teachers, who generally by now strongly supported this move, had to work out for themselves how to cope in the new situation. There was little or no official advice. Research studies had not yet penetrated the classroom to any extent; there was, therefore, little information as to what was actually happening. The Plowden Committee, while recommending unstreaming, did not tangle with the issue as to *how* the unstreamed class should be organised and *how* its teaching should be structured, except in the most general way. What took the place of the streamed, 'homogeneous' classes for whom didactic, whole-class teaching had been seen as appropriate, was the so-called 'informal' classroom where children worked as individuals or in groups under the aegis of the teacher. New, more flexible, techniques had to be developed. What followed was a period of experiment, of trial and error, by hundreds, indeed thousands, of individual teachers, assisted, for the most part, by local advisers (who were learning from the teachers' experience as much as vice versa).

There was a powerful shift in these years towards creative activities of all kinds, but especially in the field of music, dance, drama, art and crafts, and writing. Many primary schools were transformed as ideas, long current, could actually now be implemented (by now the size of classes had been reduced). There was, however, certainly less emphasis on intellectual, cognitive or concept development as an educational goal, even though much effort was made to bring a new understanding of mathematics into the primary school. There is no doubt also that pupil–teacher relations became easier, more friendly and informal. Researchers have shown, however, that it would be wrong to over-emphasise the significance of the transformation. The great mass of primary schools did not suddenly transform themselves – far from it. Surveys have shown that the old-established emphasis on 'the basics' continued in most schools, that the traditional narrowness that marked elementary education still persisted. The ideal 'Plowden-type' primary schools identified by the Committee in their report formed only a small proportion of all such schools.[1] Nevertheless, there certainly had been an important shift of emphasis.

The Plowden Report (1967) – the most recent and massive examination of primary school procedures and practices – has been criticised for the emphasis given to the uniqueness of each individual child, and therefore for too great a stress on the need to *individualise* the teaching–learning process. If each child has to be treated individually, it is argued, the complexity of classroom organisation becomes overwhelming, while, at the same time, it becomes impossible to develop effective pedagogic means relevant to the needs of children generally. It was criticism of this kind which was to come to the fore in the new circumstances created by the passage of the Education Reform Act of 1988 and subsequent developments.

This Act created a new situation in English (and Welsh) education through its imposition of a National Curriculum defined in terms of nine separate subjects, together with their programmes of study, attainment targets and standard assessment tasks (SATs). Primary schools, while certainly retaining subject teaching in some areas (for instance, English and mathematics), also relied extensively on topic and project work, interdisciplinary in nature, to cover other areas of knowledge and skills. For the latter, group and individual work tended to predominate. The requirements of the National Curriculum, however, clearly challenged classroom procedures which had developed following the 1960s. As mentioned at the start of this chapter, a widespread discussion now took place on primary school practices, led, in part, unusually by the Secretary of State himself, who encouraged a re-think though suggesting a return to the more directly didactic approaches of the past.[2]

The outcome was the appointment of the committee of inquiry into primary education late in 1991, with a brief to report in six weeks. This they achieved. Their report recognised that the imposition of the National Curriculum, together with its attendant assessment requirements, has set quite new problems for schools and their teachers. These problems will certainly require new solutions and the report itself made many suggestions. Some quite radical revision of the National Curriculum was also suggested and, it is generally agreed, this also is necessary. Primary teachers were known to be under excessive pressure in their attempts to carry it through as proposed.

In facing the new situation, thinking based on over-simplified reduction of differences of view to that of the crude dichotomy between 'traditional' and 'progressive' approaches is less than helpful. The primary teacher has enormous responsibilities, involving promoting both the social and the intellectual development of young children. But a great deal more is known about the nature of children's mental development than was the case 50 or more years ago.

The teacher, and her advisers, need now to work out, in the new situation, approaches which are most relevant, and most effective, in promoting learning, and in developing pupils' abilities and skills across a very wide range of activities. What also has to be worked out in the new situation relates to the search for the most effective forms of classroom organisation to achieve these aims.

There is not likely to be any simple answer. Over the years the teaching profession has built up an enormous fund of experience and so of knowledge as to different approaches. This provides a firm base for the future given that there is a readiness to jettison obsolete practices in the light of evidence, and to continue the search for new and more effective ways of promoting growth, intellectual and other, among those most resilient and rewarding of subjects, the primary school pupils.

NOTES

1 For an analysis of the Plowden Committee's findings on this question, see Brian Simon, 'The primary school revolution: myth or reality?' in Brian Simon and John Willcocks (eds) *Research and Practice in the Primary Classroom*, London: Routledge & Kegan Paul (1981).
2 'Primary Education – a Statement' by Secretary of State for Education and Science Kenneth Clarke, DES 412/91, 3 December 1991.

REFERENCES

Alexander, R., Rose, J. and Woodhead, C. (1992) *Curriculum Organisation and Classroom Practice in Primary Schools: a Discussion Paper*, London: DES.
Hadow Report (1926) *The Education of the Adolescent*, London: HMSO.
—— (1931) *The Primary School*, London: HMSO.
—— (1933) *Infant and Nursery Schools*, London: HMSO.
Jackson, B. (1964) *Streaming: an Education System in Miniature*, London: Routledge & Kegan Paul.
Plowden Report (1967) *Children and their Primary Schools*, 2 vols, London: HMSO.
Selleck, R. J. W. (1972) *English Primary Education and the Progressives, 1914–1939*, London: Routledge & Kegan Paul.

Chapter 2

Analysing practice

Robin Alexander

Robin Alexander was one of the authors of the 'Three Wise Men' report on primary practice referred to in the last chapter. This short extract (taken from a longer chapter) is drawn from the author's study of primary practice based on the Leeds Primary Needs Programme, published soon afterwards. In it he lays out clearly his own framework for thinking through practice, and it is offered here for discussion both as a framework for the analysis of the Report itself, and as a potential approach for analysing classroom teaching. In this extract the author identifies five dimensions which need consideration in analysing practice. In the original chapter, Alexander goes on to argue that of these, while political and pragmatic considerations of course mould practice, value, conceptual and empirical considerations are central to the definition of good practice.

How can we begin to draw up a map of the vast territory of educational practice? In absolute terms it is an impossible enterprise. However, there may be a level at which such a map is not only possible but might also serve as a useful prompt to those involved in the examination, execution and judgement of practice.

My own shot at such a framework starts with what one encounters on entering a classroom: a *context* comprising first the physical and organisational features of furniture, resources and participants, and second, the relationships observable as existing among and between these participants. This, then, is the setting.

Looking closer, one notes that most of the relationships and interactions are not random, but are framed by *pedagogic process*: teachers adopt particular strategies, particular combinations of class, group and individual work, particular patterns of interaction; and pupils are organised so as to facilitate these.

Next, we note that these processes are focused upon specific tasks and the acquisition of specific knowledge, skill, understanding or attribute: the *content* of teaching and learning.

Finally, we recognise that what we see and what the participants experience is subject to the teacher's *management*: it is planned, implemented and evaluated.

Thus far, we are dealing with what can be observed. However, to make sense of what we see we need to encounter the educational ideas and assumptions in which the observable practice is grounded. Without them practice is mindless, purposeless and random. It is reasonable to assume that, although we may not necessarily agree with such ideas as an explanation and justification of what a teacher does, ideas of some kind are the basis for all observable practice. Talking with teachers about their practice, I find I can group such ideas under three broad headings.

The first concerns *children*. Most teaching rests on assumptions about what they can or cannot do, what they need, how they develop, how they learn, how best they can be motivated and encouraged.

The second collection of ideas concerns *society*. Teachers usually have some sense of the demands and expectations which emanate from outside the school, of the needs of society or particular sections of it, and of the needs of the individual in relation to that society. Reconciling and balancing these is one of the central challenges of every teacher and every school, and many primary teachers have a powerful sense of having moved from the era of Plowden in which the needs of the individual were paramount to one in which these are made subservient to, or are redefined in terms of, economic and political imperatives.

Finally, all teaching rests upon ideas about the nature of *knowledge*: its structure, its character, its source (whether newly created by each individual and culturally evolved or handed on from one generation to the next), and its content.

It will probably be apparent that at this point I have telescoped a line of analysis which deserves to be greatly extended, and indeed it derives from a conceptual framework which I have developed for a higher degree course on primary education which I run at Leeds University. However, for present purposes the intention is not to provide in fine detail a fully comprehensive framework for analysing and exploring classroom practice, but simply to illustrate that some such framework is perfectly feasible.

Thus my own framework has two main dimensions and seven main components, as shown in Figure 2.1 below. The categories are of course not discrete, but are simply presented as such for analytical purposes. More important, the two dimensions, here presented as a sequential list, interact: each aspect of practice is to a greater or lesser extent informed by one, two or all of the areas of ideas, values and beliefs.

These seem to constitute not so much the totality as the minimum: whatever else classroom practice encompasses, it contains these elements.

Armed with such a framework we can return to any good practice statement, test its emphasis and scope, and examine the thrust of the ideas and justifications, if any, in which it is rooted. The model, incidentally, has

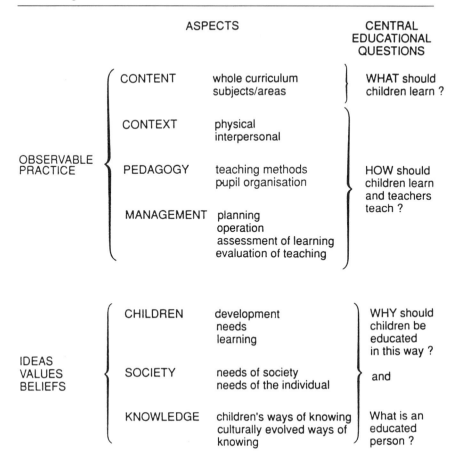

Figure 2.1 Educational practice: a conceptual framework

its parallel version at whole-school level. There the *observable practice* components include *context, management* and *external relations*, but because the focus of this discussion is the classroom I am not elaborating that part of the framework in the same way.

WHERE IS GOOD PRACTICE TO BE FOUND?

When we say of something we do, see or wish to commend 'this is good educational practice', what are we *really* asserting? There seem to be four possibilities:

1   *This is the practice which I like, and which accords with my personal philosophy of education.*
2   *This is the practice which works for me, and which I feel most comfortable with.*
3   *This is the practice which I can prove is effective in enabling children to learn.*
4   *This is the practice which I (or others) expect to see, and it should therefore be adopted.*

The status of each of these statements is significantly different:

Statement 1 is a statement of *value* or *belief*.
Statement 2 is a *pragmatic* statement.
Statement 3 is an *empirical* statement.
Statement 4 is a *political* statement.

Pursuing our quest for good primary practice in this way, therefore, we can see that while in a physical sense it resides in primary schools and classrooms, to know what we are looking for and to begin to understand how we might define and judge it, we need to recognise that it lies, *conceptually*, at the intersection of the five considerations or dimensions which we have explored: value, pragmatic, empirical, political and conceptual. Figure 2.2 represents this relationship.

The quest for good primary practice, then, is as much a conceptual as a geographical one. Before we can ask an LEA or a head to show us schools or classrooms in which good practice is to be found, we need to be clear what we, and they, mean by good primary practice, and whether there is sufficient agreement to make the journey worthwhile. 'What do we mean by good practice?' must precede 'Where is good practice to be found?'

In other words, to provide a reasonably defensible view of good practice we need to be able to answer the following questions:

Conceptual. Am I clear what practice I am talking about? Is my version of practice as balanced and as comprehensive as it ought to be, or am I operating on the basis of a rather limited view of practice, missing out some aspects and over-emphasising others?

Value. Why do I value or believe in this particular practice? Can I defend my value-position in terms of basic ideas and principles about what it is to be educated? Are these sustainable values or are they merely blinkered prejudices? Do I value this practice not so much because I have good reasons as because I've always done it this way – do I like what I know rather than know what I like?

Pragmatic. Does the practice work for me? Why? Is it reasonable to assume that it will work for others? If not, should I be commending it in this form? What are the necessary classroom conditions for making this practice practicable?

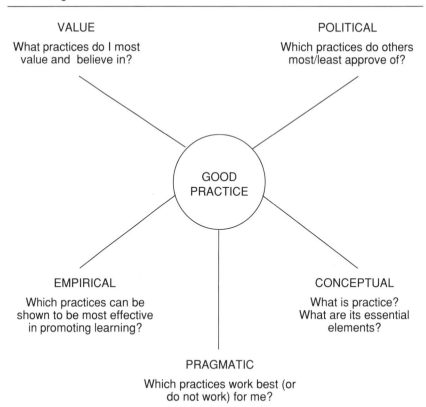

Figure 2.2 What is good practice? Reconciling competing imperatives

Empirical. Do I actually have evidence that the practice I am commending or adopting promotes learning? What kind of evidence? My own experience? Research findings? Am I prepared to allow for the possibility that there might be contrary evidence? Am I prepared to allow for the empirical perspective or am I going to press my view of good practice regardless?

Political. (1) Am I expecting people to adopt this practice not so much on its merits but because I say they should? Am I taking refuge in my authority because I haven't really thought through the arguments for the practices I am pressing for (or against)? Am I pressing for (or opposing) particular practices for other than educational reasons? Is this, in effect, an abuse of my power? (2) Does the view of good practice *x* is expecting me to adopt have good arguments and evidence to sustain it? Or if I am simply expected to adopt the practice because *x* says so, what can I do about it? Assuming *x* to be reasonable, am I prepared to argue the toss? How far am I prepared to compromise my own judgements in order to gain approval and advancement? When I achieve similar eminence, how will I use the power I shall then have to influence the practice of others?

Good primary practice, like education itself, is as much an aspiration as an achievement; but at least we can try to become clearer about what it is we aspire to, and why; and in confronting the various considerations which bear upon classroom practice we can inject a greater degree of honesty and realism into professional discourse and thereby make the gap between achievement and aspiration a diminishing one. Moreover, thus armed we may be able to counter the journalistic and political hijacking of the debate about pedagogy rather more convincingly than we have hitherto.

Chapter 3

What we know about effective primary teaching

Caroline Gipps

This chapter provides an authoritative survey of research on primary practice. To draw on the conceptual framework offered in Chapter 2, the review offers empirical and pragmatic evidence against which to analyse practice in specific classrooms. As well as setting out the main findings, it indicates the range of questions that researchers have chosen to study over the past decades, and therefore also indicates areas which have not, as yet, been investigated. A number of the issues for effective practice which the author draws from the research will be discussed and illustrated in greater detail in the other chapters of this book.

Primary education stands at a water-shed, with the National Curriculum increasing the breadth and depth of what must be taught beyond many teachers' felt competence; national assessment and its changing requirements altering profoundly many teachers' understanding of and interaction with assessment; calls from ministers to move away from 'topic teaching' towards formal class teaching; and suggestions from the National Association of Head Teachers (NAHT) that teaching for 10- and 11-year-olds be subject-specialist based on a secondary model. It seems therefore that this is an appropriate time to take stock, and look at what we know about effective primary teaching.

Although there appears to be little consensus, within or outside the profession, about appropriate teaching methods, we do in fact have a fairly clear picture from research on classroom practice. What I want to do in this chapter is to cull from theory and from research on practice what it is we know about good primary teaching. What is it that we know and what would a model of primary practice be? These are crucial questions which will not disappear simply because we have a common National Curriculum, as the recent 'debate' has shown: a National Curriculum, after all, needs a method of 'delivery'.

THE CONTRIBUTION OF THEORY AND THEORISTS

Traditionally, primary education has looked to child development and psychology for theoretical guidance and underpinning.

Probably the most famous psychologist as far as education is concerned is Piaget. His work has had an enormous influence on primary education, some of it, in retrospect, undesirable. Piaget's model is one in which the child develops thought through interaction with the environment. It is now widely accepted that Piaget under-estimated the role of language in learning and over-estimated the role of play; Barbara Tizard, for example, maintains that one result of this is large, open-plan nurseries, so that children can have free access to a range of activities, when in fact what they need is sustained conversation with an interested adult (Tizard and Hughes 1984). The other relevant aspect of Piaget's model is that children go through stages of intellectual development; this was widely interpreted as meaning that it is not possible to teach young children some things until they are 'ready' – that is, that there are limits to their capacity to learn – the corollary of this being that certain concepts emerge spontaneously and by implication cannot be taught (Walkerdine 1984). Though disputed by Bruner, who made the now famous statement that it is possible to teach children anything at any stage in an intellectually honest way, this element of Piaget's work has left us with a legacy, as Alexander (1984) and others have argued, of low expectations for primary-aged children.

Piaget's positive contribution, however, was both to start a theoretical debate about young children's intellectual development and to encourage the close observation of children. Thus, for example, the work of Margaret Donaldson (1978) – who tested Piaget's model by observing children and reworking his experiments – shows us how what is important in the child's performance of a task is, not only his or her stage of development, but also how the task makes sense to the child, and his or her perception of the sort of answer the adult wants. Both these factors have been shown to be central to children's performance in the classroom, as the next section will show.

Bruner, another psychologist of crucial importance for primary education, considered the question, what is it that makes school learning so difficult? His answer was that it is because it is separated from children's real lives, and so he incorporated into his theory of learning children's understanding of the situations in which they are asked to perform or learn (Bruner 1966). For Bruner the essence of learning is that individuals actively select, retain and transform information to a psychological frame of reference (that is, an internal model or system of representation on the basis of which we understand the world). He also sees learning as taking place through interaction with an interested adult and, as children get older, through texts.

Bruner's theory of learning is essentially a 'constructivist' one.

Constructivist models of learning assume that knowledge is built up by the child in the form of connected schemata; the child is seen as an agent in his or her own learning actively constructing knowledge. In this model, what is 'taught' to the child is only one of the factors which influence what children learn. By contrast, at the opposite extreme, is the 'transmission' model of learning in which the assumption is that the teacher transmits knowledge or information to the student; the child is seen as an empty vessel, a recipient of information, and children learn what they are taught. The model of learning which we hold has profound implications for how we teach. The latter model is linked with more formal didactic teaching methods and the former with more open and active teaching methods. Constructivist models are currently generally accepted as being more appropriate, and of course there are a range of positions along the continuum.

While constructivist views of learning may be in vogue, it has proved difficult to develop a pedagogy based on its principles which primary teachers can use consistently successfully with groups of 25–30 children. In the next section I shall describe the progress made by Neville Bennett and Maurice Galton towards framing such a pedagogy.

Vygotsky, the Russian psychologist, has given us a number of crucial insights into how children learn, of which two have particular consequences for classrooms (Vygotsky 1978). First, that speech in infancy is the direct antecedent of thinking. Very young children discover, so Vygotsky's theory goes, that it is helpful to speak aloud about what they are doing; thus they begin to use 'speech for oneself'. From the ages of 3 to 7 children's speech changes and diversifies so that they develop conversational speech, for communication, in addition to 'speech for oneself'. Piaget's view was that this latter form of speech withers away, while Vygotsky, on the other hand, suggested that this form is internalised, developing into inner speech and eventually into thought. The child then becomes capable of carrying out mental operations more subtle than anything which he or she can put into words (Britton 1989). As Britton says, if speech in childhood lays the foundations for a lifetime of thinking the implication for pedagogy is enormous, and talking should have a major role in classroom life, particularly at infant level.

The second key feature of Vygotsky's theory is that of the 'zone of proximal development'. This refers to the gap that exists for children between what they can do alone and what they can do with help from someone more knowledgeable or skilled than themselves. Here of course the role of the teacher is crucial in the case of young children, and co-operative activity or peer tutoring additionally for older children. The teacher's role then is to make the classroom as rich an interactive learning community as she or he can (Britton 1989) and through language to lead children into new zones of proximal development (Edwards and Mercer 1989). Another implication from Vygotsky's model of the zone of proximal development is to do with match: Vygotsky's model would suggest that not all tasks should be perfectly matched to the child's current level of development and skill. Quite the reverse in fact, that some tasks need to be able to shift the child into the next zone, *but* what is crucial to this idea is that interaction with another person is required – whether teacher or peer – to help in this moving-on process.

The 'social' constructivist model of learning (see Wood 1988 and Pollard 1990) sees children as social beings who construct their understandings from social interaction within the dynamics and constraints of the contexts in which learning takes place. This model focuses on the importance of the degree of control which the learner has over the process of constructing meaning. However, it also recognises the importance of the adult as an agent in the learning process – helping the child to 'make sense' and to move to the next zone of development.

From social psychology we can make use of attribution theory (Gammage 1984). The life of the classroom is busy, full of interactions and less systematic than the uninitiated would believe. Attribution theory deals with the way in which we make causal inferences about people and events, in other words, that in the absence of actual knowledge or facts we attribute causes of behaviour, understandings, states and so on to people. Within the classroom, Gammage argues, life is so busy and interactions so numerous that the teacher, who cannot assess the exact psychological characteristics which the child brings to any given task, infers, assumes and makes judgements. Indeed, without this process of attribution teachers could not operate for they would be constantly having to use diagnostic assessments of one sort or another. As human beings we attribute cause and effect, often on the most slender of evidence. Since teachers attribute much to pupils which they cannot directly ascertain, they need to be aware that this is what they are doing. Of course, in the absence of diagnosis, particularly in regard to match, sensitive attribution based on sensible awareness, Gammage argues, can be helpful.

Another feature of attribution theory is that people often explain their actions by factors that lie outside their control; this means therefore that they are powerless to effect change. Galton (1989) argues that this is one of the reasons why elements of the 'Plowden model' (DES 1967) were not taken up. For example, very low levels of adult/child interaction are widely observed in classrooms (but this is the antithesis of what the 'Plowden model' stood for), and are explained by teachers as being due to class size. This of course is beyond the teachers' control. In fact, Galton argues, the low levels of interaction are due to classroom organisation and are well within teachers' control.

Something else we can take from psychology is an understanding that children come to the learning experience with their own individual qualities, experiences, conceptions and mental states. Children differ in their prior learning and conceptual level, their rate of learning, their motivation, confidence and self-esteem: all these affect their ability to do the task, to absorb the information on offer, to learn the concept, to carry out the process. Every teacher knows this to be the case and it is one of the difficulties with the transmission model of learning: children are not identical empty vessels. The adult must understand what the child knows and the level at which she knows it in order to help the child to move on to the next stage. The child must also be interested in and committed to the material if real learning is to take place; first-hand experience and involvement are major motivators for learning.

In fact, because teaching takes place in large groups, the ideal of knowing each child's entry characteristics and modifying teaching and the curriculum to suit, or having and using some perception of the child's system of representation (cf. Bruner 1966) in order to present information in a form likely to be amenable to the child's frame of reference, is clearly not always possible.

However, as well as considering the characteristics of the children and the interaction between these and particular learning experiences or subject matter we need to put into the equation the teacher's own style: which subjects does he/she enjoy teaching, feel most confident in teaching and what is his or her preferred teaching style? To assume that there is one best method for all children and all teachers is to under-estimate significantly the complexity of the teaching situation and the interactions involved. Clearly at the heart of the educational process lie the teacher, the child and the curriculum.

One of the limitations of relying on theory, or using research which is explicitly theory-based, is that such work tends to focus on one part, or aspect, of the thing which is of concern. For example psychology has traditionally focused on children's learning and abilities, social psychology and sociology on the classroom or school, while studies of curriculum areas have concentrated on the subjects or processes taught. In fact, we need to consider all of these, that is, we need to look at children's mental processes in relation to subject matter and the whole learning context.

Another problem with theory in relation to education is that it has not always attempted to understand the daily practice of teachers before going on to make recommendations about that practice (Golby 1988). It is now more widely accepted that we need to generate educational theory out of good educational practice (e.g. Hirst 1984) rather than from the foundation disciplines of psychology, philosophy and sociology. The notion of the 'reflective practitioner' is one (Schon 1983) that is particularly helpful in viewing the relation between theory and practice in teaching. This is not to say that 'outsiders' such as researchers (with a thorough knowledge of teaching and classrooms) cannot observe good practice in action and help to build up a pedagogic theory.

In fact, as both Simon (1981) and Galton (1989) point out, education in this country is characterised by an absence of any serious discussion of pedagogy – the science of teaching – and official documents are characterised by their absence of any theory. Simon considers that one of the manifestations of this was the Schools Council approach to curriculum development and reform which he describes as essentially pragmatic and atheoretical. National Curriculum and assessment developments today suffer from a similar lack of theoretical framework or consideration of pedagogy.

One of Simon's key points is that we need to move away from the Plowden view which focused on the individual child and individual differences – a view which Walkerdine also takes, but for different reasons (1984) – because to develop pedagogy we need to start from what children have in common as members of the human species in order to establish the general principles of teaching and then to determine what modifications are needed to meet the individual's needs. If the view is that each child requires a specific pedagogical approach, then the construction of general principles of teaching becomes impossible. Simon argues (and research shows) that teachers who set up tasks for individual children then have a complex management problem which takes up all their energies (Simon 1981: 142).

So theory's contribution lies in the insights that it can give us: not for any one theory's ability to give us all, or indeed any, of the right answers, but to offer a range of insights which we can use to build up an understanding of the science *and* art of teaching within the complex classroom setting.

THE CONTRIBUTION OF RESEARCH

What does research tell us about effective primary teaching? Neville Bennett, Maurice Galton and colleagues have been researching primary classrooms for over 15 years and their writings are enormously important in the search for a primary pedagogy. Two major research studies carried out in London of junior schools, by Peter Mortimore and colleagues, and of infant schools by Barbara Tizard and colleagues, throw more light on effective teaching and learning. I shall concentrate here on these four researchers and their work.

Bennett's was the first attempt in the post-Plowden era to work towards an effective model of teaching for primary schools. *Teaching Styles and Pupil Progress* (1976) framed the debate in terms of teachers' styles categorised as formal, informal and mixed. He studied the effect these had on children's performance in maths and English. This study only looked at fourth-year junior teachers and classes, relied mostly on self-report by teachers and did not control for curriculum activity. There were also considerable problems with the design and analysis of the study – perhaps inevitable in the first of a series of studies of this sort, being a major new model.[1]

Bennett concluded that *teachers' style* did make a difference to performance on the tests used, and *time on task* seemed to be an important intervening variable.

The limitations with this approach became evident, however (Bennett 1987), since it did not focus on the pupils (who not only influence their own learning through their interactions with the teacher, but also bring their personal and cognitive styles to the classroom) and since this broad classification of teachers was too gross to be meaningful. Bennett's work then moved towards focusing on the pupils' learning experiences (Bennett *et al.* 1984). Time on task and 'match' – that is, the matching of level of difficulty of task to the level of attainment of the child – were key issues within what Bennett refers to as the 'opportunity to learn' paradigm (Bennett 1987). The assumption within this paradigm is that pupil activity is central to the effect of teaching on learning, in other words there is no *direct* relationship between teacher behaviour and pupil achievement since the pupil mediates by his or her activities. The teachers' crucial contribution is in managing the pupils' attention and time.

Bennett concluded that, contrary to the earlier work within this paradigm, time on task was not alone a sufficient condition for learning. Despite the fact that research indicates consistently that length of the school day, the amount of time spent on learning activities and homework all relate to pupil achievement: 'There is little to be gained from high pupil involvement on tasks that are either not comprehensible or worthwhile' (Bennett 1987). Thus the *quality and level of the task set* entered the debate.

Unhappily, the next study by Bennett, Desforges and colleagues (1984) showed that, even in the classrooms of teachers who were identified as being good class-teachers, only 40 per cent of tasks matched pupils' capabilities. Furthermore, the tasks set by the teacher did not always embody their intentions. Now, given that these were experienced, good teachers, we need to consider why the 'match' was poor. This, we cannot fail to notice, is a regular theme of the HMI: they report poor match with an awesome regularity (HMI 1978, 1983, 1985). Desforges and Cockburn (1987) point to the logistics of the teacher's task. We may believe that 'the single most important factor influencing learning is what the learner already knows. Ascertain this and teach him accordingly' (Ausubel 1968), but with a class of 30 pupils if the teacher did nothing else she would have slightly less than 10 minutes a day to focus on each individual child. Given the dynamics of large groups of young children, the fact that the state of children's knowledge is changing all the time, and the number of curriculum areas covered, actually to diagnose correctly on a regular basis the understanding of every child and to set work at an appropriate level is clearly impossible, as Simon pointed out. Thus the teacher must limit her diagnostic activity and aim her teaching (albeit unwittingly) 'down the middle'. So one of the necessary conditions for learning, the appropriate level of the task set, is problematic within large mixed-ability classes.

Bennett's next move was to bring *teachers' subject knowledge* into the arena. How can teachers teach well knowledge which they themselves do not thoroughly understand; how can they identify pupil misconceptions or misunderstandings or make decisions about what counts as development in content areas with which they are not thoroughly conversant? Is teachers' poor subject knowledge part of the problem in lack of diagnosis, which for Bennett means identifying appropriate tasks for children? Findings from this research indicate that only a third of primary teachers feel competent to teach science, 27 per cent to teach music and 14 per cent design and technology in the National Curriculum (Wragg *et al.* 1989). Findings which did not bode well for the teaching of some National Curriculum subjects (Bennett and Carré 1991).

Bennett now concludes that teachers need a range of teaching styles, and his current model is one which includes *interactions of teacher, pupil and task within the complex social setting of the classroom*. Here Bennett draws on Doyle's ecological model of the classroom as a complex environment and information system to which teacher and pupil must adapt (Doyle 1986).

> To understand the degree to which teaching prospers learning it is necessary to ascertain the extent to which the intellectual demand in assigned work is appropriate or matched to pupils' capabilities. Further, since classroom learning takes place within a complex social environment it is necessary to understand the impact of social processes on children's task performances.
>
> (Bennett 1988)

The first major study by Maurice Galton and his colleagues, ORACLE (Galton and Simon 1980), used systematic classroom observation to study teacher and pupil behaviour in the classroom. What this study showed was that primary teachers were involved in interaction with pupils for nearly 80 per cent of the time they were observed. What was significant, however, was the pattern of these interactions: 70 per cent were with individual children, 20 per cent with the whole class and under 10 per cent with groups. Since there is little group interaction and given the proportion of teachers to children, what this interaction pattern means is that for children their main contact with the teacher is when she is interacting with the whole class – this accounted for nearly three-quarters of the attention that an individual pupil received from the teacher. Again, because there was little co-operative group work observed, pupils did not interact with other pupils either, thus the interaction pattern for pupils was the opposite of that for teachers, with almost 80 per cent of their time not interacting with anybody. Galton pointed out that the teachers' decision to work with individual children meant that tasks had to be set which did not make too many demands on the teacher, hence the widespread use of published schemes and work sheets. This strategy in turn led to a greater emphasis on the traditional areas of the curriculum, or the basics, than was assumed to be the case in the post-Plowden era. Another consequence of this pattern of classroom organisation and the high number of interactions was that the majority were lower-order interactions, that is, to do with organisational matters, giving guidance on routine and factual statements. Nearly 45 per cent of exchanges were teacher statements and there was little discussion, higher-order questioning or sustained interaction observed. Another study with a slightly different time sampling observation technique indicated that the interactions with individual pupils were short (that is, a high proportion of interactions were with a different pupil 5 seconds later), thus giving little opportunity to engage in challenging discussion which of necessity requires sustained interaction (Galton 1989). This picture again does not fit with the assumed post-Plowden picture of the modern primary classroom, based on questioning, discovery methods and group activities.

Galton and colleagues also classified their teachers into types and investigated pupils' progress in relation to these types. What this part of the research indicated was that two groups of teachers were more successful. The first group were those who were able to sustain high levels of questioning, eliciting factual information and challenging responses from the children and providing feedback to the pupils about their work. They made conscious switches of strategy from class to individual teaching in order to maintain their desired pattern of teaching tactics. The second group was those who worked with the class as a whole regularly and had the highest level of challenging questions, cultivated a positive climate in the classroom by using praise more often than other teachers, often demonstrated tasks and showed things to the whole class so that the children were to an extent learning by example.

What comes through again and again from Galton's work is the importance of *high levels of questioning* and the need to engage in strategies which allow *maximum levels of sustained interaction* with all pupils. This is a finding which has been replicated in the ILEA Junior School Study (see below), and would of course be consistent with Vygotsky's theory. Wood (1988), however, shows how too much teacher questioning is 'closed' and leads to low-level responses from the children. What raises the level of response is offering a longer response time (which many teachers find difficult) or teacher input which is high in cognitive level itself – for example, offering speculations, hypotheses and conjectures; this stimulates more talk, questions and ideas from pupils and generates discussion between them.

Galton also discusses children's own contribution to poor match. During the later stages of the ORACLE work – Delamont and Galton (1986) and Galton (1987) – Galton used informal qualitative observations and interviews with pupils to help explain the quantitative data. He concluded that pupils are anxious to please the teacher and to do what she wants, so they find high-risk situations (such as being called upon to answer questions) threatening. They thus attempt to avoid being picked on to answer questions, or to get the teacher to give as many clues as possible until the 'correct' answer is framed for them. Galton maintains that pupils offer good behaviour and a reasonable amount of work in exchange for tasks which have low ambiguity and are well within their capability, so that they do not have to expose their ignorance to the class or the teacher (see also Holt 1984). Work by Pollard further suggests that the children are trying to maintain good relationships with their peers while at the same time coping with shared social understandings of routines, conventions and expectations (Pollard 1987). Galton argues that in some classroom settings children develop a variety of strategies to slow down their work rate. For example, faced with the possibility that completing one work sheet will ensure another containing more difficult examples, pupils, understandably, prefer to take as long as possible to complete the first one (Galton 1989: 118). He suggests that a concerted effort of this kind by a class, particularly during the first few weeks of the school year, creates a situation in which the 'new' teacher expects these children to manage only a certain amount of work during a session. Thus mismatch occurs in that the pupils do not get any quicker when doing practice tasks, and Galton argues that the children have contributed to this mismatch.

Galton concludes that if teachers are to be able to question individual pupils in a sustained way about their work in order to diagnose their learning problems, then the children must have independent learning strategies, be less dependent on the teacher and not find the questioning threatening. Galton's view is that children need to have the confidence to think for themselves, and not to be dependent on the teacher if they are to engage in independent learning. However, many teachers exert their authority by using power over the children, particularly when there are conflicts over behaviour. Pupils then conform out of fear (of embarrassment or loss of status and self-esteem). This requires them to be dependent upon the teacher for clues to acceptable behaviour and this dependency is transmitted to their work. Edwards and Mercer (1989) argue similarly that even within a 'Plowden-type discovery' approach children must come up with spontaneous solutions to 'problems' which are at the same time the teachers' solutions. The child tries to discern in the teachers' cues, clues and questions what the required answer is; so the child is not discovering knowledge for herself, it is merely a different way of coming to the teachers' knowledge. This again increases the child's dependence on the teacher and limits their autonomy. Alexander (1991) describes life in Leeds primary classrooms as running on a similar model, with low-level questioning and teacher-determined classroom dialogue.

An alternative approach (Galton 1989) involves an open negotiation between teacher and pupils so that consideration is given within a shared framework of behaviour to both teachers' and pupils' needs. Thus Galton's work, too, now looks at the *interaction between teacher, pupil and task within the complex social setting of the classroom.*

Other research has looked at effective schools rather than effective teachers. Peter Mortimore and colleagues, at the then ILEA Research and Statistics Branch, carried out a longitudinal study of 2,000 junior school children in 50 schools. This study was designed to replicate, though in a modified and technically improved way, the secondary school study *Fifteen Thousand Hours.* Both studies had the major aim of investigating the issue of what makes an effective school. The junior school study, published as *School Matters* (Mortimore *et al.* 1988), collected an enormous amount of data: detailed information about the children's age, social class, sex, race and attainment on entry to school; detailed information about the children's attainment in cognitive and non-cognitive areas in each of the four years of junior school; and detailed evidence about school organisation collected by researchers as well as through questionnaires and self-report by the teachers. This use of more than one technique to look at teaching practice is important since there is often a gap between what teachers do and what they say they do, and equally observers' interpretations of events need checking with the actors'. Mortimore and colleagues found, for example, that the majority of teachers reported in interviews that they spent most of their time dealing with the class as a whole rather than with individuals or groups. The observations, however, showed that this was not the case – teachers spent much more time communicating with individual children than with the class or groups.

What the study found was that, once differences in pupil intake were taken into account, some schools were definitely more effective – in terms of pupil progress – than others. Because of the complex nature of the analysis it was possible to identify a range of factors that contributed to this effectiveness.

At the classroom level the effective features were these: teacher responsibility for ordering activities during the day for pupils – that is, teachers took the responsibility for structuring the day, facilitating balance and variety; some pupil responsibility for their work and independence *within* sessions; covering only one curriculum area at a time; high levels of interaction with the class as a whole (these two were related); use of higher-order questions and statements (that is, those which encourage responses which are of an imaginative or problem-solving kind); provision of ample challenging work (which resulted in high levels of pupil involvement); a positive atmosphere in the classroom with high levels of praise and encouragement.

The findings in relation to teachers using higher-order questions, giving encouragement and praise and working with the class as a whole in order to maximise and sustain interactions, replicate Galton's findings. Mortimore and colleagues were able to show that for teachers who spent a lot of time on contacts with individual pupils, much of this interaction was about routine (that is, non-work) matters and there was less use of higher-order questioning, while teachers who used class discussions as a teaching strategy also tended to make rather more use of higher-order communication. Teachers who used mixed activity sessions and integrated curriculum areas in a topic approach also spent more time on non-work contacts with pupils; these pupils showed higher levels of noise and movement, but also higher levels of inter-pupil co-operation. Mortimore concludes that classroom factors which contribute to effective teaching are: structured sessions, intellectually challenging teaching, a work-centred environment, maximum communication between teacher and pupils and a limited focus within sessions. The recent Leeds report (Alexander 1991) serves to confirm the findings of Galton and Mortimore in this area.

It seems that it is the amount, nature and content of teacher–pupil talk which is crucial to pupil learning and that communicating with groups and the whole class enables more children to experience sustained, higher-order, work-related interactions with the teacher. Focusing on one curriculum activity at a time enables the teacher to raise intellectually challenging points with pupils and class discussions, which, when handled well, can be challenging and stimulating.

Barbara Tizard and colleagues carried out a similar study in 33 London infant schools (Tizard et al. 1988) trying to find out what it is that schools and teachers contribute to children's progress. A specific focus of their work was, in addition, the differences in performance between boys and girls and the achievement of children of Afro-Caribbean origin. Like the Junior School Study this was longitudinal: it looked at the children's attainment on entry to school, it looked at home and school factors during the infant school years (carrying out observational studies in school and interviewing parents) and measured the children's progress in the basic skills in each of the three years of the study.

Apart from the finding that the strongest predictor of attainment at age 7 was the amount of '3R' knowledge the children had even before they started school, Tizard's study showed that there were strong relationships between curriculum coverage, the teachers' expectations of individual children and their progress. Curriculum coverage varied widely among schools and this was also related to progress regardless of teacher expectations: the more the children were exposed to, the more progress they made. When teachers with limited curriculum coverage were asked why they had not introduced certain items to their classes, they replied that these things were too difficult for children of that age, or in that school. Yet, as Tizard and colleagues point out, teachers in other schools in the study with children of very similar ability had introduced these items. Classrooms were well ordered and busy, and children did not spend much time in play (14 per cent and 2 per cent of classroom time at reception and top infant respectively) but they also spent very little time actually engaged in reading (only 4 per cent of the working time – that is, 8 minutes a day approximately, at top infant level) which the researchers cite as the cause of low levels of reading attainment in the schools. Those classes where children were reading for considerably longer were using techniques such as reading to each other or reading in groups rather than always to the teacher individually. Another disquieting finding was that the children spent almost half their school day (43 per cent) on dinner time, playtime, lining up, register and other non-work activities. A quarter of their time is spent at dinner and in the playground. Less than half the day (46 per cent) was devoted to learning activities in the classroom – of this 64 per cent was spent on the '3Rs'. Overall, children observed were engaged in their tasks 61 per cent of the time. Given the evidence that these were fairly low-level, repetitive activities, one is amazed at children's ability to stick docilely at the task in hand, although there are echoes of the contract between teacher and children which Galton and Pollard describe: we will behave well and work hard if you give us work that is predictable and easy.

What this study points out, in common with the Junior School Study, is that children need to be exposed to an ample range of challenging and interesting tasks. To summarise, teacher expectation for this sample of inner-city children was, for whole classes, too low; where teachers had higher expectations for individual children they were exposed to a wider range of curriculum and learning experiences; there was wide variation in curriculum coverage and this affected progress; much of the school day was spent on non-work activities; very little of the children's time was spent on reading by the top infant class and this affected progress; there was also very little maths teaching observed in the reception classes of almost all schools. The lack of balance in time spent on various curriculum areas will, of course, be changing with the introduction of the National Curriculum. In the first year of its introduction, however, HMI found many schools were spending a disproportionate amount of time on the core subjects, which caused concern about their ability to devote 'reasonable time' to all National Curriculum subjects (HMI 1989).

CONCLUSIONS: LOOKING TO THE FUTURE

What are the conclusions that we can take from this research? What does it tell us about good primary teaching which can help us to frame an effective pedagogy?

All the evidence points to the fact that when teachers take as their main focus individual children, most of their interactions are routine, organisational and low-level; the children, by contrast, get little teacher attention, working mostly on their own. As a result, extended discussions with children about the tasks – including higher-order questions and statements – are severely limited. In order to achieve this sustained interaction more use needs to be made of class and group work. Where class work is common, this is usually accompanied by a reduction in the amount of subject integration and the integrated day. Indeed, structuring the day for pupils and focusing on one curriculum area at a time were strong factors in effective teaching. So too is the provision of a plentiful and wide range of work tasks, which need to be matched to the child's level of attainment and understanding so that a balance of practice/consolidation tasks and learning/extension tasks is achieved. Important too is a good, positive, atmosphere in the classroom with plenty of encouragement and praise, high levels of expectation for all children and high levels of work-related talk and discussion.

What does 'theory' tell us about good teaching? What the 'theorists' tell us is that children are capable of more than we tend to give them credit for, provided that they understand what is required by the task; that interaction with others is of crucial importance, as is language; that through language the young child learns, among other things, to think;[2] that through interaction with others children can explore their own knowledge and understand how the new knowledge they are 'learning' fits in with this prior knowledge. But research tells us that the adult–child interactions need to be sustained, challenging and extended rather than fragmented and routine. The picture is thus of classrooms with an emphasis on language and challenge rather than quiet 'busy work'. This picture matches the one provided by research on classrooms, and we need to continue to get this message over to teachers.

It is clear then, in our model of good practice, that we need to emphasise strategies for increasing levels of interaction between teachers and children and higher-order questions and statements; as Vygotsky and Bruner both point out, the younger the child, the more they learn from language and the less from texts. We also need to work on ways of enabling teachers to assess children's levels of understanding or attainment so as to enable tasks to be appropriately matched. The teacher assessment element of National Curriculum assessment, if we can get to a model which is manageable and for which teachers are properly prepared and trained, could be an important element in the 'matching' process. Of course, informal assessment is also the way in which, following constructivist models of learning, one finds out how children think about things before developing those ideas.

Given that in classes of 25–30 teachers cannot match every task to every child's ability, one fairly common tactic is to present material and tasks to the class, discuss it altogether so that all children are listening to the teacher and are an audience, if not participants, in the sustained interaction, then for the teacher to go around and modify the task and/or give further explanation to individuals or groups. Another tactic is to develop co-operative or collaborative group work so that children interact with one another, and both Galton and Bennett have turned their attention to this. However, as the ORACLE research showed, children dislike group work because of the high levels of ambiguity and risk perceived in it, so teachers also need to know how to develop a classroom climate in which children have some control over their learning and are not dependent on the teacher so that such situations are not threatening to them. Early results indicate that when co-operative group work is facilitated, there are high levels of task-related talk in the group and the demands on the teacher decrease significantly; when interactions do take place they tend to be higher-order rather than routine (Dunne and Bennett 1990).

Thus we have two strategies – a version of 'traditional' class teaching which is modified around the edges to match some individual needs, and co-operative group work – both of which aim to reduce individual demands on the teacher and allow pupils to engage in increased amounts of task-related interaction. It is also possible that teachers need a mix of approaches to suit their own style and that of the children; just such a range of strategies has been recommended by Alexander et al. (1992). Classrooms should have a shared responsibility for learning: the teacher structures the session and allocates the task, but the child has responsibility for how the task is carried out and has some responsibility for his or her learning, thus reducing dependency on the teacher (see Yeomans 1987).

One reality that we need to face is that we will have to work within current, or increased, class size. All teaching would be easier in smaller classes. However, given the likelihood of future problems in teacher supply, it seems unlikely that class size can be expected to decrease in the near future. As Lawton (1990) points out, the unhappy coincidence of the increase in primary school pupil numbers (over half a million from 1990 to 2000) combined with the fall in numbers of school leavers during the same decade leading to a diminished pool of young people for teacher training, the lowered status of teaching as a profession and unattractive salary levels compared with other graduate careers, together with the proportion of practising teachers who are leaving the profession,[3] together present a picture of teacher shortages of frightening proportion. Recent improvement in the teacher supply figures seems to be the result of the recession rather than any more positive factors. As Professor Smithers has put it, 'Government has solved the teacher supply crisis by closing down the economy' (TES 1991).

So, as well as looking for ways of improving the status and morale of the teaching profession and looking at alternative models of training, we will need to cope, certainly in the interim, with current or increased class size. It is clear then that we cannot encourage an approach which focuses mainly or solely on the individual child. One possibility – as well as more class work and co-operative group work – would be to employ classroom assistants who can take the routine and organisational tasks away from the teacher leaving him or her free to concentrate on work tasks and higher-order interactions, assessment and curriculum planning. One version of the two-tier model put forward by Lawton (1990) is based on three different levels of qualification, training and experience with initial/licensing trainees, probationer/induction teachers, and those with fully qualified teacher status (perhaps with an MA) all working in classrooms but with clear differences in the roles and tasks which they undertake.

Teachers reading this chapter may feel that there has been an undue emphasis on problems and difficulties. There are, of course, many effective and exciting schools and teachers, and, at its best, being a primary teacher is extremely satisfying, though demanding. All those who have been in primary classrooms can point to the rewards, excitements and deep satisfaction that working with young children bring. Indeed as Nias' account shows (Nias 1989), many teachers derive intense satisfaction from feeling natural and whole in their relationship with children and from creating a sense of community within classes and schools. This is not sentimental anecdote, it is part of the long-held view of teaching as education, not of teaching as direct instruction. Similarly, Woods' (1987) account of relationships between teachers and children and the caring, friendly and cheerful atmosphere which is a feature of all good primary schools answers his own question: why do teachers carry on teaching?

We know much about effective teaching strategies, research has done much to show us what these strategies are, while theories have helped us to make sense of the findings. It is important now to make sure that what we know about effective primary teaching does not get lost under the weight of National Curriculum folders, statements of attainment and statements from ministers.

The problem with externally imposed change is that it devalues people's previous practice – they cannot have been right, otherwise there would be no need to change. In the area of curriculum coverage and match this may have been true for a number of teachers, but it is only part of the picture. Framing the model from a basis of research on good classroom practice should be one element in restoring morale and felt worth for teachers since our information on effective practice has come, as it only can, from observing effective teachers at work.

NOTES

1 Although Joan Barker Lunn's earlier work, *Streaming in the Primary School* (1970), also categorised teachers into types on the basis of whether their lessons and attitudes were mostly traditional or progressive.
2 It was Bertrand Russell who said, 'Most people would die sooner than think, and most people do.'
3 Professor Smithers' survey for the Leverhulme Trust indicates that teachers are leaving at about five times the rate of official DES figures (Smithers *et al.* 1989), and more recently that teacher turnover in London and the South-east is worryingly high (Smithers and Robinson 1991).

REFERENCES

Alexander, R. (1984) *Primary Teaching*, London: Holt, Rinehart & Winston.
—— (1991) *Primary Education in Leeds*, Leeds: University of Leeds.
Alexander, R., Rose, J. and Woodhead, C. (1992) *Curriculum Organisation and Classroom Practice in Primary Schools*, London: DES.
Ausubel, D. (1968) *Educational Psychology: a Cognitive View*, New York: Holt, Rinehart & Winston.
Barker Lunn, J. (1970) *Streaming in the Primary School*, NFER.
Bennett, N. (1976) *Teaching Styles and Pupil Progress*, Open Books.
—— (1987) 'Changing perspectives on teaching learning processes', *Oxford Review of Education*, 13, 1.
—— (1988) 'The effective primary school teacher: the search for a theory of pedagogy', *Teaching and Teacher Education*, 4,1.
Bennett, N. *et al.* (1984) *The Quality of Pupil Learning Experiences*, Lawrence Erlbaum.
Bennett, N. and Carré, C. (1991) 'No substitutes for a base of knowledge', *Times Educational Supplement*, 8 Nov.
Britton, J. (1989) 'Vygotsky's contribution to pedagogical theory', in P. Murphy and B. Moon (eds) *Developments in Learning and Assessment*, London: Hodder & Stoughton.
Bruner, J. (1966) *Towards a Theory of Instruction*, Cambridge, MA: Harvard University Press.
Delamont, S. and Galton, M. (1986) *Inside the Secondary Classroom*, London: Routledge & Kegan Paul.
DES (Department of Education and Science) (1967) 'Children at their primary schools' (Plowden Report), London: HMSO.
Desforges, C. and Cockburn, R. (1987) *Understanding the Mathematics Teacher*, London: Falmer.
Donaldson, M. (1978) *Children's Minds*, London: Fontana.
Doyle, W. (1986) 'Classroom organisation and management', in M.C. Wittrock (ed.) *Handbook of Research on Teaching*, New York: Macmillan (3rd edn).
Dunne, E. and Bennett, N. (1990) *Talking and Learning in Groups*, London: Macmillan Education.
Edwards, D. and Mercer, N. (1989) *Common Knowledge*, London: Routledge.
Galton, M. (1987) 'An ORACLE chronicle: a decade of classroom research', *Teaching and Teacher Education*, 3,4.
—— (1989) *Teaching in the Primary School*, David Fulton Publishers.
Galton, M. and Simon, B. (1980) *Progress and Performance in the Primary Classroom*, London: Routledge & Kegan Paul.
Gammage, P. (1984) 'The curriculum and its participants: perspectives of interaction', in M. Skilbeck (ed.) *Readings in School-based Curriculum Development*, Paul Chapman Publishing.
Golby, M. (1988) 'Traditions in primary education', in M. Clarkson (ed.) *Emerging Issues in Primary Education*, Falmer.
Hirst, P. (1984) 'Educational theory', in P. Hirst (ed.) *Educational Theory and its Foundation Disciplines*, London: Routledge & Kegan Paul.
HMI (1978) *Primary Education in England*, London: HMSO.
—— (1983) *9–13 Middle Schools: an Illustrative Survey*, London: HMSO.
—— (1985) *Education 8–12 in Combined and Middle Schools*, London: HMSO.
—— (1989) *The Implementation of the National Curriculum in Primary Schools*, London: HMSO.

Holt, J. (1984) *How Children Fail*, Harmondsworth: Penguin.

Lawton, D. (1990) 'The future of teacher education in England and Wales', Paper given to ATEE conference, Aug. 1990, in N. Graves (ed.) *Initial Teacher Education: Policies and Progress*, Kogan Page (London Educational Studies, ULIE).

Mortimore, P. *et al.* (1988) *School Matters: the Junior Years*, Open Books.

Nias, J. (1989) *Primary Teachers Talking*, London: Routledge.

Pollard, A. (ed.) (1987) *Children and their Primary Schools*, London: Falmer.

—— (1990) 'Towards a sociology of learning in primary schools', *British Journal of Sociology of Education*, 11,3.

Schon, D. (1983) *The Reflective Practitioner*, London: Temple Smith.

Simon, B. (1981) 'Why no pedagogy in England?', in B. Simon and W. Taylor (eds) *Education in the Eighties*, London: Batsford.

Smithers, A. *et al.* (1989) *A Study of Teacher Loss*, Leverhulme Trust.

Smithers, A. and Robinson, P. (1991) *Teacher Provision*, University of Manchester.

TES (Times Educational Supplement) (1991), 27 Dec.

Tizard, B. and Hughes, M. (1984) *Young Children Learning*, Fontana.

Tizard, B. *et al.* (1988) *Young Children at School in the Inner City*, Lawrence Erlbaum Associates.

Vygotsky, L. (1978) *Mind in Society*, Cambridge, MA: Harvard University Press.

Walkerdine, V. (1984) 'Developmental psychology and the child centred pedagogy', in J. Henriques *et al.* (eds) *Changing the Subject*, London: Methuen.

Wood, D. (1988) *How Children Think and Learn*, Oxford: Blackwell.

Woods, P. (1987) 'Managing the primary teacher's role', in S. Delamont (ed.) *The Primary School Teacher*, Falmer.

Wragg, E., Bennett, N. and Carré, C. (1989) 'Primary teachers and the National Curriculum', *Research Papers in Education*, 4,3.

Yeomans, R. (1987) 'Making the large group feel small', *Cambridge Journal of Education*, 17,3.

Part II

Managing learning and the curriculum

Chapter 4

Managing learning in the primary classroom

Neville Bennett

This chapter is an extract taken from one of the working papers of the Association for Primary Education. In it, Neville Bennett applies the research findings outlined by Caroline Gipps in Chapter 3 to the concrete task of teaching. He breaks this down into four discrete elements: planning and preparation, presentation, implementation and assessment. Working through each stage in turn, he draws on social constructivist theories of learning as well as research evidence to set out the implications for effective practice. Critical of much contemporary practice, the extract challenges teachers to experiment with new ways of classroom organisation.

A constructivist view of learning perceives children as intellectually active learners already holding ideas or schemata which they use to make sense of their everyday experiences. Learning in classrooms involves the extension, elaboration or modification of their schemata. This process is one in which learners actively make sense of the world by constructing meanings. Learning is believed to be optimised in settings where social interaction, particularly between a learner and more knowledgeable others, is encouraged, and where co-operatively achieved success is a major aim. The medium for this success is talk, which is now widely accepted as a means of promoting pupils' understandings, and of evaluating their progress.

IMPLICATIONS FOR CLASSROOM PRACTICE

The classroom implications of the above conceptions of children's learning are now considered in the light of contemporary practice. Divergences between implications and practice will show clearly where current practice might be reconsidered. For this purpose a simple model of a teaching cycle is used as shown below (Figure 4.1).

The cycle begins with the teacher planning and preparing tasks and activities for children which are then presented in some way, for example, through discussion, an experiment, a TV programme, and so on. The children then engage with their work within a classroom management system set

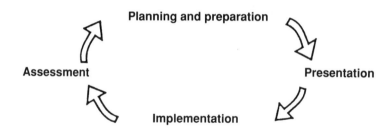

Figure 4.1 A teaching cycle

up by the teacher: for example, individuals working on individual tasks; mixed-ability groups in an integrated day arrangement; the whole class working in small co-operative groups on the same technology task, and so on. Once this work has been completed, it would be expected that teachers would assess or diagnose it, using that information to feed back to pupils, and to feed forward to inform their next round of planning.

PLANNING AND PREPARATION

A crucial part of planning is the selection or design of tasks, with associated materials, appropriate to children's capabilities. There are two aspects of this – choosing appropriate content, and the appropriate level, both of which assume an understanding by the teacher of the children's conceptions.

Choosing the content relies heavily on the teacher's knowledge of the subject unless there is a set scheme or textbook which is to be followed. Even here, however, teachers need to choose these carefully. Recent research on primary school texts in history (Beck and McKeown 1988) indicates that they fail to enable many pupils to develop a coherent representation or theme for a sequence of events. The major deficiency in these texts was that they made inadequate or unfounded assumptions about pupils' background knowledge.

Another aspect of content selection is the appropriate choice of content from National Curriculum programmes of study to fulfil particular statements of attainment.

Choosing the appropriate level of a task in relation to individual pupils means avoiding 'the twin pitfalls of demanding too much or expecting too little' (Plowden 1967). HMI have long expressed concern about poor levels of matching, particularly in areas like science and project work. They have argued that the level of demand, and pace of work, is most often directed towards children of average ability in the class, and that high attainers in the class tend to be under-estimated and low attainers over-estimated. These professional judgements of the Inspectorate are borne out by research studies (Bennett *et al.* 1984 and 1987).

In this context the notion of the zone of proximal development is also important. This is based on the view that optimal learning is that which involves the acquisition of cognitive skills slightly beyond the child's independent grasp in a co-operative setting. This conception of matching is not common in current practice and its implementation has implications both for teachers' planning and for classroom management.

PRESENTATION

The tasks, when planned, are presented by the teacher to an individual child, a group or the whole class. This presentation could simply take the form of a general direction to 'get on from where you left off yesterday', or it could be a discussion, a class written task, a TV programme, a science experiment, and so on. Whatever mode of working is decided upon, it is critical that children are clear about the requirements, have the necessary information, and any relevant materials.

It is becoming increasingly clear how crucial presentation is in terms of children's learning. The presentation of bits of knowledge or fragmented information supplied either by text or by teachers is not likely to encourage pupils to construct new understandings. Similarly, learners are much more likely to make sense of new input if it is clearly structured and organised. Two aspects of contemporary practice bear on this: the manner in which tasks are specified, and the nature of teacher questions.

Recent studies have shown that although teachers are very good at telling children *what* to do, they very rarely tell them *why* they are doing it. Thus although the immediate task may be clear the overall purpose, or curricular sequence within which the task is located, is unknown to them.

Although teachers in general are good at specifying tasks, about one in six tasks are poorly presented. These create problems for teachers and learners because the manner in which a task is specified confers importance on certain aspects of it, and ignores others. A simple example will suffice. A reception class teacher had the intention of helping children to think logically, and to give them the idea of direction. The task she chose to fulfil this intention was picture sequencing, integral to which was the colouring of each picture to add interest. However, the task was presented to the children with the words 'now we are going to do some colouring and cutting'. Observing and talking to these children after they had finished their activity made it abundantly clear that they had done what they had been asked to do – colouring in. No picture sequencing took place. The teacher's presentation had dictated the children's activity, thereby subverting the teacher's own good intentions (Bennett and Kell 1989).

Another important aspect of presentation is teacher questioning. It has been argued (Edwards and Mercer 1987) that 'it is essentially in the discourse between teacher and pupils that education is done, or fails to be done'. Recent studies (Galton *et al.* 1980; Tizard *et al.* 1988; PRINDEP 1990) of teacher–pupil talk have presented pictures of the pattern, nature and quality of this discourse. Not surprisingly there appears to be a marked asymmetry in teacher–pupil interaction. Teachers typically spend most of their time talking to, and with, pupils, whereas any individual pupil talks with the teacher for only a very small proportion of his or her time. Most often the individual pupil experiences being talked *to*, by the teacher, as a member of a group or class, rather than being talked *with*. From the child's point of view therefore, although individual work is common in primary schools, individual teaching is not.

With regard to the nature of teacher talk, the most recent study (PRINDEP 1990) classified interactions into five categories – work, monitoring, routine, disciplinary and other. Over a third of the interactions were about the content of the tasks which had been set, about a fifth were concerned with checking, marking and monitoring progress. Routine matters accounted for just over a quarter of the interactions, and discipline and control about 10 per cent. However, of most importance in considering the impact of teachers' presentation of children's learning is the quality of that interaction. If the patterns found in this study are at all typical then there are no grounds for complacency. The main points were as follows:

1 Teachers ask a great many questions. However, there were few questions which encouraged children to work through an idea or a problem or to build on previous learning. Many were rhetorical or pseudo-questions. Others were closed, requiring simple one- or two-word responses, and yet others were inappropriately pitched. 'Although questions were indeed prevalent, it was nearly always the teacher who asked them.'
2 A problem of matching arises with questions. Generating questions, the demands in which match children's differing abilities, is virtually impossible. Genuine dialogue with the whole class did not therefore occur despite the fact that some teachers attempted to maintain that illusion. The most common expedient was to pitch genuine questions at a very low level, and accept pupil responses which were barely adequate or relevant.
3 There is a reluctance to pronounce any child's response as wrong. The other factor which often determined the teacher's treatment of pupil response was its relation to the teacher's train of thought, and the extent to which it enabled her to say what she wanted to say, irrespective of its correctness or relevance.

The fostering of children's capabilities to talk and listen emerged as a particular issue, and supported the view of HMI (DES 1990) that 'Where the work is less effective than it should be, it is the development of oracy that is often impoverished and given too little time'. This issue is considered in more detail below.

IMPLEMENTATION

The view that learning is optimised through talk in co-operative settings has implications for presentation, as well as for classroom management. The nature of the teacher's talk needs to be carefully considered, as does the kind of classroom settings which allow for peer tutoring and co-operative working between pupils.

The most explicit advice on this aspect of classroom practice is to be found in the National Curriculum Council (NCC 1989) guidance on the English curriculum, particularly that on speaking and listening. Here the guidance prescribes classrooms where children feel sufficiently encouraged and secure to be able to express and explore their thoughts and feelings and emotions; where teachers encourage talk which is genuinely tentative and explanatory, whilst demonstrating that talk is a rigorous activity. Drawing clearly from constructivist ideas, the guidance argues that children should be able to make connections between what they already know and new experiences and ideas, and that the main vehicle for this will be their own talk. Teachers are also asked to reflect on their own questioning strategies.

For example, in talking with children the teacher should ensure that questions are genuinely open-ended, that children have problems to solve without a subtly indicated, expected answer, and that they are encouraged to speculate, hypothesise, predict and test out ideas with one another and with the teacher. The emphasis should be on language being used, not to communicate what is known, but as an instrument of learning. 'It is time for children to think aloud, to grapple with ideas and to clarify thoughts.' The guidance argues that once children have developed new understandings they will need to reflect and exchange ideas and views with other pupils and the teacher in order to consolidate their learning. Such talk does of course also indicate to the teacher the state of the child's understanding; that is, it is an aid to diagnosis.

This guidance, although in line with current views on children's learning, is not in line with current primary practice in Britain, which is ostensibly based on the individualisation of learning. The Plowden Report (1967) advocated individualisation of learning, but recognised a practical difficulty. If all teaching were on an individual basis only 7 or 8 minutes a day would be available for each child. The report therefore advised teachers to economise by 'teaching together a small group of children who are roughly at the same stage'. Further, these groups should change in accordance with children's needs, the implication being that the class would be organised flexibly, with groups forming and re-forming according to children's needs and activities. Various advantages were perceived for group work: it would help children learn to get along together in a context where peers could help one another and realise their own strengths and weaknesses as well as those of others; making their meaning clearer to themselves by having to explain it to others;

and gaining some opportunity to teach as well as to learn. It was hoped that apathetic children would be infected by the enthusiasms of a group, while able children would benefit by being caught up in the thrust and counter-thrust of conversation in a small group of children similar to themselves.

Unfortunately, research on classroom grouping practices provides little support for this rosy picture. In arguing that children in the group should be 'roughly at the same stage', the Plowden Report was, in modern parlance, calling for ability grouping – and that is what tends to happen. Three-quarters of classes are grouped according to ability for maths, and for reading two-thirds of 7-year-olds and over one-half of 9-year-olds are grouped this way (DES 1978). When the focus has been narrowed to observe what actually happens in such groups some sobering findings have been reported, particularly in junior classes. A major finding is that although most children sit in groups, for the great majority of the time they work as individuals on their own, individual, tasks. In other words, pupils work *in* groups, but not *as* groups. Further, whilst working in groups the amount of task-related talk is low, interactions tend to be short, and the opportunity to co-operate is slim. Finally, there appears to be a clear sex effect in inter-action. The great majority of talk is between pupils of the same sex, even in mixed-sex groups (Galton *et al.* 1980).

The small amount of research carried out at infant level indicates that there too children work in, not as groups, but that the sex effect is far less noticeable. Levels of task-related talk are higher, but little of it is task-enhancing – namely, aids the children in understanding their work (Bennett *et al.* 1984).

What seems to have happened is that teachers have taken note of Plowden's views in having children work in groups, but have preferred to retain individualisation rather than to introduce co-operation in that con-text. The unfortunate outcome of that is a high level of low-quality talk and a dearth of co-operative endeavour.

These outcomes could have serious implications both for children's learn-ing and for the fulfilment of National Curriculum attainment targets. In the English curriculum, for example, the attainment targets for speaking and listening include a specific demand for the assessment of co-operation. At level 2, children must present real and imaginary events in a connected narrative to a small group of peers. At level 4, the demands are far more extensive. Children must describe an event or experience to a group of peers, clearly and audibly and in detail; give and receive precise instructions and follow them; ask relevant questions with increasing confidence; offer a reasoned explanation of how a task has been done or a problem has been solved; take part effectively in a small group discussion and respond to others in the group.

It is not that primary teachers do not appreciate or understand the importance of talk. It may be that the link between talk and grouping has not previously been made explicit, or it may be, as Alexander (1984) argued, that grouping has emerged 'as an organisational device rather than as a means of promoting more effective learning, or perhaps exists for no reason other than that fashion and ideology dictate it'. But practice is slowly catching up with belief, aided and abetted by research studies and by HMI. Recent studies on co-operative group work in classrooms have shown clearly that achievement improves and pupil involvement increases, as do the development of such valued social outcomes as enhanced self-esteem and better understanding of different races and cultures – see Slavin (1983); Bennett and Dunne (1992). HMI too have observed the improvements that co-operative group work can bring. 'Co-operative work was a strong and distinctive feature of the best mathematics seen, with pupils seeking together a solution to an intellectual or practical problem' (DES 1989).

ASSESSMENT

That pupils bring schemata of their own to bear on any given topic, and that some of these will be shared and others idiosyncratic, has to be taken into account by teachers in their planning of classroom tasks. In order to take these schemata adequately into account a clear understanding of what they are is necessary; that is, it requires the teacher to take on the role of diagnostician. A useful metaphor for gaining access to children's conceptions is that of creating 'a window into the child's mind'. To draw back the curtains of that window often needs far more than a rudimentary look at a child's work. It demands a sophisticated combination of observation and careful questioning, and this is likely to need a great deal of time.

However, as was pointed out in the previous section, any individual child spends very little time interacting with the teacher, so how is effective diagnosis happening? What, in fact, is often found in contemporary classrooms is a great deal of assessment, some informal and unrecorded, and much assessment characterised by ticks, crosses and brief comments. There is a lack of diagnosis, and this is often accompanied by teachers concentrating on what children produce (for example, a page of completed sums), rather than on how it has been achieved. Yet both are necessary for diagnosis. An analysis of common errors in written work, or in number work, gives teachers a first glimpse through the 'window'; further questioning of the child concerning strategies used when coming to those typical errors opens the 'curtains' even wider (Bennett et al. 1984; Bennett and Kell 1989).

Poor diagnosis has serious implications. No teacher can decide on the next optimal step for a child or children without a clear view of where they are now. It is not possible to extend or modify schemata without knowledge of those schemata. Lack of diagnosis also has substantial implications for the quality of matching. It has been argued (Bennett et al. 1984) that at the root of poor matching is inadequate diagnosis, and this view is supported by

HMI (DES 1980): 'Generally, schools that had good procedures for the assessment of individual children's needs, abilities and attainments were, not surprisingly, markedly more successful in providing appropriate work for their pupils than were those schools without such procedures.' It is not difficult to agree with the conclusion of the Task Group on Assessment (DES 1988) that 'Assessment should be an integral part of the assessment process, continually providing both "feedback" and "feedforward"'. It therefore needs to be incorporated systematically into teaching strategies and purposes. But systematic, diagnostic assessment takes time, which is an extremely scarce resource in classrooms. Marking a page of sums may be relatively speedy, but probing children's understandings of their work takes considerably longer.

This demand for diagnostic assessment has to be considered in the light of ever-increasing demands on teachers for continuous assessment, record-keeping and reporting. That diagnosis is not as evident as it should be is thus understandable. However, efforts to improve this through the creation of time via alternative methods of classroom organisation are under way (see Dunne and Bennett 1990).

TEACHER KNOWLEDGE

For teachers effectively to diagnose children's conceptions, to plan appropriate classroom tasks, to present quality explanations and demonstrations and to make curricular choices, requires knowledge and understandings of subject matter. Recent research indicates that teachers have a better chance of being able to help their pupils develop flexible understandings of subject matter if they understand it well themselves. Moreover, such understandings enable teachers to develop a variety of ways of representing their understanding to pupils, who bring very different experiences and knowledge with them – see, for example, Reynolds (1989).

This argument may seem self-evident, but there is increasing evidence from Britain and the United States that teachers in training, and experienced teachers, both elementary and secondary, do not understand subjects in depth. In Britain, the Department of Education and Science has recently argued, for example, that the greatest obstacle to the continued improvement of science in primary schools is that many existing teachers lack a working knowledge of elementary science. This has been supported in a set of studies (Kruger and Summers 1989) on primary teachers' understanding of science concepts. It was reported that the majority of teachers' views were based on a 'mixture of intuitive beliefs and half-remembered textbook science from their school days, sometimes with incorrect or imprecise use of scientific language'. Another, smaller group of teachers seemed not to possess any theoretical understanding of phenomena presented. This group had received little education in science at school and of necessity were able to explain the instances only at a perceptual level, or not at all. The researchers concluded that the scientific thinking of many of the teachers studied resembled that of children, being limited to perceptual and observable entities.

CONCLUSION

Learning has here been defined as the extension, elaboration or modification of children's schemata. Children achieve this by making sense of new knowledge in the light of their existing knowledge. The construction of this sense-making is a continuous intellectual process, an essential input to which is social interaction. Talk aids the organisation of experience into thought, and is thus central to learning.

For teachers the major implication is for the structuring of classroom environments which offer the best opportunity for pupils to be involved in the social and cognitive activities entailed in building knowledge and understanding. Indeed, one theorist (Glaser 1991) has characterised classrooms as knowledge-building communities. This requires the translation of beliefs about pupils as 'social beings' into modes of classroom organisation which encourage talk within co-operative endeavours.

Managing such classroom environments needs high levels of organisational and diagnostic skill. From the perspective of current thinking about learning, diagnosis is the corner-stone of effective pupil development. As Ausubel (1968) put it, 'the single most important factor influencing learning is what the learner already knows. Ascertain this and teach him accordingly.' But diagnosis requires time, skill and knowledge, and, as the evidence indicates, there is room for improvement in each of these areas. Teachers' knowledge bases are of particular contemporary interest because effectively to diagnose children's conceptions or schemata, to plan appropriate classroom tasks, to present quality explanations and demonstrations and to make appropriate curricular choices, all require knowledge and understandings of subject matter.

REFERENCES

Alexander, R.J. (1984) *Primary Teaching*, London: Holt, Rinehart & Winston.
Ausubel, D.P. (1968) *Educational Psychology: a Cognitive View*, New York: Holt, Rinehart & Winston.
Beck, I.L. and McKeown, M.G. (1988) 'Toward meaningful accounts in history texts for young learners', *Educational Researcher*, 17: 31–9.
Bennett, N., Desforges, C., Cockburn, A. and Wilkinson, B. (1984) *The Quality of Pupil Learning Experiences*, London: Erlbaum.
Bennett, N. and Dunne, E. (1992) *Managing Classroom Groups*, Hemel Hempstead: Simon & Schuster.
Bennett, N. and Kell, J. (1989) *A Good Start? Four-year-olds in Infant Schools*, Oxford: Blackwell.

Bennett, N., Roth, E. and Dunne, R. (1987) 'Task processes in mixed and single age classes', *Education 3–13*, 15: 43–50.

DES (1978) *Primary Education in England*, London: HMSO.

—— (1980) *Education 5–9*, London: HMSO.

—— Task Group on Assessment and Testing (1988) *National Curriculum*, London: HMSO.

—— (1989) *Aspects of Primary Education: the Teaching of Mathematics*, London: HMSO.

—— (1990) *The Implementation of the National Curriculum in Primary Schools*, London: HMSO.

Dunne, E. and Bennett, N. (1990) *Talking and Learning in Groups*, London: Macmillan.

Edwards, D. and Mercer, N. (1987) *Common Knowledge: the Development of Understanding in the Classroom*, London: Methuen.

Galton, M., Simon, B. and Croll, P. (1980) *Inside the Primary Classroom*, London: Routledge & Kegan Paul.

Glaser, R. (1991) 'The maturing of the relationship between the science of learning and cognition and educational practice', *Learning and Instruction*, 1, 2.

Kruger, C. and Summers, M. (1989) 'An investigation of some primary teachers' understandings of changes in materials', *School Science Review*, 71: 17–27.

NCC (National Curriculum Council) (1989) *English in the National Curriculum: Key Stage 1*, York: NCC.

Plowden Report (1967) *Children and their Primary Schools*, London: HMSO.

PRINDEP (1990) *Teachers and Children in PNP Classrooms*, Evaluation Report 11, University of Leeds.

Reynolds, M.C. (1989) *Knowledge Base for the Beginning Teacher*, Oxford: AACTE/Pergamon.

Slavin, R.E. (1983) *Co-operative Learning*, New York: Longman.

Tizard, B., Blatchford, P., Burke, J., Farquhar, C. and Plewis, I. (1988) *Young Children at School in the Inner City*, London: Erlbaum.

Chapter 5

Negotiating learning, negotiating control

Maurice Galton

In Chapter 3, Caroline Gipps referred to the way in which Maurice Galton's research had shown the ambiguity of classroom demands, with children asked to be independent in their work, but with a classroom ethos such that they find risk-taking and independence threatening. The extract reprinted here is a highly edited version taken from two rich chapters in Maurice Galton's book Teaching in the Primary School. *In editing the chapters, I have tried to bring together just those sections which relate to the negotiation of learning and the negotiation of control, and to show how the author argues that the two need to be interrelated in classroom practice, so as to encourage shared responsibility for learning.*

The importance of a child's self-concept in learning has generally been recognised (Burns 1982) but, as Kutnick (1988: 166) points out in his review of the literature, there is a tendency to equate the construct largely in terms of academic self-concept. An equally important component concerns the child's self-image in regard to interpersonal relationships with both the teacher and his peers. Teachers in primary schools have always attempted to build up good personal relationships between themselves and their pupils in the hope of improving the children's academic self-concept. Paradoxically, the strength of this relationship may be in itself problematic – the more that a pupil's self-concept is dependent upon a strong relationship with the teacher, the greater the risk involved should the pupil fail to satisfy the teacher's demands publicly in front of the other pupils. Hence the widespread strategy used by pupils during class discussion and questioning of trying to avoid answering the question until they are certain of the answer that the teacher requires.

ANSWERING QUESTIONS TO PLEASE THE TEACHER

The pupils' need to please the teacher by attempting to offer the answer that they think the teacher wants is illustrated by the experiments reported by Donaldson with respect to 6-year-old children who were being tested to discover whether they were able to conserve number. In one experiment carried out by McGarrigle, children were shown two rows of equal length each containing five buttons. Having confirmed that the children knew that there were the same number of buttons in each of the rows, the researcher then rearranged one row so that the spaces between the buttons were no longer the same, thereby making one row longer than the other. When pupils were then asked if there were the same number of buttons in both rows, 84 per cent of the children appeared not to understand number conservation, confusing the number of buttons on each of the rows with the length of the row. This finding confirmed the earlier work of Piaget concerning the age levels at which children might be expected to reach this developmental stage. However, when the researcher no longer asked the question directly but instead introduced a small mischievous teddy bear who 'messed things up' by moving the buttons, the children's responses changed. McGarrigle told the children that 'naughty teddy often got things wrong' and 'needed help'. Naughty teddy wanted to know whether the two rows of buttons were still the same. When the question was put in this way 63 per cent of the children were able to conserve number (McGarrigle and Donaldson 1975).

Although, as Meadows (1986) points out, the reasons for failing to make satisfactory comparisons between the two sets of buttons are complex, one factor clearly concerns the effect of the perceived relationship between the adult researcher who was asking the questions and the child. The children in this experiment appeared to offer the adult the answer that they thought was wanted, whereas with the 'naughty teddy' they felt able to be more open in their response. There is evidence that the response of the child is not simply a function of an adult presence but relates to the perceived role of the adult in the learning situation, since the teddy bear can be replaced by a friendly, clumsy adult who comes into the room and accidentally upsets the buttons (Hargreaves *et al.* 1982). Thus it is the social context that largely determines the pupils' response. A teacher may be warm and friendly, as prescribed by the direct instruction model, but this classroom climate may induce in the children a dependency upon the teacher and an unwillingness to take risks when answering the teacher's questions or working independently on a challenging problem.

FEAR OF FAILURE AND PUPILS' SELF-CONCEPT

One striking example of this kind of pupil behaviour occurs in John Holt's book *How Children Fail*. From descriptions of his lessons, Holt is obviously a very charismatic teacher with a warm relationship with his pupils. They often engage in friendly banter and talk, particularly towards the end of a teaching session when things are relaxed and the work has been satisfactorily completed. On one of these occasions Holt describes how he jokingly asked the students in a matter-of-fact way what it felt like when he asked them a question. He recounts how he saw suspicion in every child's eyes and how the relaxed atmosphere in the class suddenly evaporated. Eventually one child responded, 'We gulp.' Holt goes on to comment:

> He [the child] spoke for everyone. They all began to clamour and all said the same thing, that when the teacher asked them a question and they didn't know the answer they were scared half to death. I was flabbergasted. . . . I asked them why they felt gulpish. They said they were afraid of failing, afraid of being kept back, afraid of being called stupid, afraid of feeling themselves stupid.
>
> What is most surprising of all is how much fear there is in school. . . . Most children in school are very scared. Like good soldiers they control their fears, live with them and adjust to them. But the trouble is, and here is a vital difference between school and war, the adjustments children make to their fears are almost wholly bad, destructive of their intelligence and capacity.
>
> (Holt 1984: 70–1)

The exchanges with 9-year-olds who were part of the follow-up project of the first ORACLE study, 'Effective group work in the primary classroom', describe similar feelings. In response to the same question that Holt asked his students – 'What do you feel like when the teacher asks you a question?' – these pupils replied:

FIRST PUPIL: It's like walking on a tightrope.
SECOND PUPIL: We guess.
FIRST PUPIL: And then we get found out and you don't know the answer.
THIRD PUPIL: Then you wait until the teacher tells you and says, 'Oh yes, that's it.'

Here the third pupil goes to extraordinary lengths to save face in front of the teacher and the other children, thus preserving his self-image as a competent student.

Kutnick (1988), however, argues that the global concept of self, with its components of 'self-identity, self-worth, self-esteem' may not be solely academic or socially related as the above exchange would suggest. It may also be influenced by the pupils' 'sense of control over the environment and the quality of the relationships' (Kutnick 1988: 167). There is support for this view from the open education studies in the United States. Giaconia and Hedges (1982) found a consistent effect of enhancing the student's self-concept when comparisons were made between the more successful open education systems and those where there were only small differences between the classrooms practising the open education and the controls. In the successful classes, not only were teachers able to provide a warm, co-operative atmosphere but pupils also made good progress and the pupils' self-concepts were enhanced. In English classrooms it may also be that the pupils' feeling of control over their immediate environment exerts as important an effect on the way in which the children perceive themselves as does avoiding getting things wrong.

OWNERSHIP AND CONTROL OF THE LEARNING PROCESS

Certainly, this view is supported by researchers such as Michael Armstrong (1980, 1981) and Stephen Rowland (1984, 1987). Rowland, the teacher in whose class Armstrong carried out his observations, rejects the main assumption of the direct instruction model 'that the teacher should be in control' of the learning environment. Instead he wishes to reconceptualise teaching as being principally 'a task of active observation and interpretation, rather than one of informing and instilling' (Rowland 1987: 121).

Unlike earlier forms of progressivism which emphasise freedom of choice, either child or teacher may provide the initial stimulus for the activity, although the child must be free to interpret the stimulus in a way that excites their interest. In this way the pupil is not trying to guess what is in the teacher's mind as in the earlier examples of questioning.

Rowland illustrates this notion that children should take control of their learning by relating a story about Dean, a 10-year-old boy who was engaged in examining and making homes for a collection of caterpillars. Rowland describes how, initially, Dean decided to call his caterpillars by special names rather than the real names of the different varieties. Some were called 'Mr Diet' while some were called 'Arthur' or 'Cyril' and others 'Stannage'. While watching another pupil draw the caterpillars, Dean noticed that one of his 'Cyril' varieties had six legs and ten suckers, whereas most of the other 'Cyrils' had only four suckers. Rowland, thinking to use this difference in order to suggest a criterion for classification, proposed that together he and Dean list the different varieties and make up a table on which they record the number of legs, the number of suckers and other characteristics.

However, after the conversation, Dean went away and recorded in his table a totally different set of categories based upon colour, fatness, degree of hairiness, the location in which they were found and a further category called 'sameness'. Rowland was puzzled by the need for the column 'sameness', having assumed that 'the purpose of such a table was to list the attributes of different classes of caterpillar', whereas 'Dean, apparently, saw it as a way of recording the attributes of his different individual creatures'. Dean decided to put the caterpillars in pairs and then say whether they were identical, at which point Rowland questioned the need for the column 'sameness'.

On the following day the reasoning behind Dean's classification became clear. It appeared that sameness was defined solely in terms of the entries into the column and did not relate 'directly to the appearance of the insects or whether, on some evidence, he thought they were of the same type'. Having selected a pair with the same attributes of colour, fatness, hairiness and location, Dean then decided he needed a name, not like those he had invented but 'their real names'. At this point, according to Rowland,

> Dean seemed to have discovered a need for a taxonomy. Having selected (what he considered to be) criterion attributes by which to describe the caterpillars, he saw that a class could be made of those creatures with identical attributes, and that such a class should be given a name. It was this identity of selected attributes rather than direct appearances which characterised Dean's conception of class and is indeed central to any such system of classification.
>
> (Rowland 1987: 125)

From this account, Rowland argues that, although Dean's approach may seem somewhat eccentric (and therefore unpredictable) to us, Dean 'would never have confronted problems of classification and taxonomy in such depth' if he had followed the teacher's suggestions of tabulating his inventive names for the caterpillars against the teacher's selection of attributes. More importantly, when Rowland looked back on the episode he was able to say that Dean's search for understanding 'actually sharpened my own understanding of what a taxonomy is about' so that 'these three ideas of inventing, discovering a need and the teacher acting as a reflective agent are crucial elements in the learning process' (Rowland 1987: 126).

During this 'reflecting' process the roles of the teacher and pupil are often exchanged, so that sometimes the teacher reverts to the position of an instructor. Following on from the early observations, Dean decided to weigh the caterpillars and devised a method for doing so. This involved the use of fractions, which Dean had not yet reached in his graded primary mathematics scheme, so Rowland carried out a small lesson on the blackboard. After this Dean was able to add various fractions in order to record the weight of each caterpillar. Rowland then suggested that Dean did some more work on fractions and Dean made use of books that were two to three years ahead of his age group. Dean had 'no difficulty in tackling the tasks set so long as such tasks bear a direct and understood relationship to the activity over which he has recently exercised control' (Rowland 1987: 128).

The results of interviews carried out with pupils during the second stage of the ORACLE project, 'Effective group work in the primary classroom', confirm the importance of this idea of 'ownership'. In the classroom where pupils rated working in groups in the absence of the teacher as the 'most liked' activity – unlike the remainder of the sample – the children said this was because:

PUPIL 1:   When you are in groups you can discuss it, can't you, instead of working on your own. It's better working on your own than working with the class.

PUPIL 2:   I think it is best when the teacher comes because they don't want you to mess about. Because when you are on your own you are always talking about other things but when you are with the teacher you start working harder.

PUPIL 3:   Yes, the teacher helps you. She gives you different ideas.

PUPIL 1:   I think the teacher wants to put her view into what you are thinking which might make you change your mind about something. You know, instead of keeping to your own idea.

PUPIL 4:   Teachers stop you if you are right. Say you get, say your answer's right and they think it is wrong, well they will stop you and put what they think they want you to do. They don't like you to do your own work but sometimes they do.

PUPIL 2:   When you have to do something, like we have had that before and you have got to do a certain number of things, when the teacher comes up telling you you've got a right good idea you go away and do it and they will come back and alter it all and they will make you do something else and [tell you] it's got to be like this.

INTERVIEWER: Now, why do you think that is?

PUPIL 1:   Because they think it is best.

INTERVIEWER: Because they think it's best?

PUPIL 1:   Because they think it could be improved.

INTERVIEWER: Does that stop you putting your ideas as well?

CHORUS OF
PUPILS: No.

INTERVIEWER: You can still put your ideas forward then?

CHORUS OF
PUPILS: Yes.

INTERVIEWER: OK. So what do you feel like if you think your idea is a good idea and then it happens like you say and the teacher comes and changes it?

PUPIL 2:   You feel a bit upset. You have put all that work into it and then the teacher suddenly changes it.

PUPIL 3:   You get a bit mad with her?

PUPIL 1:   You don't feel it is your piece of work. You feel as if it is the teacher's. When you have done everything to it and you think, that's my piece of work and no one else has done owt to it. But when the teacher has done something to it it don't feel as good.

In this school, many of the teachers were considered outstanding and there were frequent visits by other teachers from the local authority to see the staff at work. They shared a determination to provide children with opportunities for ownership of their ideas. They saw the learning experience as something to be shared with children and also, as with Rowland, saw the importance of their taking the role of 'critic rather than assessor'. Yet even in this school there still remained some of the uncertainties in the teacher–pupil relationship described by John Holt. This reflects the way in which the child in the conservation of number experiment responded to McGarrigle's question about whether there were more or fewer buttons in the rearranged row.

This uncertainty emerged later on in the interview described earlier, when the pupils began to argue that working in groups helped to prevent the teacher from imposing their ideas:

PUPIL 1: When the teacher comes over and they disagree with something that you are doing, if all the group agrees with it then the teacher has got no point of view really because if all the children don't agree with the teacher then there is just one person and they end up just not doing it. When there is just one teacher and one child working together, if the teacher says something and the child goes opposite, it's the teacher that gets their own way because the child's a bit frightened of the teacher.

OTHER PUPILS: Yes.

INTERVIEWER: Do you all think that is true?

CHORUS OF PUPILS: Yes.

INTERVIEWER: But the teachers here are very friendly so why would you be frightened?

CHORUS OF PUPILS: (All shouting out and interrupting each other.)

PUPIL 2: You get nervous when someone is around. You feel uncomfortable. . . . If you do anything wrong you think 'Oh No'.

INTERVIEWER: So it is fear of doing things wrong, is that what it is?

CHORUS OF PUPILS: Yes.

PUPIL 1: You get a book and start reading because you know the teachers are watching you.

INTERVIEWER: OK. So why can't we have a system, which is what I think the teachers would like, where, when they come to the group and sit down they just listen to what you are saying? They just listen and therefore learn what you are thinking about. They say, let me tell you what they say, that if they try to do that you all shut up and wait for them to take over

PUPIL 3:

the discussion group and tell them things. They find that's a problem. Is it true?

Some teachers try to do that but we won't let them listen because they [the pupils] think they [the teacher] will change your ideas about something.

One weakness of Rowland's account of teaching by negotiation is that the presentation of this key concept of ownership is relatively unproblematic. The teacher is seen as someone who helps to facilitate ownership by supporting and promoting pupils' ideas. Yet although the teacher's intention is to provide the appropriate amount of guidance and help so that the pupils produce outcomes of quality that increase their 'self-confidence and self-esteem', thereby 'motivating them to undertake further tasks' (Nias 1988: 130), it seems from the above extract that the pupils found it difficult to distinguish between the different roles of the teacher as helper and guide on some occasions and as arbiter of behaviour on others. [In Nias' 1988 study, all] six teachers, for example, argued that when they were engaged in purposeful learning based upon negotiation, their relationship with the children had to be 'authentic' and 'reciprocal . . . a two way thing' (Nias 1988: 135). They had to feel secure: that is, 'in control' and 'free from the constant need to shout'. In contrast, whenever they felt they were in a state of latent, potential or actual conflict with their pupils, they were aware of the need to 'act a role, to be a policeman, a boss figure, the teacher'. Only 'when they felt relaxed, easy, not frightened any more – that is, when they could be themselves in the classroom – were they ready to pass more and more responsibility for learning to their pupils' (Nias 1988: 133). But for the pupils in the ORACLE studies taking part in the interview about group work, there was still a problem:

PUPIL 1:

You never know when they are going to shout at you. Sometimes you can be saying something and they like agree with you but like next minute they can just turn against you and shout at you for something like that.

AMBIGUITY THEORY AND PROGRESSIVE PRACTICE

Thus one explanation for the failure fully to implement progressive or informal practice can be termed the 'ambiguity' theory. A crucial stage of this concerns the setting or negotiating of new tasks and activities. As Doyle (1979, 1986) points out, when setting tasks in the classroom teachers have in mind a variety of purposes, based partly on their perception of the needs of individual children. The more complex the task, the greater the possible range of purposes and therefore the greater the ambiguity, with the risk that the child will misinterpret the teacher's intention. For example, in a recent observation of creative writing, a teacher encouraged the children to draft and redraft stories using the approach recommended by Graves (1983). When the stories were finally completed the children were allowed to use the word processor to produce a final version for inclusion in a book of stories. Seen from the pupils' eyes, the teacher displayed a remarkable degree of inconsistency. Some children, having produced pages of writing, were made to redraft it further, while others who produced six lines were allowed to use the computer. The teacher was able in each case to justify these decisions in terms of the pupils' special needs. One child who had written several pages was at a stage where the teacher felt 'she needed to develop her ideas further, they were becoming stereotyped', while the child who wrote six lines 'had concentrated well, which was unusual for him and had also worked well with the other children in his group'. The children, however, were not party to these deliberations. When asked by the observer how they knew when their work was ready to be published, they replied 'we take it to the teacher and he tells us'.

There is considerable evidence that tasks, such as story-writing, do indeed appear to be carried out more successfully if the children can feel that they have ownership over their ideas (Cowie 1989). However, in taking on this ownership, children have to accept the risk of having their ideas evaluated critically. This risk can be reduced if the child has some idea of the criteria being used for this evaluation. During the 'Effective group work in the primary classroom' project, it was very noticeable how repeatedly children complained about not understanding why teachers made certain decisions. As one pupil put it,

> If I could see what it was learning me I could do it but I don't see what it's learning me. I am not really bothered because I want to know what it's learning me. One teacher, Miss Preston, did say that if you don't like what we are giving you come and tell us about it but I think lots of people are frightened to do that.

Teachers would emphasise the importance of the processes rather than the product of the learning, but rarely tried to explain to children why they were being asked to do certain activities at times when there was a need to direct the learning or to introduce a new topic. Indeed, some teachers made a point of saying that they thought that 'children of this age don't need to under- stand why they do things'. In one example children were investigating various ways of measuring time, using an assortment of materials such as sand, water and plastic bottles. Both teachers under observation began by emphasising the importance of time and gave very precise instructions about *how* the children were to proceed with the task and *how* they were to not worry too much about results because what mattered was their ideas. As the children began to assemble the apparatus, it was noticeable that almost every pupil had on their wrist a cheap digital watch; to some of them, at least, it must have seemed strange that they should need to engage in an attempt to measure time in a variety of crude ways when a more accurate method was immediately to hand. With hindsight it would have been relatively easy for the teacher to explain that the main purpose of the exercise was not to measure time but to provide a problem-solving exercise where certain science skills could be developed. However, in the earlier example of developing children's writing skills through publishing, it would have been less easy for the teacher to explain the reasons for what appeared to be unfair treatment of some children as compared to others, without embarrassing the child who was allowed to publish only six lines. None the less, the pupils have eventually to face up to their limitations. The pupil who was allowed to publish six lines told the observer: 'When we have finished we have to read each other's stories. I watch what the others are reading but no one reads mine.'

DO AS YOU THINK AND DO AS YOU'RE TOLD

An even greater ambiguity in setting classroom tasks stems from the fact, as Doyle (1983) points out, that tasks have not only an academic content but also a behavioural purpose. The teacher's main purpose during a question and answer session may be to tease out the children's ideas so that the lesson may be shaped in terms of the pupils' concerns rather than the teacher's. At any one time a question may also be used to see if a child is paying attention. The pupil therefore has to work out what kind of question they are being asked. Is it the kind where a speculative answer will be praised or where a wrong answer will be seized upon as evidence of inattention? This sort of dilemma offers another excuse for pupils to adopt a strategy of avoidance – they leave someone else to make the initial responses until the purpose behind the teacher's questions becomes clear. Similarly, when writing it may not always be clear to the pupil what the difference is between redrafting and being made to do corrections.

Rowland (1987) argues that in negotiating ownership with children one removes the need to exercise authoritarian control over behaviour. Nias (1988) is more cautious and admits uncertainty about the causality of this process. It may be, therefore, that the form of the control exercised over the pupils' behaviour by the teacher largely determines whether pupils perceive the teacher's interventions as collaboration or as a 'take-over'. Thus when children regard control of the classroom organisation and of their behaviour as primarily the teacher's responsibility, then, because they are unable to distinguish easily between the teacher's role as 'policeman' and as 'negotiator', they play safe and seek to hand back responsibility for the learning to the teacher. Only in circumstances where the teacher is seen in a similar light to 'the mischievous friendly teddy bear' do the children appear able to resolve this basic ambiguity between a desire for 'ownership' and 'fear of getting things wrong' – which was so strikingly revealed in the interview transcripts earlier in the chapter. The strength of this 'fear of wrong-doing' is confirmed by other studies, notably that by Barrett (1986), who interviewed 5-year-old children during their first few weeks in the reception class. She reported the children's impressions when shown a series of photographs:

> A boy doesn't know what to do. He is sucking his pencil. He cannot do his work. He must tell the teacher.

> I don't know how to do it. I didn't know how to paint or mix colours properly.

> I didn't like to write when I came to school. I couldn't make a snail. I couldn't draw a picture. It was too hard. I was too little. I feel miserable when I can't do it. I am frightened I might get it wrong.

> (Barrett 1986: 82)

Social learning theorists, such as Bandura (1986), point out that all learning is influenced by the way in which the learner views what he is being asked to learn. If learners are to reconstruct knowledge, they require suitable explanations not only of *what* they are being asked to do but also of *why* they are being asked to do it.

It appears that many teachers have, intuitively, modified the original prescriptions for progressivism as contained in the Plowden Committee's Report (1967), with its emphasis on a curriculum based upon choice and the interests of the children, an organisation largely devoted to individual work, and a teaching method providing individual attention and emphasising discovery learning. In the 'revised form of progressivism', choice is no longer about *what* task to do but more importantly about *how* to do it. Whether the teacher or the pupil initiates the activity, it is important that the pupil feels they retain a degree of control over the way in which the task should be carried out. During this process the teacher tries to build upon the child's partial understandings so that the pupil can reconstruct their knowledge and ideas in ways that make them more generally applicable to a wider range of problems. The teacher also has a role as an instructor in this process, but it is likely, on the evidence of the research findings on direct instruction, that this help will generally relate to lower-order cognitive tasks to do with areas such as reading, computation and study skills. During complex challenging tasks the introduction of these periods of instruction must be carried out skilfully so that children see them as useful additions to their own activities rather than as something imposed unilaterally by the teacher.

For children to feel in control of their learning, teachers need to explain not only what children are required to do but why a particular instruction is relevant to the activity. As part of this better understanding by children of the 'why' as well as the 'what', the teacher's role in relation to the outcomes of the activity changes. Rather than simply assessing the child's work, there is a need for a critical dialogue in which the teacher's and other pupils' views are offered as part of an ongoing debate about the quality of the final product. This is a most difficult area because the teacher needs to be simultaneously supportive of what the child has achieved but also critical so that clear standards are set and agreed between all participants in the learning process.

A crucial factor in ensuring that such evaluation is seen by pupils as a positive contribution to the development of their ideas, rather than as an indication of the teacher's displeasure, is the way in which the relationship between the teacher and the children extends beyond the learning activity to the management of behaviour and control in the classroom. It would appear that when setting out to implement the Plowden ideology, many teachers did so within a traditional framework of control. This created much ambiguity as children attempted to assimilate the teacher's hidden message – when it's learning 'do as you think', but when it's behaviour 'do as I say'. Children are particularly vulnerable at an early stage of an activity when they are uncertain about the status of the response that they can expect from the teacher. In these circumstances the pupils will return to well-tried strategies of avoidance in which responsibility for control of the learning is returned to the teacher. The evidence suggests that teachers who can successfully implement a 'negotiated' learning model also seem able to use similar strategies to control the children's behaviour.

Teachers who wish children to engage in independent learning require pupils who are unafraid, self-reliant and self-disciplined, but it is precisely pupils with these kinds of qualities who are likely to react badly to the teacher's imposition of control over their behaviour. If the teacher continually exercises power, particularly when conflicts occur over matters of behaviour, pupils will conform either out of fear of embarrassment or fear that they will lose status and therefore self-esteem. This strategy of avoidance requires them to be dependent upon the teacher for clues about what constitutes acceptable behaviour and this dependency transmits itself to their work.

SHARING RESPONSIBILITY FOR THE TEACHER'S NEEDS

The alternative approach involves, whenever necessary, shared decision-making, with consideration given to both the teacher's and pupils' needs. This differs from the behaviour modification process where the emphasis is on the teacher's wants. Initially, this negotiated approach requires teachers to face their pupils with explanations of their needs so that the children can accept their share of responsibility. Thus teachers try to say not 'I want quiet' but 'I need quiet because I can't give out these instructions'.

It cannot be said too often that the negotiated approach does not hand over control to the children. Children need to exercise their freedoms within a framework, so they need to know which solutions to problems that they suggest are unacceptable to the teacher because they do not meet the teacher's needs. Nor does the approach mean that teachers should never tell children what to do. Telling a class to sit down or to work quietly only becomes a problem if the children decide to exert their power by reason of their numbers and refuse to comply. It is at this juncture that the non-evaluative 'I' messages are required.

Over the years a number of schools in the various ORACLE studies have developed procedures that make use of these principles. One teacher devotes Friday afternoons to 'an open discussion', in which issues of rules and procedures are debated. Another school constructed a paper brick wall with a face appearing over the top and the caption 'It isn't fair'. Both children and teachers could take a yellow paper brick and write about something that wasn't fair and place it on the wall. Each week the yellow bricks would be collected and form part of class discussion.

When teachers use their authority to control the class and are unable to resolve the conflict at their first attempt the only recourse is to increase the power. This process can be stressful because the individual is on trial, in the eyes of both the pupils and the other teachers. Negotiating rules of behaviour has one great advantage. Although it may take time to agree the rules, the rules are everybody's so that if they are broken it is no longer a defeat, in personal terms, for the teacher. One teacher described this reduction in stress after she had undergone Gordon's programme:

> I was ready to quit teaching because of the constant need to be a disciplinarian. The course showed me that the real problem was my rules. I made them and I had to enforce them. That's all I accomplished most of the time. When I let the class set the rules this changed. I have time to teach now and the students like me more because I am a teacher instead of a disciplinarian. I don't know if they learn any more but we have a lot more fun learning it.
>
> (Gordon 1974: 272)

REFERENCES

Armstrong, M. (1980) *Closely Observed Children*, London: Writers and Readers Co-operative and Chameleon Press.
—— (1981) 'The case of Louise and the painting of landscape', in J. Nixon (ed.) *A Teacher's Guide to Action Research*, London: Grant McIntyre.
Bandura, A. (1986) *Social Foundations of Thought and Action*, Englewood Cliffs, NJ: Prentice-Hall.
Barrett, G. (1986) *Starting School: an Evaluation of the Experience*, Final Report to the AMMA (Assistant Masters and Mistresses Association), CARE (Centre for Applied Research in Education), University of East Anglia.
Burns, R. (1982) *Self-concept, Development and Education*, London: Holt, Rinehart & Winston.

Cowie, M. (1989) 'Children as writers', in D. Hargreaves (ed.) *Children and the Arts*, Milton Keynes: Open University Press.

Doyle, W. (1979) 'Classroom tasks and student abilities', in P. Peterson and H.J. Walberg (eds) *Research on Teaching: Concepts, Findings and Implications*, Berkeley, CA: McCutchan.

—— (1983) 'Academic work', *Review of Educational Research*, 53(2): 159–99.

—— (1986) 'Classroom organisation and management', in M. Wittrock (ed.) *Third Handbook of Research on Teaching*, New York: Macmillan.

Giaconia, R.M. and Hedges, L. (1982) 'Identifying features of effective open education', *Review of Educational Research*, 52: 579–602.

Gordon, T. (1974) *TET: Teacher Effectiveness Training*, New York: Peter Wyden.

Graves, D. (1983) *Writing: Teachers and Children at Work*, Exeter, NH: Heinemann.

Hargreaves, D., Molloy, C. and Pratt, A. (1982) 'Social factors in conservation', *British Journal of Psychology*, 73: 231–4.

Holt, J. (1984) *How Children Fail*, rev. edn, Harmondsworth: Penguin.

Kutnick, P. (1988) *Relationships in the Primary School Classroom*, London: Paul Chapman.

McGarrigle, J. and Donaldson, M. (1975) 'Conservation accidents', *Cognition*, 3: 314–50.

Meadows, S. (1986) *Understanding Child Development*, London: Hutchinson.

Nias, J. (1988) 'Informal education in action: teachers' accounts', in A. Blyth (ed.) *Informal Primary Education Today*, London: Falmer Press.

Rowland, S. (1984) *The Enquiring Classroom*, Lewes: Falmer Press.

—— (1987) 'An interpretative model of teaching and learning', in A. Pollard (ed.) *Children and their Primary Schools*, London: Falmer Press.

The use of primary teachers' time
Some implications for beginning teachers

R.J. Campbell and S.R. St J. Neill

Although there has been a great deal of research on how pupils spend their time in class, until recently very little was known about how primary teachers used their time. Chapter 6 provides detailed quantitative evidence of the varied demands on teachers' time, both in and, increasingly, outside the classroom. Perhaps surprisingly to those new to teaching, it shows that less than half the teachers' working week is spent in contact with children, and less than a third is spent teaching the curriculum. Essential reading for beginning teachers who want to find out exactly what the job of primary teaching entails, Campbell and Neill include details of how teachers have been managing the curriculum, the time spent on each subject and the time spent on assessment.

BACKGROUND

In this chapter we attempt to draw some implications, for those beginning teaching, from research we carried out in 1991 into the work of primary teachers. The research describes and analyses quantitative data about teachers' time – what activities teachers spent their time on when working, and how much time they spent on them – in order to draw a picture of the typical pattern of teachers' work. In using the research evidence as our starting point, we have a different approach to the issues from that of the Council for the Accreditation of Teacher Education (CATE) which has tended to produce a specification of criteria or competencies that beginning teachers should possess. These embody qualitative values. For example, a DFE Circular proposes that:

2.3 Newly qualified teachers should be able to:
    2.3.1 produce coherent lesson plans which take account of NCATs [National Curriculum Attainment Targets] and of the school's curriculum policies; [. . .]
    2.3.4 employ a range of teaching strategies appropriate to the age, ability and attainment level of pupils;

2.3.5   present subject content in clear language and in a stimulating
        manner.

(DFE Circular 9/90, Annex A, para. 2.3)

CATE does not say how much time teachers should devote to each activity,
nor does it specify clearly how these skills should be learned (Neill 1991).
Our approach is much less ambitious than that of CATE, but we see it as
complementary, rather than oppositional, to it. Our approach may be of
especial interest to beginning teachers concerned to manage their time
effectively, in so far as that is a realisable ambition.

There is a large and sophisticated research literature on how primary
pupils spend their time in classrooms (e.g. Bennett *et al.* 1980; Galton and
Simon 1980; Alexander 1992), but relatively little is known about how
primary teachers spend their time on work, whether inside or outside
classrooms. The 'baseline' study in the field (Hilsum and Cane 1971) used
direct observational techniques in order to develop a picture of the work of
129 junior teachers in Surrey in 1969. The study claimed to have exploded
the myth of teaching as a 9 to 4 job, since it showed the teachers working a
44.5-hour week, 42 per cent of which was in the teachers' 'own' time. The
researchers drew particular attention to the finding that much of teachers'
work was outside the classroom, and that if all that was involved in the true
nature of teachers' work was to be understood, focusing exclusively or
principally on classrooms was inappropriate. They summarised this point (in
their now unfashionably sexist language) as follows:

> Teachers have often protested that their work outside the classroom goes
> unrecognised, and that the image of the teacher held by many outside the
> profession is far too narrow, in that he is thought of primarily as a
> practitioner in a classroom. Our figures show that less than three-fifths of
> the teacher's working day was spent in direct contact with classes: 15 per
> cent of the day was spent in the school but without class contact, and a
> quarter of the working day was spent entirely outside school hours.
> These facts lend weight to the suggestion that an understanding and
> appreciation of the teacher's role as a professional person will not come
> from a study of the classroom alone: his work and interaction with pupils
> in the classroom setting may be an important, perhaps the most import-
> ant, aspect of his professional life, but it must be seen in the wider context
> of the totality of his work.

(Hilsum and Cane 1971: 91)

Since Hilsum and Cane conducted their research, the framework within
which teachers work has been altered by statute, in two fundamental ways.
One concerns teacher time and the other concerns the curriculum.

Directed and non-directed time

The Teachers' Pay and Conditions Act 1987, and the annual orders flowing from it, specified that teachers could be required to work on not more than 195 days a year, of which 190 were days on which they could be required to teach pupils. The other five 'non-pupil' days are normally used for in-service training, but may be used for other purposes. Teachers can be required to work at the direction of their head for a maximum of 1,265 hours per year. Colloquially known as 'directed time', this is equivalent to about 33 hours per week, in an assumed 39-week working year. Any other time spent on work – 'non-directed time' – is discretionary in the sense that it is not directed by the headteacher. It was specified loosely: 'such additional hours as may be necessary to enable them to discharge effectively their professional duties' (School Teachers' Pay and Conditions Document, 1989, para. 36(1)(f)). It might be thought that the specification that teachers can be directed to work only 33 hours a week in a 39-week year reinforces the public image of teaching as a job with short hours and long holidays.

Curriculum

The Education Reform Act 1988 laid down criteria that the curriculum in a maintained school should meet, and in the orders that flowed from the Act, established central control over the content of the curriculum (programmes of study) and indicators of progress (attainment targets and statements of attainment), and assessment arrangements – including the assessment of performance in the three core subjects by means of Standard Assessment Tasks (SATs) – at the end of each Key Stage.

The 1988 Act also altered certain conditions of employment of teachers (the governing body of a school was given the power to appoint and to dismiss teachers) and the basis upon which schools were funded and managed.

We were interested to see whether these changes in the legal and political framework had altered the nature of the teacher's job, and we undertook at Warwick University a series of studies, funded by the Assistant Masters and Mistresses Association and the Association of Education Committees Trust, into the nature of primary teaching in the post-ERA period. The studies involved 401 Key Stage 1 and Key Stage 2 teachers, who provided records of just over 4,000 working days, in 1990, 1991 and 1992. The teachers were not observed teaching, but they each kept a specially devised record of the time they spent on work for seven or fourteen continuous days, between 7 in the morning and midnight.

The record had five main categories of activity: namely, Teaching, Preparation, Administration, Professional Development and Other Activities. These main categories were broken down into twenty-five sub-categories. We thus had a record of work that included weekdays and weekends, and time in school and out of school.

At the end of the recording period the teachers completed a questionnaire covering their professional biography, working conditions and their perceptions of their work. (For fuller details see Campbell and Neill 1990, 1992; Campbell *et al.* 1991.) Except where stated otherwise, the data used in this chapter were collected across one whole year (1991) from 192 Key Stage 1 and 2 teachers from three local authorities. All were full-time class teachers.

HOW DO PRIMARY TEACHERS SPEND THEIR TIME?

Total time on work

We were able to show that the teachers were working an average total of 53.5 hours a week. Of this time, 41 hours were spent on school premises, and 12.5 off them, mostly at home. The teachers spent 5.5 hours on work at weekends, and 48 hours during the five weekdays. These overall figures are similar to those found in three other studies (Coopers and Lybrand Deloitte 1991; Lowe 1991; NAS/UWT 1991) also carried out in 1991. Despite different samples and methodologies, these studies reported teachers working between 51 and 55 hours a week. Thus the first thing that a beginning teacher might note about primary teaching as a job is that it consumes large amounts of time during term time; on average the teachers worked a nine-and-a-half-hour working day during the week, and a further two and a half hours each day at the weekend. Another way to think of the overall time is to imagine that the teachers had their weekends free of work, and had carried out all their work during the five weekdays. If this happened, they would spend an average of over ten hours on work each weekday.

The figures above are averages, and disguise considerable individual variation. At the extremes one teacher spent 36.75 hours, whilst another spent 77.0 hours per week on work; the 'top' 20 per cent of teachers worked on average 62.3 hours and the 'bottom' 20 per cent worked for 43.9 hours per week. Yet all were involved in the same basic job: namely, class teaching. This shows the great extent of discretion teachers exercise over how much time to spend on their work. What influenced teachers in this respect was not *positional* variables, such as the number of responsibilities they held, or incentive allowances, or size of class, but *personal* sense of obligation, or conscientiousness. The more of their own time they thought it was reasonable for them to be expected to devote to work, the more time they actually spent. Despite the new statutory frameworks within which they work, primary teachers are vocationally, rather than contractually, driven. For beginning teachers the implication is that how much of their own time to spend on work is a matter for their individual sense of obligation, but they will be entering an occupational culture which lays heavy stress on conscience rather than contract; they will be expected to work as long as is necessary to meet children's needs rather than to meet the letter of the law.

However, a third point needs stressing at this stage. The amount of time that the teachers were spending on work was almost ten hours a week more than they thought was reasonable. When we interviewed a group of infant teachers (see Campbell *et al.* 1991), we found that the long hours they were spending on work were causing stress, mainly due to the conflicting time demands of their domestic and work situations. Not all the stress is directly attributable to the 1988 Act, since research predating the Act (Nias 1989; PSRDG 1989) suggests that primary teaching is intrinsically stressful. However, beginning teachers with heavy domestic responsibilities may expect to face conflicting demands of this kind, and it is as well to be aware of the possibility in advance.

Distribution of teachers' time

We were able to show the way the teachers' time was distributed among the five main categories of work (see Table 6.1).

Table 6.1 Time spent on 5 main categories of work, expressed (a) in hours, and (b) as percentages of the total time on work

Category	(a) Hrs	(b) %
Teaching	18.7	35
Preparation	15.9	30
Administration	14.1	26
Professional development	5.9	11
Other activities	5.5	10
Total time on work	53.5	100

Three points emerge. First the sum of the hours spent on the individual categories (60.1 hours) is greater than the total time on work. This is because teachers often carried out two or more activities simultaneously (such as teaching mathematics (Teaching) and mounting a display (Administration)). The work of primary teachers is characterised by frequently having to do two different things at once, a feature that explains why the teachers felt pressured during the school day. Column (b) of Table 6.1 shows that teachers' work is a '112 per cent' job. We also found that two-fifths of their breaktimes, including lunchtimes, were taken up with work. It should be added here that we found two-thirds of teachers saying consistently across the years 1990–92 that 'lack of time' was the main obstacle to their implementing the National Curriculum.

Second, teaching the curriculum occupies only just over a third of teachers' time. Our category 'teaching' excludes some activities when

(a)

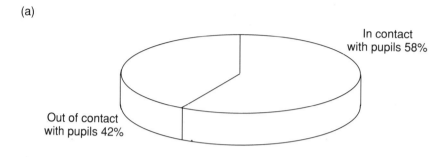

In contact
with pupils 58%

Out of contact
with pupils 42%

(b)

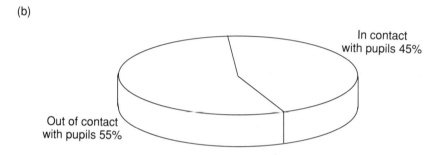

In contact
with pupils 45%

Out of contact
with pupils 55%

Figure 6.1 Proportions of time spent: (a) 1971; (b) 1991

teachers are in contact with pupils, such as registration and transition (that is, moving children from one place to another), attending assembly and supervision.

If these other activities, which in combination amounted to 5.4 hours a week, are added to the time spent on teaching, the sum of this time spent by teachers in contact with pupils amounts to 45 per cent of their total working time. This is a dramatic shift from 1971, when Hilsum and Cane found that 58 per cent of teachers' time was spent in contact with pupils, as Figure 6.1 illustrates.

The point to be drawn from the two pie charts is not that in 1991 teachers were spending less time with pupils in absolute terms, but that the job had been fundamentally restructured, with time away from pupils having increased compared to 1971, so that work with pupils was a smaller proportion of teachers' total work.

Two points need to be made here. Primary teachers gain most job satisfaction from the intrinsic psychic rewards of working with children (see Lortie 1971; Nias 1989), and thus the restructuring of the balance of their work towards more activities away from children is likely to be seen as comparatively unrewarding. Moreover, the restructuring reveals a shift towards a more 'extended professionality' (see Hoyle 1975) with time spent in professional development activities, such as in-service training, and in the 'collegial' (see Campbell 1985) working relations of staff meetings and meetings with other adults. In support of this, recent evidence (Muschamp *et al.* 1992; Campbell *et al.* 1991; NCC 1992; Core Subjects Association 1991; DES 1990) suggests that the introduction of the National Curriculum has led to increased amounts of whole-school planning, other school-based professional development and in-service training. Thus for all teachers, including beginners, small but substantial parts of the working week of teachers are spent working with other adults. The skills and sensitivities needed for this aspect of work are different from those needed to organise children's work.

The third point arising from Table 6.1 is of great significance for the beginning teacher who wishes to plan her time effectively. Preparation in our categorisation includes three sub-categories: lesson planning, marking and recording results, and organising resources. The amount of time spent on preparation in this sense was 15.9 hours a week. To this might be added 1.9 hours a week spent on professional reading (of curriculum documents, journals, and so on), giving a total of 17.8 hours. The ratio of teaching to preparation is 1:0.95. This means that for every hour that a teacher spends teaching, she spends very nearly another hour in planning, organising and follow-up marking and recording results. Hardly any teachers were able to do less preparation than an hour a day, and most averaged between two and three hours a day across the seven days.

THE DETAILED WORK PROFILE

The distribution of time shown in Table 6.1 is at a rather general level. We were able to show a more detailed profile using the 25 sub-categories that went to make up the five main categories. This is given as a bar chart below (Figure 6.2) and in tabular form as Table 6.2.

There are many points arising from Figure 6.2, but space permits us to deal only with the most salient to beginning teachers. We have clustered them under four main headings: the delivery of the National Curriculum and assessment, school routines, professional development and other activities.

Delivering the National Curriculum and assessment

The sum of time on the different subjects and assessment (31.8 hours) exceeded the 18.7 hours total time spent teaching by 70 per cent. It gives the '170 per cent curriculum'. This is because teachers taught more than one subject in many teaching sessions. For example, they might have a class topic integrating several subjects, or they might have one group doing maths, another doing English, and so on. A DES discussion paper (Alexander *et al.* 1992) raised the issue of whether the organisation in many classes was too

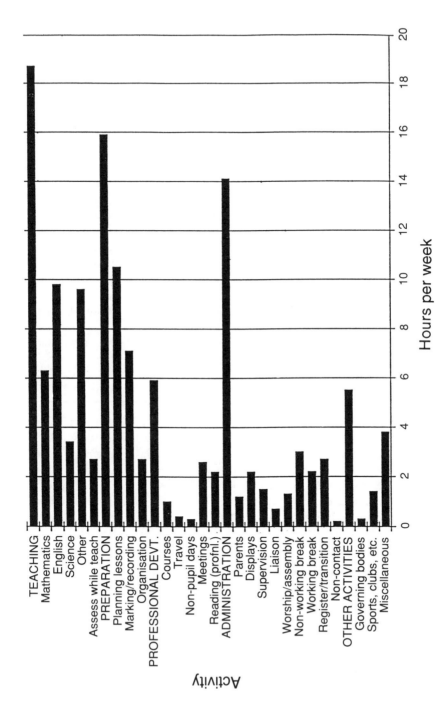

Figure 6.2 A profile of primary teachers' work in 25 sub-categories

Table 6.2 A profile of primary teachers' work in 25 sub-categories (time in hours per week)

Category	Hours/week
TEACHING (total)	18.7
English	9.8
Mathematics	6.3
Science	3.4
Other subjects	9.6
Assessing while teaching	2.7
PREPARATION (total)	15.9
Planning lessons	10.5
Marking/recording	7.1
Organising	2.7
ADMINISTRATION (total)	14.1
Parents	1.2
Displays	2.2
Liaison	0.7
Breaks (non-work)	3.0
Breaks (working)	2.2
Non-contact time (non-working)	0.2
Registration/transition	2.7
Supervision	1.5
Worship/assembly	1.3
PROFESSIONAL DEVELOPMENT (total)	5.9
In-service courses	1.0
Travel to in-service courses	0.4
Non-pupil days	0.3
Meetings	2.6
Professional reading	2.2
OTHER ACTIVITIES (total)	5.5
Governing bodies	0.3
Extra-curricular (sports, clubs, orchestras, etc.)	1.4
Miscellaneous	3.8

complex for effective class management. Our evidence does not bear directly upon that issue, but there are two points we would make. First, the Key Stage 1 teachers had more complex curricular organisation (they had a '200 per cent curriculum') than the Key Stage 2 teachers; and second, that integrated approaches are more time-consuming to plan, assess and record for National Curriculum purposes. This is because lesson planning for work involving integrated topics has to start from orders specified as single subjects, then combine parts of the subjects into the topic, then disaggregate them again for assessment and record-keeping purposes.

A second issue relates to the delivery of the broad and balanced curriculum required by the Act. Circular 5/89 (DES 1989) required that, from August 1989, all the foundation subjects and RE should have a 'reasonable' amount of time devoted to them to enable worthwhile study to take place. (The Secretary of State is not allowed to specify the time that must be given to any subject.) One of the problems is that there is no definition of what is reasonable, and it is therefore a matter of judgement that has to be made by each teacher, in the light of school policies and the needs of her pupils as she sees them. Some guidance was given to the National Curriculum subject working groups, and this is provided as Table 6.3. From this it can be seen that the three core subjects were expected to take about 50 per cent of the timetabled time, and the other foundation subjects, RE, other teaching, and assessment, were expected to occupy the remaining 50 per cent.

Table 6.3 Notional time for curriculum subjects

	KS1	KS2
MATHEMATICS	20	20
ENGLISH	20	20
SCIENCE AND TECHNOLOGY	12.5	12.5
HISTORY	7.5–10	7.5–10
GEOGRAPHY	7.5–10	7.5–10
ART	7.5	6
MUSIC	5	5
PHYSICAL EDUCATION	5	5
RELIGIOUS EDUCATION	5	5
OTHER TEACHING	5–10	6–11

Note: The figures are percentages of the time available for lessons, and exclude time in assembly, registration and breaks. The minimum lesson times suggested in DES Circular 7/90 were: for Key Stage 1, 21 hours per week, and for Key Stage 2, 23.5 hours per week.
Source: *Education*, 3 April 1992

We have constructed Table 6.4 below from the data in Table 6.2, which showed the actual time within which teaching of particular subjects was recorded. In Table 6.4 this time is shown as a percentage of two totals. In column (a) the time is expressed as a percentage of the total time spent teaching (18.7 hours), and represents the maximum possible time the teacher taught the subject. Because they taught several subjects simultaneously, it is greater than the time any one pupil would be learning the subject. In column (b) the time is expressed as a percentage of the sum of all the subjects. Column (b) is the nearest guide to the proportion of time spent by pupils on aspects of the curriculum, since it assumes that when more than one subject is being taught simultaneously, the subjects are evenly distributed among the pupils.

From Table 6.4, column (b), a problem of curriculum management is immediately obvious. There was only 30 per cent of the curriculum available for the delivery of the 6 non-core subjects, RE and any other teaching. Thirty per cent of the time at Key Stage 1 is 6.3 hours (0.8 hours per subject);

Table 6.4 Proportions of time recorded as spent on different aspects of teaching: time spent as a proportion of (a) total hours spent teaching, (b) the sum of all subjects and assessment

Subject	(a) (%)	(b) (%)
English	52	31
Mathematics	34	20
Science	18	11
Other subjects	51	30
Assessment	14	9

Total time spent teaching = 18.7 hours
Sum of all subjects and assessment = 31.8 hours

at Key Stage 2 it is 7.1 hours (0.9 hours per subject). The broad and balanced curriculum was not being delivered according to the 'reasonable time' expectation of DES Circular 5/89, or the assumptions shown in Table 6.3.

The explanation for this is partly that the teachers were spending so much time on the three core subjects, especially English and mathematics, and assessment. This is understandable, since the primary curriculum has always emphasised these two subjects (see Alexander 1984), and this characteristic was being reinforced by government policy on publication of results, at the end of the Key Stage, when the three core subjects were assessed by SATs. The curriculum dilemma for teachers, however, is that they are also faced with the statutory requirement to deliver a broad and balanced curriculum incorporating reasonable time on all the foundation subjects and RE, yet this is impossible given the time currently and historically allocated to English and mathematics. (For a more detailed analysis of this dilemma at Key Stage 1, see Campbell and Neill 1992.) This dilemma is not restricted to beginning teachers, but is particularly acute for them since they have to find ways of balancing the whole curriculum whilst continuing to develop their early skills of classroom organisation.

A second explanation for lack of curriculum time is 'evaporated' time (ILEA 1989) – that is, time allocated for teaching but actually spent on transition and supervision, such as when teachers take a class of pupils from their classroom area to the hall, or to the swimming pool. This amounts to at least 1.75 hours per week, according to our evidence. At the time of writing the National Curriculum Council is reviewing the 'collective weight' of the National Curriculum orders and RE upon class teachers, but it will remain a basic curriculum management responsibility for individual teachers to monitor the balance of time across the different subjects.

Time spent on assessment was spent on two activities: teacher assessment (TA) and administering SATs. At the time of writing there is considerable confusion in government policy on the nature and purpose of assessment and testing, and most research evidence concerns Key Stage 1 only, since end-of-Key Stage testing had not yet occurred at age 11. What is involved in each is discussed in a training document from SEAC (1990), but the early evidence (e.g. DES 1991) was that teachers were engaging in 'fervent but unfocused' recording of pupil performance in classroom for TA, often using very detailed checklists, and sometimes checking each pupil against statements of attainment every day. Teachers will need to do far less than this if they are to teach pupils as well as assess them, and beginning teachers will need to keep simple records of pupil progress in their own record books, save some pieces of work as 'evidence' about attainment in some attainment targets, and enter a level for each pupil in each attainment target in each subject once or twice a term. The important issue here is not the frequency of records nor the nature of evidence, since this will normally be decided on a whole-school basis, but the adoption of a systematic approach to assessment, using the National Curriculum statements of attainment as the criteria.

What has to be done in administering SATs at the end of the Key Stage applies to only some of the attainment targets in the three core subjects. It is an important task, and the targets and tests vary each year, but for most teachers the ongoing TA and record-keeping each year for each attainment target in each subject is a more substantial and pervasive aspect of their work. Our estimate, based on the evidence in Table 6.4, is that TA takes up the equivalent of 9 per cent of teaching time; that is, about 1.7 hours per week.

School routines

Teachers spend considerable amounts of time on routine matters that enable the school to run smoothly. For example, they take registers, collect dinner money, move the class around the school (for instance, to the hall for assembly), attend assembly, supervise children at the end of lessons and sometimes during breaks, and put up displays of children's work. The time spent on these activities by our teachers averaged 7.7 hours per week, equivalent to over a third of the time they spent teaching. It is sometimes argued that the time spent in this way is especially valuable for children's personal and social development, because it provides opportunities for teachers to talk to and listen to the pupils' concerns and interests. Moreover, it is part of the way children learn to become part of the school as a community. None the less, it might be asked whether this is the best use of teacher time, and, when teachers have non-teaching assistants to support them, whether the assistants should take on the bulk of this routine work, guided by the teachers. As a matter of fact we found that teachers who had more time with non-teaching support actually spent significantly more time than others on display and supervision. This pattern of teachers' time sits rather oddly with their view that 'lack of time' was the major obstacle to their implementing the cognitive objectives of the National Curriculum. The skilled use of non-teaching assistants is an essential part of the teacher's job, but an aspect on which there is little hard evidence (see Mortimore 1992 for the most recent study).

Professional development

We have included in this category, not only in-service training and the non-pupil days, often referred to as 'Baker days', but also meetings with other adults, including staff meetings, and reading curriculum documents and professional journals. If we take the strictest view of professional development, beginning teachers might draw the conclusion that despite being in the van of educational reform, only a minute proportion of their time (2 per cent) will be taken up with in-service training. This is because the dominant model of training has been the cascade model, where senior teachers go for training and are expected to disseminate it to the rest of the staff. Thus part of the time spent in staff meetings would involve professional development, as would informal meetings with advisers and inspectors. The relatively large amounts of time given over to professional reading include time spent reading National Curriculum documents, which it is essential for teachers to use in planning and recording pupil progress.

Other activities

Even having finished teaching, preparing, developing professionally, and spending time in school routines, the modern primary teacher's task is incomplete. Some small amounts of time by some teachers are spent in governors' meetings, and about 1.4 hours a week are given over to extra-curricular activities such as clubs, orchestras, plays, sports teams and other activities outside the timetabled time. Moreover, a substantial amount of time is spent in miscellaneous activities that the teachers could not fit into our category system. Some of these mentioned to us by teachers were: school administration, appraisal interviews, writing school policy statements, case conferences with welfare workers and educational psychologists; others are interruptions to routine life in school such as moving furniture because the classroom is due to be painted. Although beginning teachers are unlikely to be involved in governors' meetings, they can be expected to spend time on voluntary extra-curricular activities, and a range of other less easily categorised tasks.

CONCLUSION

The teacher's working week is characterised by five dominant characteristics.

1 It is both extensive (typically stretching to about 53 hours per week including weekends and evenings), and intensive (with much time spent doing more than one task simultaneously, in a pressured climate where lack of time inhibits effectiveness).

2 Teaching the curriculum is the most important task, though occupying only about a third of the working time. The delivery of the whole curriculum is problematic, since there is not enough time available after evaporated time is taken into account, and because of the concentration upon the core subjects.

3 Working with other adults, including teachers and non-teachers, is a small but increasingly important aspect of teachers' work, requiring a collegial, rather than an individualised, orientation.

4 Less than half the working week is spent in contact with children, and a substantial minority of this time is spent in low-level activities of a routine kind, important though these are for children's development.

5 Preparation (including lesson planning, marking and recording results, and organising learning materials) takes as much time as teaching and is necessary for the systematic delivery of the National Curriculum. Teacher Assessment is a continuing part of the teaching task and is necessary to provide the basis for annual reporting of pupil progress, across the whole curriculum, to parents.

Finally, we found that teachers reported high levels of stress because of the overload of work, and the conflict between time demands of work and those of family and personal life. Beginning teachers may help to reduce at least part of such stress by considering data such as those presented in this chapter in order to see whether they can manage the use of their time more effectively. There is, of course, a limit to the benefits of time management. It cannot make the unmanageable manageable, but it might help beginning teachers to allocate priorities to different components of their working time.

REFERENCES

Alexander, R.J. (1984) *Primary Teaching*, London: Holt, Rinehart & Winston.
—— (1992) *Policy and Practice in Primary Education*, London: Routledge.
Alexander, R.J., Rose, J. and Woodhead, C. (1992) *Curriculum Organisation and Classroom Practice in Primary Schools: a Discussion Paper*, London: DES.
Bennett, S.N., Andreae, J., Hegarty, P. and Wade, B. (1980) *Open Plan Schools: Teaching, Curriculum, Design*, Windsor: NFER for the Schools Council.
Campbell, R.J. (1985) *Developing the Primary School Curriculum*, London: Holt, Rinehart & Winston.
Campbell, R.J. and Neill, S.R. St J. (1990) *1330 Days*, Final report of a pilot study of teacher time in Key Stage 1, London: Assistant Masters and Mistresses Association.
—— (1992) *Teacher Time and Curriculum Manageability*, London: Assistant Masters and Mistresses Association.

Campbell, R.J., Evans, L., Packwood, A. and Neill, S.R. St J. (1991) *Workloads, Achievement and Stress*, London: Assistant Masters and Mistresses Association.

Coopers and Lybrand Deloitte (1991) *Costs of the National Curriculum in Primary Schools*, London: National Union of Teachers.

Core Subjects Association (1991) *Monitoring the Implementation of the National Curriculum, 1989–90*, English Studies Centre, Sheffield LEA.

DES (1989) *Circular 5/89*, London: HMSO.

—— (1990) *The Implementation of the National Curriculum in Primary Schools*, London: HMSO.

—— (1991) *The Implementation of the Curricular Requirements of the Education Reform Act: Science, Key Stages 1 and 3*, London: DES.

Galton, M. and Simon, B. (1980) *Progress and Performance in the Primary Classroom*, London: Routledge.

Hilsum, S. and Cane, B. (1971) *The Teacher's Day*, Windsor: National Foundation for Educational Research.

Hoyle, E. (1975) 'Professionality, professionalism and control in teaching', in V. Houghton, R. McHugh and C. Morgan (eds) *Management in Education*, London: Ward Lock/Open University.

Inner London Education Authority (ILEA) (1989) *The National Curriculum: a Planning Guide for Schools*, London: ILEA.

Lortie, D. (1971) *Schoolteacher*, Chicago: University of Chicago Press.

Lowe, B. (1991) *Activity Sampling*, Humberside County Council, Hull.

Mortimore, P. (1992) *The Innovative Uses of Non-teaching Staff in Primary and Secondary Schools Project: Final Report*, London: Institute of Education, London University.

Muschamp, Y., Pollard, A. and Sharpe, R. (1992) 'Curriculum management in primary schools', PACE Project, Bristol University.

NAS/UWT (1991) *Teacher Workload Survey*, Birmingham: NAS/UWT.

National Curriculum Council (1992) *Report on Regional Primary Seminars*, York: NCC.

Neill, S.R. St J. (1991) *Classroom Non-verbal Communication*, London: Routledge.

Nias, J. (1989) *Primary Teachers Talking: a Study of Teaching as Work*, London: Routledge.

PSRDG (1989) *Primary Teachers: a Profession in Distress*, Birmingham: Primary Schools Research and Development Group, School of Education, Birmingham University.

SEAC (1990) *Guide to Teacher Assessment: Packs A, B & C*, London: School Examination and Assessment Council.

Part III

Developing the curriculum

The earlier parts of the book have concentrated on classroom organisation and teaching methods, the 'how' of teaching. This part focuses on the 'what', issues of curriculum content. Rather than introduce each chapter separately, this introduction will bring the chapters together. In choosing the majority of the papers, I have chosen to focus on the ways in which different subjects are defining themselves in relation to primary teaching. I have left open the discussion of 'subject teaching' versus the 'integrated curriculum', which is being handled elsewhere within the Open University Primary PGCE. It seemed to me that as a basis for such discussion, it would be useful to know what the fundamental questions and approaches in the different subject areas were. From this, it would be possible to see how far the different 'disciplines' had their own ways of thinking, talking and operating, and how far the issues seemed to be common, and capable of being dealt with effectively within an integrated theme-based approach. Referring back to Chapter 5, by Maurice Galton, in which ways would it be best to develop 'ownership' and a 'shared responsibility for learning'?

For this reason, I hope that the reader will approach the chapters from at least two perspectives, first in using the articles as a stimulus for considering the nature of the discrete subjects and ways to approach them in the primary classroom; secondly, to draw out any fundamental differences, to consider any different conceptual and linguistic demands of the different subjects, and to see in what ways the processes of developing shared understandings in each are common.

Another useful question to ask would be, in what ways would the understandings of this subject area differ if it was presented to children as a subject in its own right, or as an approach to a wider theme? To support such analysis, as well as for its importance in its own right, I have begun Part III with a chapter by Neil Mercer. In it, he explains the concept of 'common knowledge' or the 'educational ground rules', through which children learn to take part successfully in the discourse of the curriculum. This chapter offers an explanation of how teachers help children to acquire certain 'educational language practices' in the classroom, and indicates the practices are to which they are introducing children. Readers may want to consider how far the educational practices in their classrooms admit the children to the practices and discourses aimed for in the other subject-based chapters in this part of the book.

Chapter 14, the final paper in Part III, takes up and extends the cross-curricular themes which have begun to emerge through the chapters. In it Peter Woods defines as 'critical events' those rare but important teaching/learning experiences which reach out of the classroom and the timetable into the wider community, and become significant moments in both pupils' and teachers' development. He shows how such events do not simply 'happen', but pass through six well-defined stages, including careful preparation, opportunities for divergent thinking, consolidation of skills, and a final celebration of the achievements. His chapter is a reminder of the necessity to ensure that space is left in the curriculum for sustained work which draws on the specific skills and interests of teachers and children in different classrooms.

Chapter 7

Language in educational practice

Neil Mercer

In English, we have the words 'teaching' and 'learning', but no single word for the process of 'teaching-and-learning'. (The term 'education' usually refers to something more general, and at an institutional level.) Perhaps this is why in Britain we get so little discussion of the quality of the process as a whole, but only of its supposed constituent parts. For example, explanations of why individual children succeed or fail in school are commonly couched in terms of individual intelligence, motivation or aptitudes for learning; while critical comments by politicians on the quality of British education seem to focus inexorably on the attributes and competences of teachers.

For anyone interested in what really goes on in schools or homes or any other educational settings, there are very good reasons for rejecting such partial perspectives on teaching-and-learning. The most obvious is that people do most of their learning by talking and interacting with other people. Another is that children's responses to tests of their aptitudes and competences have been found to be strongly influenced by the particular social, interpersonal circumstances in which the tests are carried out. Education at the classroom level needs to be recognised as a communicative process, in which the outcomes in terms of learning are jointly determined by the efforts of teachers and learners. It also needs to be recognised that this is a process for sharing knowledge, not simply acquiring it or transmitting it, and the prime medium for that sharing is language.

Language is at the heart of education not only because it is the principal means of communication between teachers and learners, but also for at least two other reasons. One is that language is a vital means by which we represent our own thoughts to ourselves. The Russian psychologist Vygotsky (1978) described language as a *psychological tool*, something each of us uses to make sense of experience. The second reason is that language is also our prime *cultural tool*. It is mainly through the medium of spoken and written language that successive generations of a society benefit from the experience of their forebears, and it is also through language that each new generation shares, disputes, resolves and refines its own experience. Education is – or should be – a process for developing the effective use of both these language functions, psychological and cultural.

Becoming 'educated' essentially involves gaining entrance to an intellectual community. It is not simply a matter of acquiring a body of knowledge, and it certainly cannot be achieved through personal, unaided discovery. An educated person not only has access to a certain body of knowledge, but also has acquired a set of procedures for solving problems and a set of language practices for describing and discussing ideas, problems and the relationships between them. Becoming a 'scientist', for example, is not really about becoming more independent, detached, or abstract in one's manner of analysis and representation, but instead is largely a matter of learning to think, talk and write like other members of the scientific community. Of course, fields of knowledge are not static, and emergent scientists may use their entry into the discourse of the community to challenge and change established theories and practices. But education is always primarily a matter of social and linguistic enculturation.

IN THE CLASSROOM

To move from generalities to classroom events, consider the following piece of classroom discourse (Sequence 1, below). It was recorded in a primary school in the West Midlands in 1989. Two children, one 11 and one 5, were working together without their teacher. They were doing an activity of a kind which is increasingly common in British primary schools, in which an older and younger child work together as 'talk partners' on some specific task – see Madeley and Lautman (1991), and Meyer (1991), for fuller accounts of such activities: Sequence 1 can be heard on the audiocassette of the Open University INSET pack which contains these two articles. On this occasion (at which I was present), the older child (a girl called Michelle) and the younger (a boy called Ashley) were engaged in the retelling of his favourite picture-book story, *The Very Hungry Caterpillar* by Eric Carle (1986). Both Ashley and Michelle had read the book, but they did not have a copy of it with them during the activity. [*Note:* pauses of more than three seconds are indicated by //.]

Sequence 1: *The Very Hungry Caterpillar*

ASHLEY	MICHELLE
	1 Right what's your favourite book Ashley?
2 The Very Hungry Caterpillar	
	3 Is it a good book?
4 Yea	
	5 Can you tell me the story please?
6 Yea//in the light of the moon a egg lay on a leaf//	

7 What happened next?

8 Um//

9 Did he wake up?

10 No

11 He didn't? What happened then? Was it on a Sunday morning?

12 Yea

13 Right, can you carry on then? On a Sunday morning//did he pop out of the little egg?//

14 Yea

15 And what happened after that, then?

16 He started to look for food// and on Monday, he ate through one apple, and on Tuesday he ate through two pears, and //on Wednesday he ate through three plums

17 He was greedy, weren't he? What did he eat on Thursday?

18 Four strawberries

19 Friday?

20 Four//five oranges

21 What else did he eat?

22 //Don't know

23 On Saturday what did he eat?

24 On Saturday he ate a slice of cherry chocolate cake, one ice cream, one pickle, one Swiss cheese, one// one slice of salami

25 Did he eat anything else?

26 One lollipop//

27 Any pie?

28 Some cherry pie//one cup cake// and a sausage

29 And a sausage. He was greedy wasn't he? What else happened?

30 And the next and that night he had a belly ache and the next day was Monday again and he ate through one nice green leaf and after that he felt much better. Now he wasn't small any more he was a big fat caterpillar. He built a house

round himself called a cocoon// and
he stayed in there for more than two
weeks and he nibbled an 'ole and he
pushed his way out and he was a
beautiful butterfly

31 Lovely

In this episode we see Michelle helping Ashley to reconstruct the text of a book. This is accomplished through a conversation. We can infer some interesting things about Ashley's education from this conversation. In his re-telling, he reproduces not only the plot of the story, but also much of the actual written language of the book. He shows that he has learned the story as a piece of literature, an item of contemporary literary culture.

And by providing this kind of re-telling he also shows that he is aware of what can be called an *educational ground rule*; namely, that when asked to re-tell the story of a book you do so by keeping as closely as possible to the original text. Although he is not working here with a teacher, Ashley recognises the key contextual features of the situation, and so is able to act accordingly. It is important to note that developing this kind of awareness is not necessarily unproblematic for children. For example, the anthropologist Shirley Brice Heath (1982, 1983) has shown that differences between what counts as 'storytelling' in school and in their home community can be an important and enduring source of educational problems for children of some cultural backgrounds. I will say more about 'educational ground rules' later.

Sequence 1 also shows that both Ashley and Michelle have learned the discourse requirements for doing one kind of educational activity: they seem to have few problems in making a 'talk partners' activity happen as a joint enterprise. It is also very apparent that Michelle has developed the ability to engage in some other educational language practices: she has learned how to take a teacher's role. We see her 'setting up' the activity through her initial remarks. She asks questions in order to stimulate Ashley's recall (for example, lines 7, 15, 21) rather than to elicit information of which she is truly ignorant. She gives him a series of 'prompts', switching from general questions to providing more specific clues from the story when she feels he is struggling (lines 7–13, 21–7). She reiterates what he has said (line 29) and provides supportive, evaluative feedback (lines 17, 29, 31). One way in which she perhaps behaves differently from most adult teachers is that she tolerates very long pauses before offering him further prompts (Edwards 1992; Wood 1992).

'Scaffolding' learning

In her role as surrogate teacher, Michelle elicits the whole story from Ashley: she demonstrates that he really knew it all himself. But his realisation of his knowledge for the purpose of this activity is achieved by her careful management and support of what could have been for Ashley too difficult and too daunting a task. A useful concept for describing what she does is that of '*scaffolding*', of which Jerome Bruner says, 'it refers to the steps taken to reduce the degrees of freedom in carrying out some task so that the child can concentrate on the difficult skill she is in the process of acquiring' (Bruner 1978: 19). It represents the kind and quality of cognitive support which an adult or more competent peer can provide for a child's learning – a form of 'vicarious consciousness' (as Bruner also put it) which anticipates the child's own internalisation of mental function. (See Maybin *et al.* 1992 for a fuller discussion of 'scaffolding' in the classroom.)

Michelle and Ashley's activity is dependent on a great deal of prior, shared educational knowledge and experience. That knowledge and experience provides a *contextual framework* for their conversation and the task in hand. Although no teacher is directly involved, the sequence illustrates well how activity, and hence learning, in the classroom is accomplished through dialogue which is heavily context-dependent, with the context being constructed by speakers from their current and past shared experience. A person's education proceeds by the extension and revision of such contextual frameworks. The way in which Michelle highlights aspects of the structure and content of the story for Ashley may help him learn more about storytelling and books, and so guide his future literary, and literate, experience. He will almost certainly come away with his assumptions about educationally appropriate modes of storytelling confirmed. An activity of this kind, successfully completed, could also be expected to increase Ashley's confidence and fluency in demonstrating his knowledge and understanding through talk (a field of competence now formally included in the English National Curriculum).

TEACHERS' COMMUNICATIONS WITH PUPILS

Vygotsky proposed that 'the very essence of cultural development is in the collision between mature cultural forms of behaviour with the primitive forms which characterise the child's behaviour' (Vygotsky 1981: 151). If this is true, then the quality of interactions between adults and children is a crucial issue for any society. More specifically, the quality of communication between teachers and pupils is crucial for the quality of education.

Try asking someone why teachers need to talk to children. They will probably say because teachers must tell children what to do, how to do it, when to start and when to stop. Teachers certainly do those things, but they do much more. They assess children's learning through talking to children and listening to what they say, they provide children with educational experiences which would be hard to provide by any other means other than talk (for example, telling stories, reading poetry, describing events, supplying factual information at the right time and in an accessible form). And, of course, one very important function of talk for teachers is to control the behaviour of children. There has been a good deal of educational research on classroom talk as a medium for 'social control'. But only quite recently has there been much research into its function as a medium for sharing knowledge, and one through which adults influence the representations of reality, the interpretations of experience, which children eventually adopt.

At the classroom level, education proceeds by *the development of shared understanding*. Through talk and joint action, participants in the process of teaching and learning can build a body of common knowledge which provides a contextual basis for further educational activity. This applies to activities in which a teacher is talking with pupils, and to those in which pupils are working together. The extent to which educational knowledge becomes 'common' to teachers and pupils is one measure of the effectiveness of the educational process. One important and problematic aspect of the 'common knowledge' of classroom education is what I referred to earlier as *educational ground rules* (Edwards and Mercer 1987; Sheeran and Barnes 1991). By this is meant the implicit norms and expectations that it is necessary to take account of in order to participate successfully in educational discourse. Ground rules of this kind govern the language practices we observed Michelle and Ashley following in Sequence 1. Becoming educated means becoming able to follow the ground rules: but having acquired these rules, people then tend to assume that what is involved is no more than 'common sense'. As Sheeran and Barnes say, 'In spite of their importance, these tacit expectations or ground rules are seldom discussed with pupils, because the teachers themselves are largely unaware of them' (1991: 2). They go on to show how many of the requirements for providing satisfactory essays and other written work in different school subjects are never made explicit to pupils. And even when some of those requirements are made clear, teachers hardly provide justifications which will help children understand *why* they should write in particular ways. Classroom research has provided many examples of how children's interpretations of the ground rules may differ in important ways from those of their classmates and/or their teachers. For example, whereas some children may see 'discussion group' activities as an opportunity for airing problems and misunderstandings, others in the same group may see them only as occasions on which you must try to demonstrate that you know the 'right answers'. Yet other children may think that that real imperative is to talk fluently and without hesitation, rather like in the radio programme *Just a Minute!* (Mercer *et al.* 1988). Research on GCSE oral English examinations has suggested that children sometimes graft the ground rules of TV 'chat shows' on to their discussions (Hewitt 1989). There is evidence that when teachers bring ground rules for discussion out into the open for consideration with their classes, this can lead to improved motivation and levels of performance among the children (Prentice 1991; Steel 1991; Dawes *et al.* 1992).

One striking feature of the language behaviour of teachers is that they ask a great many questions. Teachers use questions to monitor children's knowledge and understanding, so that they can evaluate their teaching, assess the learning of their pupils, and so plan ahead. However, teachers also use questions to try to shape the course of children's learning, and there is some controversy about how useful questions are as a strategy for doing so (see chapters by Wood, Mercer, Edwards, Wells and Brierley *et al.* in Norman 1992). For example, Dillon (1982) and Wood (1992) argue that teachers' questions often constrain and limit the directions of classroom discussion in quite unfortunate ways. By requiring short, factual answers, teachers may actually inhibit pupils' intellectual activity. Wood (1992) shows that when teachers use other kinds of conversational strategies, such as offering their own reflective observations, this can encourage pupils to do likewise and can generate longer and more animated responses from pupils. However, although Wood provides a good example of a nursery teacher generating animated and extended responses from two 4-year-old children (1992: 211–12), it is not clear that the talk in the example is related to a curriculum! The amount of lively talk which goes on during teaching-and-learning is not, in itself, a measure of its quality. The crucial issue for primary and secondary teachers is maintaining a suitable balance between, on the one hand, offering children opportunities for open-ended exploration and discussion and, on the other, fulfilling a responsibility for achieving established curriculum goals. It is generally accepted that this is a difficult balance to achieve.

There are some interesting examples of teachers' questions in Sequence 2 (below), which was videorecorded for an Open University course in a secondary school in Derbyshire. As part of their English studies, a class of 14-year-olds were engaged in an extended computer-based communication with children in a nearby primary school. In a 'fantasy adventure' setting, the secondary students (in groups of three) were pretending to be a group of characters stranded in time and space. Explanations of their predicaments and requests for solutions were e-mailed to the primary children, whose responses were considered and developed by each group of students. Sequence 2 is one small part of a recorded session in which their English teacher was questioning them about the most recent interaction and their future plans. (*Note*: T = teacher; P1, P2 and P3 are the girls in one group. Simultaneous speech is indicated by [and [] indicates that some speech has been omitted.)

Sequence 2: guidance through questions

T: What about the word 'dimension', because you were going to include that in your message, weren't you?

P1:   Yeh. And there's going to be – if they go in the right room, then they'll find a letter in the floor and that'll spell 'dimension'. []

T: What happens if they do go in the wrong room?

P2: Well, there's no letter in the bottom, in the floor.

T: Oh God! So they've got to get it right, or that's it! (*Everyone laughs*) for ever. And Cath can't get back to her own time. What do you mean the letters are in the room, I don't quite [follow that?

P2:   [On the floor, like a tile or something.

T: Oh I see. [] Why did you choose the word 'dimension'?

P1: [Don't know (*pupils looking to each other, seeming uncertain*)

P2: [It just came up. Just said, you know, 'dimension' and everyone agreed.

P3: [Don't know.

T: Right, because it seemed to fit in with, what, the [fantasy flow, flavour?

P3:   [Yeh.

T: OK. Why do they go through the maze rather than go back? I mean what motivation do they have for going through it in the first place?

P: Um, I think that it was the king told them that Joe would be in the maze or at the end of the maze, and they didn't go back because of Joe, think it was. I'm not sure about that.

T: You've really got to sort that out. [It's got to be very, very clear.

P1:   [Yeh.

P2: Joe went through this secret passage, you see, round the edge. [And we couldn't go through there it was like a different door.

T: [OK

P2 Yeh and that was like the only way we could meet Joe.

T: OK. Do remember that anything that you don't explain adequately, the primary school children are going to pick up on, and so it's got to make sense. Particularly at this end of the project, because they're not going to have much time to reply to your messages.

              (From Videocassette 2, EH232 *Computers and Learning*)

In Sequence 2 the teacher uses questions to draw out from the students the content of their recent e-mail message, and also some justifications for what they included in it. At one level, she is simply monitoring their activity and assessing the adequacy of their attempt to continue the communication with the younger children. But her questions are not merely assessment, they are *part of her teaching*. Like many effective teachers, she is using questions not only to monitor children's activity, but also to guide it. Through questions like 'Why did you choose the word "dimension"?' and 'Why do they go through the maze rather than go back?' she directs their attention to matters requiring more thought and clarification. In much of her talk, and particularly her imperative conclusions ('You've really got to sort that out' and 'Do remember . . .'), we can see her 'scaffolding' her students' endeavours. Children can learn a lot from working together on computer-based activities, as they can from practical science activities, individual study pursuits and so on. But teachers need to highlight key points and to create continuities between past, present and future events in children's classroom experience if they are to make educational sense of it all.

Through observational research in primary schools, Derek Edwards and I (Edwards and Mercer 1987) set out to describe how teaching-and-learning, as a process of sharing and constructing knowledge, was carried out. Among other things, we identified various kinds of discourse strategies used by teachers to control the representation of educational knowledge through their talk with pupils. These were basically of two kinds: *elicitations* and *knowledge markers*

Elicitations

One obvious thing that teachers do is to *directly elicit* information from children, in order to see what the children know already. But teachers often avoid direct elicitations, and instead try to draw out the information they want – the 'right' answers to their questions – by *cued elicitations* in which they give children strong visual clues and verbal hints as to what answer is required. (I will use Sequence 3 below to illustrate some of these strategies.)

Knowledge markers

Teachers also use talk to mark particular things which are said and done as important for pupils' learning. To be more precise, they mark some items of knowledge as *significant and joint*. There are a number of features of teachers' discourse which can operate in this way: *confirmations* (as, for example, a teacher's 'Yes, that's right' to a pupil's answer) are one of the most obvious and straightforward of such features. *Repetitions* of 'correct' answers or other utterances made by children and judged by the teacher to have educational significance are another. Teachers may paraphrase or *reformulate* a pupil's remark, so as to offer the class a revised, tidied-up version of what was said. The term *'elaborations'* can be used to describe instances when a teacher picks up on a cryptic statement made by a pupil and expands and/or explains its significance to the rest of the class.

'We' statements (as in a teacher saying to a class 'last week we learned how to measure angles') are another interesting procedure for representing knowledge or experience as significant. They show how teachers represent their classes, *to* their classes, as small intellectual communities which have significant past experience in common and so have gained shared knowledge and collective understanding. Teachers also frequently *literally recap* for the benefit of the class what has gone on earlier in a lesson, and in previous lessons. More problematically, they also sometimes *reconstructively recap* what has been said and done by themselves and the children on earlier

occasions, 'rewriting history' so as to make events fit better into their pedagogic framework. (For example, a science teacher might remind pupils of 'the lesson in which we made a vacuum', even though the lesson saw more failed attempts than successes!)

We can see some of these features, in Sequence 3 (below), which was recorded in 1991 as part of the *SLANT* research project (see Mercer *et al.* 1989; Mercer and Fisher 1992; or Dawes *et al.* 1992, for more information about this project). *SLANT* (which stands for Spoken Language and New Technology) was concerned with the quality of talk in computer-based activities in primary school classrooms. In Sequence 3, the computer-based activity in question had been devised by the class teacher as part of a larger scheme of work on traditional fairy tales. From discussions with the teacher, we know that she had three main aims for this activity. She wanted her pupils (aged 6 and 7) to learn about the structure of such stories and how characters in them are typically represented. She wanted to develop her pupils' understanding of the 'language level' of young children who read such stories. And she intended this computer-based activity also to fulfil the aim of developing the computing skills of her pupils.

She therefore asked them to design and use an 'overlay' for the keyboard, transforming it into a 'concept keyboard' which the children in the nursery class of their school could use to select a limited set of words to make sentences and so create their own fairy stories. Eight pupils in the class were working on this task in pairs, and the teacher supported their activity by going round to each pair in turn. With each pair, she would observe the current state of their progress, draw attention to certain features and use them to raise issues related to the successful completion of the activity. In the sequence, she is talking with one such pair, Carol and Lesley. (*Note*: T = teacher. Simultaneous speech is marked by [.)

Sequence 3: designing a concept keyboard

T: (*standing behind the pair of pupils*) So what are you going to put in this one? (*points to a blank square on their overlay*)

CAROL: [(*inaudible mutters*)

LESLEY: [(*inaudible mutters*)

T: Come on, think about it.

LESLEY: A dragon?

T: A dragon. Right. Have you got some words to describe a dragon?

CAROL: [No.

LESLEY: [No.

T: (*reading from their overlay and pointing to the words as she does so*) 'There is a little amazing dragon.' They could say that, couldn't they?

CAROL: [Yes.

LESLEY: Yes.
           (*Carol and Lesley continue working for a short while, with the teacher making occasional comments*)
T: Now let's pretend it's working on the computer. You press a sentence and read it out for me, Lesley.
LESLEY: (*pointing to the overlay as she reads*) 'Here . . . is . . . a . . . wonderful . . .'
T: Wait a minute.
LESLEY: 'Princess . . .'
T: (*turning to Carol*) Right, now you do one. You read your sentence.
CAROL: (*pointing to overlay*) 'Here . . . is . . . a little . . . princess.'
T: Good. What do you need at the end of the sentence, so that the children learn about [how
LESLEY: [Full stop.
T: Full stop. We really should have allowed some space for a full stop. I wonder if we could arrange . . . When you actually draw the finished one up we'll include a full stop. You couldn't actually do it. We'll put it there (*she writes in a full stop on the overlay*) so that when you, can you remember to put one in? So what are the children going to learn? That a sentence starts with a . . . .?
LESLEY: Capital letter.
T: And finishes with?
LESLEY: A full stop.
T: And it's showing them? (*She moves her hand across the overlay from left to right*) What else is it showing them about sentences? That you start? On the?
LESLEY: On the left.
T: And go across the page (*she again passes her hand from left to right across the page*).

                                        (Mercer and Fisher 1992: 350–1)

Sequence 3 includes good examples of some of the teachers' discourse strategies described above. Selecting particular themes, the teacher elicits responses from the pupils which draw them along a particular line of reasoning on that theme (a line of reasoning consonant with her own goals for the activity). Moreover, she provides *cued elicitations* for some of those responses through the form of her questions (for example, 'That a sentence starts with a . . .?') and through her gestures (as when she moves her hand across the overlay, indicating the way text is laid out). By her *repetition* of Carol's answer 'full stop' she marks a 'right answer'. In her final remark, she also *elaborates* Lesley's brief, cryptic response to make the point more clearly. At a number of points in the sequence, she defines the learning experience as one which is shared by her and the children through her use of 'we' and 'let's'.

In the sequence, we can see how a teacher uses talk, gesture and the shared experience of the piece of work in progress to draw the children's attention to salient points – the things she wishes them to do, and the things she wishes them to learn. She reminds pupils of some specific requirements of the task in hand, clarifies some of those requirements, and so guides their activity along a path which is in accord with her pre-defined curriculum goals for the activity. She 'scaffolds' their participation in the activity so as to try to ensure (1) that its demands do not exceed the capabilities of the children and (2) that the activity keeps 'on track' for the specific curriculum goals she had set. (For the record, Lesley and Carol did produce a satisfactory overlay, and went on to teach the nursery children how to use it.)

CONCLUSIONS

In this chapter I have tried to describe some important educational functions of language in the classroom. I hope that some of the practical implications of my discussion of classroom language are clear: that children need to be helped to acquire certain educational language practices and – crucially – to see the point and purpose of them; and that teachers need to be aware of how, and how well, they teach through talk. However, I should say that I am very aware that I have only dealt superficially with some important matters, and left some others out entirely. For example, the issue of 'educational ground rules' leads into a cluster of thorny educational language problems, including such controversial matters as how and when children should be introduced to the technical vocabularies of school subjects and how children's competence and confidence with language should be taken into account in making assessments of their understanding of subject knowledge. (Interested readers might turn to Maclure et al. 1988; Sheeran and Barnes 1991; and Norman 1992.)

Early in the chapter I suggested that the essence of 'becoming educated' is gaining admission to an intellectual community and to a universe of discourse. I hope that I have shown some of the ways in which this process of gaining admission takes place. The talk and writing which goes on in any particular classroom only has meaning if it is embedded in a wider, less tangible but potentially very powerful discourse which links schools and other cultural institutions across time and space. It is in that broad context that the communicative process of teaching-and-learning should be studied and evaluated. I have not addressed some of the most problematic features of that process: many people who go to school do not gain proper entry to an intellectual community, or they have no good reasons to value membership of such a community, or their entry to it does not lead to any significant improvement to the quality of their lives (see, for example, Edwards 1979; Heath 1982, 1983; Carraher et al. 1985; Martin 1986; Edwards and Sienkewicz 1990). My own view is that we can only begin to address those problems seriously at a practical level when education is given the political and economic priority it deserves, as a communicative process at the heart of the cultural development of any society.

REFERENCES

Bruner, J. (1978) 'The role of dialogue in language acquisition', in A. Sinclair, R. Jarvella and W.J.M. Levelt (eds) *The Child's Conception of Language*, New York: Springer-Verlag.

Carle, E. (1986) *The Very Hungry Caterpillar*, London: Hamish Hamilton.

Carraher, T.N., Carraher, D.W. and Schliemann, A.D. (1985) 'Mathematics in the streets and in schools', *British Journal of Developmental Psychology*, 3: 21–9.

Dawes, L., Fisher, E. and Mercer, N. (1992) 'The quality of talk at the computer', *Language and Learning* (Oct.): 22–5.

Dillon, J.T. (1982) 'The effects of questions in education and other enterprises', *Journal of Curriculum Studies*, 14(2): 127–52.

Edwards, A.D. (1992) 'Teacher talk and pupil competence', in K. Norman (ed.) *Thinking Voices: the Work of the National Curriculum Project*, London: Hodder & Stoughton, for the National Curriculum Council.

Edwards, D. and Mercer, N. (1987) *Common Knowledge: the Development of Understanding in the Classroom*, London: Methuen.

Edwards, J.R. (1979) *Language and Disadvantage*, London: Edward Arnold.

Edwards, V. and Sienkewicz, T. (1990) *Oral Cultures Past and Present: Rappin' and Homer*, Oxford: Basil Blackwell.

Heath, S.B. (1982) 'What no bedtime story means: narrative skills at home and school', *Language and Society*, 11: 49–76.

—— (1983) *Ways with Words*, Cambridge: Cambridge University Press.

Hewitt, R. (1989) 'Oral assessment and the new oracy', Paper presented at the CLIE Symposium on Oracy and Assessment, Birkbeck College, University of London (Nov.).

Maclure, M., Phillips, T. and Wilkinson, A. (1988) *Oracy Matters*, Milton Keynes: Open University Press.

Madeley, B. and Lautman, A. (1991) 'I like the way we learn', in *P535 Talk and Learning 5–16: an In-service Pack on Oracy for Teachers*, Milton Keynes: The Open University.

Martin, T. (1986) 'Leslie: a reading failure talks about failing', *Reading*, 20: 43–52.

Maybin, J., Mercer, N. and Stierer, B. (1992) '"Scaffolding" learning in the classroom', in K. Norman (ed.) *Thinking Voices: the Work of the National Curriculum Project*, London: Hodder & Stoughton, for the National Curriculum Council.

Mercer, N., Edwards, D. and Maybin, J. (1988) 'Putting context into oracy', in M. Maclure, T. Phillips and A. Wilkinson (1988) *Oracy Matters*, Milton Keynes: Open University Press.

Mercer, N. and Fisher, E. (1992) 'How do teachers help children to learn? An analysis of teachers' interventions in computer-based activities', *Learning and Instruction*, 2(4): 339–55.

Mercer, N., Phillips, T. and Somekh, B. (1989) 'Research note: spoken language and new technology', *Journal of Computer Assisted Learning*, 7: 195–202.

Meyer, B. (1991) 'Talk partners in the infant classroom', in *P535 Talk and Learning 5–16: an In-service Pack on Oracy for Teachers*, Milton Keynes: The Open University.

Norman, K. (ed.) (1992) *Thinking Voices: the Work of the National Curriculum Project*, London: Hodder & Stoughton, for the National Curriculum Council.

Prentice, M. (1991) 'A community of enquiry', in *P535 Talk and Learning 5–16: an In-service Pack on Oracy for Teachers*, Milton Keynes: The Open University.

Sheeran, N. and Barnes, D. (1991) *School Writing: Discovering the Ground Rules*, Milton Keynes: Open University Press.

Steel, D. (1991) 'Granny's garden', in *P535 Talk and Learning 5–16: an In-service Pack on Oracy for Teachers*, Milton Keynes: The Open University.

Vygotsky, L.S. (1978) *Mind in Society: the Development of Higher Psychological Processes*, London: Harvard University Press.

—— (1981) 'The genesis of higher mental functions', in J. Wertsch (ed.) *The Concept of Activity in Soviet Psychology*, Anmonk, NY: Sharpe.

Wood, D. (1992) 'Teaching talk', in K. Norman (ed.) *Thinking Voices: the Work of the National Curriculum Project*, London: Hodder & Stoughton, for the National Curriculum Council.

Chapter 8

Perceptions of process and content in the science curriculum

Patricia Murphy and Eileen Scanlon

Recent changes in the content and structure of the UK science curriculum reflect a long history of debate and controversy. The chapter sets the evolving curriculum in context by briefly reviewing some of this history and critical incidents within it. We then discuss the key debates that emerged through the eighties and consider their implications for learning and teaching in science. The chapter concludes with a résumé of recent research findings about children's science learning. This research provides some useful indications of what remains problematic in the science curriculum.

BACKGROUND

In the early 1960s several influential reviews of the aims and objectives of science education were published (MoE 1960; ASE 1961). These sparked a major curriculum initiative in science which led to the development of the Nuffield science courses for secondary schools and Nuffield Junior Science and Science 5–13 for primary. The main aim of Science 5–13 was that the child should develop an inquiring mind and a scientific approach to problems. The project was to 'assist teachers to help children through discovery methods to gain experience and understanding of the environment and to develop their powers of thinking effectively about it' (Harlen 1975: 2). This focus on experimentation and inquiry learning was echoed in the Nuffield secondary science courses. However, a review of curriculum projects produced in the wake of the Nuffield initiatives revealed that practical work to produce the right answer was the norm whereas true experimentation and discovery was only rarely present in courses (ASE 1979).

It was during this review and development period that the Assessment of Performance Unit was set up. This was in response to a perceived need to find out what was happening in schools in key areas of the curriculum (DES 1974). The APU Science project (1978–90) monitored the performance of pupils aged 10–11 and 13 and 15 in primary and secondary schools in England, Wales and Northern Ireland from 1980 to 1984. The project and its findings proved to be a powerful influence on the science curriculum.

A critical part of the APU team's remit was to develop an assessment framework to represent pupils' scientific achievement. Murphy (1990), commenting on the APU experience, described the framework in the following way:

> The rationale for the science framework reflected a view of science education as an experimental, problem solving activity involving a complex interaction of demands. In this view science understanding is a product of scientific conceptual and procedural knowledge.
>
> (Murphy 1990: 188)

The APU view stressed the personal investigative nature of science and that scientific understanding had to be demonstrated across *contents* and *contexts* within and outside of school. The demands of assessment meant that the APU had to define those activities, content and contexts appropriate for the range of pupils monitored. This exercise had never previously been done and foreshadowed the National Curriculum in science.

The APU Science project was in the process of monitoring and disseminating findings when a further major UK science initiative was launched – the Secondary Science Curriculum Review (SSCR 1983). The view of science supported by the review did not differ markedly from that enshrined in the Nuffield courses except for the focus on the cultural nature of scientific activity and the view that knowledge is 'constructed rather than discovered through a method that is characterised by inherent uncertainties and is unavoidably subjective' (Bentley *et al*. 1985: 664). This social constructivist view of learning differs from the Piagetian constructivism which underpinned the discovery learning approach of the Nuffield courses and Science 5–13, particularly with regard to the role of the teacher.

The social constructivist view of learning was not, however, the only view of learning being applied to the science curriculum in the eighties. The Piagetian perspective remained influential. Shayer and Adey (1981) used Piagetian stages of development to analyse the demands of the science curriculum, particularly those of Nuffield courses. This analysis revealed considerable mismatch between course demands and the cognitive levels of pupils (as assessed by Piagetian reasoning tasks). Shayer and Adey, on the basis of their results, suggested that different 'types' of science teaching could 'influence the rate at which children's cognitive power develops' (1981: 134). The significance of the Shayer and Adey research was that it provided means for analysing curriculum demands, important when we go on to consider National Curriculum levels of attainment.

The constructivist view of learning that characterised research in the eighties remains a dominant influence in science education. It lies at the heart of many of the critiques of the Nuffield approach that influenced thinking about the curriculum. Woolnough and Allsop (1985) in their critique of the role of practical work in science education commented:

Science has two quite distinct strands. The knowledge, the important content and concepts of science and their interrelationships, and also the processes which a scientist uses in his working life. In teaching science we should be concerned both with introducing students to the important body of scientific knowledge, that they might understand and enjoy it, and also with familiarising students with the way a problem-solving scientist works, that they too might develop such habits and use them in their own lives.

Science teaching often appears to work on the assumption that scientific knowledge is objective, detached from the learner, and needs only good teaching to implant that knowledge into the learner's mind. . . . We see the students essentially active in the learning process in which they are continually enquiring, testing, speculating and building up their own personal constructs of knowledge.

(Woolnough and Allsop 1985)

In *The Pupil as Scientist*, Driver (1983), like Shayer and Adey, directed attention to problems with the science curriculum in terms of the level of conceptual achievement expected of pupils but on the basis of quite different evidence and concerns. In Driver's view the methods used by science teachers failed to take account of what was involved when pupils attempted to construct new understandings and integrate these with their existing knowledge of the world (Driver 1983). Driver was critical of the role of practical work in secondary school science. In essence, her challenge was not about the purpose of most school-based practical work (namely, to develop theories and test them out) but the time involved in it, and the structuring of it. She argued that in both these respects practical work was inadequate if its aim was to enable pupils' ideas to be made explicit, challenged and reconsidered. Her project's research (CLIS 1987) through the eighties focused on developing strategies to help teachers be more effective and provided them with a wealth of information about the nature of pupils' ideas in science.

Woolnough and Allsop (1985), while sharing many of Driver's concerns about the curriculum, concentrated on a different aspect of it, namely, the nature of practical work. They claimed three aims for practical work:

- developing practical scientific skills and techniques;
- being a problem-solving scientist;
- getting a 'feel for phenomena'.

(Woolnough and Allsop 1985: 41)

In their definition of aims and the subsequent discussion of them the strong influence of the APU Science framework is evident. The APU Science banks of practical and written test items looked at pupils' practical performance in a variety of ways: across a range of scientific skills and techniques involving reading and handling data and use of measuring instruments; on practical tests devoted to making and interpreting observations; and in a series of practical investigative tasks with associated written planning tasks to uncover the strategies used by pupils when investigating. Hence aspects of science education hitherto rarely emphasised were now both defined and exemplified in practical tasks.

Gott and Murphy developed a simple model for problem-solving activity which underpinned the APU approach to the development and analysis of investigative tasks. This model is referred to by Woolnough and Allsop and began to appear in various publications and exam syllabuses in the mid-eighties. Gott and Murphy described what they meant by a scientific problem and investigative activity in the following way:

> We have chosen to define a task for which the pupil cannot immediately see an answer or recall a routine method for finding it . . .
>
> In the investigations, science concepts and procedures are essential elements of any solution. Without some conceptual understanding the problem to be investigated will have no meaning. Even one asking pupils to, for instance, compare types of kitchen roll for their effectiveness at mopping up spills will rely on some understanding of mass and/or volume. Similarly, hypothesising, planning and interpreting are inevitably a part of the investigative process. . . . The carrying out of an investigation does not rely on the ability to explain a phenomenon, only to recognise its significant aspects and to develop an effective plan of action. In other words tacit rather than explicit understanding of the concepts involved can prove adequate. Furthermore as procedures are deployed in the course of the investigation, there are opportunities to amend that plan of the action to take into account incomplete conceptualisation or inadequate planning. Problem-solving relies on both the procedures of science and conceptual understanding but it can also act as an important vehicle for their future development.
>
> (Gott and Murphy 1987: 7, 8)

This view of the interdependence of procedural and conceptual understanding engendered considerable support in the scientific education community. Gott and Murphy distinguished between conceptual understanding, processes and procedural understanding, and provided definitions of these so that teachers and others could make sense of both the tasks and the findings.

Conceptual understanding: In scientific investigations, the concepts involved are tied closely to the identification of key variables in a system. Those variables have then to be systematically changed, measured or controlled.

Thus for instance, the concept of length, as a continuously variable quantity, has to be understood as more than a label. The idea that length can take any value and that value can be changed and measured is crucial to any practical investigation. . . . Other concepts, such as electrical resistance perhaps, are rarely introduced other than in science lessons and are equally rarely, if ever, reinforced outside those lessons.

We have then a loose division of concepts into those involving taught science and those which may well involve taught science but which will be reinforced in other areas of the curriculum or in everyday experience.

Processes and procedural understanding: There is a measure of agreement as to what is meant by the term science 'processes'. They are seen to include such *activities* as: communicating via prose, graphs, charts and tables; observing; predicting; inferring; interpreting.

We have already noted that many of these 'processes' are necessarily deployed, to a greater or lesser extent depending on the style of teaching and assessing, in any view of science and, indeed, in other subject areas of the curriculum. Within problem-solving they inevitably assume a some-what greater significance since they are intimately related to the activities of science. They will be called upon at all stages of an investigation, from the initial planning through to the interpretation, evaluation and com-munication of results.

Within such an activity as 'investigating', however, there is a set of scientific *procedures*. We use this term to describe strategies of scientific enquiry such as will occur in a many variable problem. Consider, for example, an investigation into the speed at which a number of toy cars will run down a ramp. The dependent variable, speed, will be affected by several factors – the make of the car and the height of release, for instance. Finding their effect will involve pupils in holding one factor constant and varying the other, whilst keeping any other potentially influential factors (the slope of the runway say) constant.

(Gott and Murphy 1987: 12–13)

Other procedures they referred to included knowing what to measure; how often and at what intervals; selecting an appropriate scale for an investigation – that is, matching instruments to the quantities to be measured for example, and so on.

The findings of the research we have quoted had a major impact on curriculum debate and development. Several outcomes were evident, many not anticipated. First, there were curriculum projects that built on what they saw were the insights provided by the research evidence. Some of these led to courses which focused on the processes of science independent of its content, in marked contrast to the APU's perspective. Secondly, the findings and their interpretations fuelled ongoing debate about the nature of scientific activity. This debate was focused in four main ways: *the nature and role of processes; the meaning of scientific observation; the nature of practical work; the definition and value of problem-solving activity*. In the next section we briefly characterise the main points of these particular debates.

SOME DEBATES IN SCIENCE EDUCATION

The nature and role of processes

In the past, the science curriculum in schools tended to be defined by content. Pupils would be studying and finding out about electricity or plants, for example. Curriculum innovation in the second half of the eighties saw a dramatic increase in process-led courses. In these courses lessons focused on observation, interpretation or classification, for example. Alternatively, activities were structured with pupils going through stages labelled by the dominant process, such as planning, controlling variables, and so forth. These courses received widespread criticism, even though in many instances they were welcomed by the profession. Jenkins (*TES*, 2 Jan. 1987) in his critique of 'process' science teaching identified a variety of sources responsible for the 'contemporary commitment to what has become known as the process approach to science'. These included DES policy in Science 5–16 (DES 1985), HMI criteria for judging quality in science lessons, APU Science framework categories and GCSE criteria for the assessment of practical work. In Jenkins' view, the assumption that processes can be 'identified, prescribed and taught in ways which enable pupils to acquire important and widely-applicable skills' was 'philosophically untenable, psychologically suspect and pedagogically unsound'. Jenkins' particular objection was to the notion of a set of processes which might collectively be considered to represent *a* scientific method. He did not deny the existence of scientific procedures and techniques, or 'rules' governing the conduct of scientific enterprise, but was concerned to maintain the creative nature of the scientific enterprise – an enterprise which could not be represented by a universal set of *a priori* rules.

Jenkins' other concern with the process approach was its failure to take account of content. Thus he argued the process-driven curriculum brought into question what constitutes science. For example, is classifying anything from nails to postage stamps scientific activity because of the focus on classification, or does the content have to have scientific relevance in order for it to become a 'scientific' classification? In his speculations about the attraction of the process approach Jenkins suggests that it may be seen to be more in line with a constructivist 'active' view of learning. Furthermore, given the difficulty pupils appeared to have in understanding scientific ideas, evident in the APU monitoring results (DES 1988a and b), the 'processes' of science might be a more attractive option for a curriculum that needs to be accessible to all. For Jenkins neither of these positions had much validity.

Millar and Driver (1987) published an article that brought together critiques of the process approach from a variety of sources. They, like Jenkins, argued that the 'process' approach advocated in public documents reflected both an inadequate analysis of the nature of the scientific enterprise and an inappropriate view of learning (1987: 36). They marshalled philosophical evidence against the notion of an 'algorithm for gaining or validating scientific knowledge', and went on to suggest that processes *per se* are merely common-sense ways of thinking unrelated to domains. It is, they argued, only the content and context of process-based activities which give them scientific meaning, a similar point to that made by Jenkins. The process approach in Millar and Driver's view assumes an inductivist view of learning where pupils progress as they exercise general skills observing, interpreting and experimenting and thus discovering knowledge. This model of how pupils learn is not one supported by research.

Millar and Driver also questioned the assumption that using processes to organise knowledge benefited pupils' learning as, in their view, it did not help children to make links between their experiences. This, they argued, was because of the high level of generality in the processes and their content- and context-dependency. Evidence suggests that it is through the content that links are forged between experiences rather than through the acquisition of general rules or strategies. Another argument put forward by Millar and Driver, about the inadvisability of a 'process' curriculum, was that there was no information available about children's progress in processes, in 'marked contrast to the situation for content or concept-based approaches'.

In *Skills and Processes in Science Education: a Critical Analysis* (Wellington 1989), the main thrust is a challenge to the process approach as an alternative to the over-burdened, content-led curriculum. A common theme of the articles in the book is that it is a misconception to see science as proceeding inductively and to regard processes independently of theory. The curriculum innovators of the process approach (Screen 1986) claimed that the processes of science are less provisional in nature than the concepts and more readily retained by pupils; both of these arguments are refuted in the book by reference to empirical evidence or its absence. Wellington concludes in his introductory chapter 'the aim of promoting transferable skills relevant to the twenty-first century is exceedingly problematic and in concrete terms of little value in determining the science curriculum' (1989: 15).

Out of these critiques there emerged a consensus that scientific inquiry was not about following a set of rules or a hierarchy of processes but 'the practice of a craft – in deciding what to observe, in selecting which observations to pay attention to, in interpreting and discussing inferences and in drawing conclusions from experimental data' (from Millar, in Woolnough 1990). There was also considerable agreement about the way in which scientific inquiry proceeds, an agreement evident in the various published discussions about the nature of scientific observation.

Scientific observations

The way in which observation was promoted in typical process-orientated curriculum courses assumed that it was a theory-neutral activity; that is, one observes first and interprets second, hence observation is a simple, unproblematic process open to all. This inductivist view as we have discussed is widely disputed. Research has demonstrated that observers pay attention only to those objects or features that are familiar or expected. When we observe, there is always more information than we take note of. When we observe, we select. Our knowledge of the world, our expectations and our purpose for observing, all influence the selections we make and the sense we make of them. The evidence from the APU monitoring (Gott and Welford 1987; Murphy 1989) showed that pupils' performance on observation tasks was influenced by their prior knowledge, concepts and theoretical understanding of the content of the task and science in general. Other influential factors included the pupils' level of interest and expectations of themselves with regard to the task. Hence, in order to improve pupils' ability to observe scientifically, pupils need to be made aware of the way they filter and select sensory data in different circumstances. This enables them to understand their personal view of relevance and develop an understanding of what is considered 'relevant' in scientific terms. To achieve this understanding of relevance depends on extending pupils' scientific conceptual understanding.

In spite of the evidence proffered about the intimate relationship between processes and concepts in pupil behaviour, little was articulated about the implications of this relationship for teaching and learning. Those concerned with these implications focused on the role of practical work in science.

The role of practical work

We have referred to some concerns about the way practical work was used in the curriculum. Many teachers professed a commitment to open-ended discovery learning, as advocated in Science 5–13, on the assumption that children acquire new concepts by this method. This assumption, as we have seen, is not one supported by research. However, even when this commitment existed, what happened in classrooms did not bear it out. Children were typically engaged in rediscovery with teachers concerned for them to 'discover' the right answer through practical activity. It was of this use of practical work that Driver (1983) and Woolnough and Allsop (1985) were critical, as is Hodson (1990), a long-standing critic of practical work.

For Woolnough and Allsop, practical work enabled pupils both *to learn how to do science*, as in the APU view of investigative work, and *to develop conceptual understanding* (Gott and Murphy 1987). This view is distinctly different from the process approach, in which practical work is a vehicle for teaching and developing high-level, transferable, cognitive skills. Gott and

Murphy considered that pupils needed to develop a repertoire of investigative strategies to make them more effective problem-solvers. Millar adopts a similar position in his review of the aims of practical work. Millar distinguishes between cognitive processes such as observation and classification which, in his view, cannot be taught and the practical skills which can be. He categorised those skills which can be taught into practical techniques and inquiry tactics. It is in the tactics category that he would locate the procedural understanding defined by Gott and Murphy, but he is critical of the narrow focus of Gott and Murphy's procedural understanding (Millar 1990). This definition to an extent reflected the state of understanding of the issues in the early eighties.

Several implications can be discerned in the discussion about the role of practical work in science education. One concerns what can or cannot be taught, yet another about what should be taught which reflects views about the purpose of science education. Other issues relate to how children learn. For many, especially teachers, the value of practical work is in its motivating effect; for others, it is an essential vehicle for acquiring conceptual understanding.

Problem-solving

Investigative science or problem-solving science has been advocated for a long time. The inclusion of it as a separate component in the APU assessment framework enhanced its popularity. Problem-solving science in the APU context was not about learning about the methods of science or gaining expertise in the separate processes of science. It was, rather, about using the procedures and processes of science to investigate phenomena, and solve problems that interest the learner. However, the way in which problem-solving was taken up in various curriculum initiatives and in classrooms revealed a similar disparity in purpose to that noted for practical work generally.

Critics of the problem-solving approach challenged the assumption that problem-solving was an effective teaching strategy. Indeed, in spite of the overwhelming amount of rhetoric in support of it, there is very little research evidence about its efficacy. One reason for this is people's various understandings of what constitutes a problem. Often problem-solving activities are narrowly defined, closed activities similar to traditional practical work in many respects. At other times they are very open-ended but unguided. What the pupil makes of such an open activity is determined by his or her prior understanding and motivation. There is evidence that such problem-solving activity, as with practical work, is of very little benefit to pupils in helping them to understand scientific concepts or to develop their procedural understanding.

In addition to concerns about the way problem-solving activity is put into practice, there also remain concerns about the purpose and definition of problem-solving in a domain like science. These concerns return us to dilemmas we have already discussed. Are the problems and strategies we want pupils to engage with 'scientific' ones, or are there general problem-solving strategies – that is, domain-independent – that we want them to acquire? Glaser (1984) considered whether both levels of thinking could be taught as the knowledge and skills of a subject are acquired. In his view this can be achieved by teaching 'specific knowledge domains in interactive, interrogative ways so that general self regulatory skills are exercised in the course of acquiring domain-related knowledge' (1984: 25).

SCIENCE CURRICULUM GUIDELINES IN THE NINETIES

The National Curriculum in science evolved whilst the debates we have referred to were ongoing. How did these debates influence what evolved? In the non-statutory guidance, learning science was seen to depend on 'existing ideas and on the processes by which those ideas are used and tested in new situations'. Hence there was a focus on both the concepts of science and the processes and skills of investigation. The value placed on these latter aspects of scientific behaviour was clear in that an attainment target was devoted to them. However, one would be forgiven for thinking that the original 16 content targets implied a particular view of what science was really about (DES 1988c). Interestingly, the NCC did suggest weighting across the attainment targets to indicate their relative importance, an importance that was seen to alter with age. The model of learning underlying the guidance was essentially constructivist, but the extent to which knowledge was recognised to be a social construct is unclear.

There have been numerous attempts to rewrite curriculum guidelines which help illuminate the problems that remain with the science curriculum. The alterations to the structure and content of the target devoted to scientific investigations, for example, reflect the problems with defining processes and procedures and progress in them. This was not helped by the separation of the content of science into other targets, even though progress in one dimension is dependent on progress in the other. Neither was this inter-dependence evident in the content target descriptions. Yet there appeared to be less concern about how to define progress in content areas in spite of there being very little empirical evidence to base it on. Indeed, much of the research, such as that of the APU and the CLIS project, revealed how little progress pupils made in this regard as they went through school. The main problem with the content targets in the curriculum guidelines had been their number and extent, revealing again the tenacity of the content-led science curriculum. The rewritten guidelines substantially reduced these, and in so doing had to tackle the problem of defining an appropriate and acceptable core of content for all pupils. This definition continues to have its critics.

Next we consider the rationale for the National Curriculum, by looking at the research evidence. We will review in the first instance issues related to attainment target 1, then explore what is known about children's conceptual understanding.

RESEARCH EVIDENCE

Children's procedural understanding

The APU project identified those aspects of procedural understanding that provided some indication of how pupils' investigative strategies progressed (DES 1988a and 1988b; DES 1989). For example, a significant proportion of 11- and 13-year-old pupils have difficulty understanding variables as continuous; that is, that they can take any value and that value can be changed and measured. Hence many 11-year-olds could successfully deal with a categoric variable like two pieces of material and test their insulating properties in an investigation, but most would be unable to set up an investigation to find the effect of, say, temperature or volume of a liquid.

Pupils' success at controlling variables in an investigation was dependent on their understanding their effect. Hence, as children's understanding of science concepts develops, so too does their ability to control a range of variables. However, in simple investigations most 11-year-olds understand the need for control, and practise it to some extent. There was also a difference between 11-year-olds and 13-year-olds in their understanding about measurement. About 20 per cent of 13-year-olds across investigations did not see the need for, nor the advantage of, quantified data, and this figure reached about 50 per cent at age 11. Eleven-year-olds were also less experienced than older pupils in estimating quantities which could adversely affect the scale of their investigation and limit their ability to observe any effect. Murphy (1988) also commented on the way progress in procedural understanding could inhibit pupils' approach to investigations. In an investigation to find the best kitchen towel to use, 8-year-olds

> automatically tore off whole pieces at the perforations. This unconscious choice of scale allowed them to obtain readings on the insensitive balance provided. Eleven-year-olds, in developing a thoughtful, scientific strategy, noticed that the pieces were of different sizes and carefully measured smaller, equal-sized pieces. These did not register on the balance. The older pupils modified their strategy, which got progressively worse, trying to deal with the difficult issues of scale and control.
>
> (Murphy 1988: 335)

Murphy provided evidence of the context- and content-dependency of pupils' investigative strategies even when the conceptual demands in the tasks had been reduced (see, for example, Murphy 1988). These initial findings about pupil performance were elaborated in reports published after the monitoring phase of the programme. In these reports a clearer breakdown of the successes and difficulties that pupils of 11 years of age experience is provided. The reports cover graphing skills, measurement, planning and carrying out investigations, data interpretation and observation (see SEAC 1990a and b; 1991a, b, c and d). The reports vary in the extent to which they provide evidence regarding the structure of attainment target 1, but in all cases it is clear that the content and context of tasks affects pupils' performance. This makes it difficult to interpret performance on process skill outcomes isolated from content. However, this is what teachers have to do when judging children's achievement using current curriculum guidance. The interdependence of subject knowledge is also an issue with the National Curriculum. Processes in science such as graphing, observation and investigation obviously depend on pupils' mathematical and linguistic understanding. The isolation of subjects in the curriculum guidelines makes it difficult to take this interdependence into account to develop an overview of pupil progress.

In the report on Observation in School Science (SEAC 1991d), an attempt is made to define progress in observation. The authors note, however, that

> Observation is implicit throughout the programmes of study . . . [then] becomes separated into three related processes – measurement, interpretation and control of variables. Progression in observation is 'hidden' within these other processes as they are defined in statements of attainment.
>
> (SEAC 1991d: 9)

In the amendments to the guidelines some attempt was made to address this problem. It does, however, indicate the difficulty with definitions again and the little understood relationship between the more general cognitive processes and the procedures of science. One of the benefits of the National Curriculum to the profession is in the attempt to articulate these definitions and relate them. These reports all provide useful advice to teachers about when and how to introduce various process-related activities and ideas about appropriate tasks.

The APU Science project mounted an in-depth study after the monitoring phase to look across pupil performance. A sample of pupils were given a range of questions across the assessment framework to provide a 'profile' of performance. This sample was then retested using the same questions two years later. This study is of considerable significance given the influence that the APU framework exerted on the evolution of the National Curriculum and the lack of research into pupil progress. The report of the APU profile study (SEAC 1991a) revealed that the assumptions in the National Curriculum about a hierarchy of levels in pupils' performance was often not realised in practice. Pupils could achieve higher-level criteria but not satisfy one of the lower-level criteria. Consequently, to assume a hierarchy of levels meant that pupils' success could be under-estimated. Another assumption of level difference is that the higher level is characterised by a more generalised expression. However, it was found that older pupils provide more detail, whereas when younger, the same pupil is more likely to respond in general terms. Hence the definition of levels was such that younger pupils' typical performance was judged to be superior to that of older pupils. The other phenomenon observed was similar in nature to that noted by Murphy (1988); that is, that pupils' 'newly acquired knowledge appeared to disrupt existing knowledge' (SEAC 1991a: 66). In other words, as pupils progress, their overt performance can show an apparent decline as they struggle to integrate new understanding with old. Such evidence throws into question simple hierarchical representations of progress such as the National Curriculum attainment targets.

The evidence that has emerged from secondary analysis of APU data and further APU studies indicates problems both within the definition of attainment target 1 and between the definition of the content and 'process' attainment targets of science. These problems were recognised by the National Curriculum Council who commissioned the development of in-service material and research into investigative work in science under the direction of Gott (NCC 1991; Foulds et al. 1992). This research provided a picture of the performance of primary children at Key Stages 1 and 2. Of particular significance was the finding that the concepts underlying investigations were more influential (on pupil performance) than the complexity of the variable structure within the investigation. Hence the progress defined in attainment target 1 could be over-ridden by pupils' conceptual difficulties. Pupils' performance on investigations can therefore only be judged and interpreted in the context of the range of concepts required. What remained unclear in the research study was the implications of this finding for children's learning rather than the assessment of it.

We will now consider research about children's conceptual understanding. We refer to two British projects which have developed over the last ten years out of the APU sphere of influence.

Children's conceptual understanding

We referred to Driver's research in the Children's Learning in Science Project (CLISP). Brook et al. summarise the findings of the CLISP project about children's ideas:

> Even before encountering formal school science children have constructed their own ideas of aspects of how the world works. These alternative conceptions of the scientific environment are constructed and developed through personal experience with physical phenomena

(dropping toys, touching hot objects, playing with sand and water) and through shared language and social understandings (in particular the everyday meanings given to words such as 'energy', 'force', 'food' which have very specific meanings in science).

Thus even young children are likely to have beliefs about the behaviour of objects in the world around them. These include notions about air (for example that it is weightless, that it exerts force only when moving), energy (something which humans have which gets used up in human activity), forces (necessary to sustain motion of any kind): these are just a few examples from a large body of research into children's ideas.

(Brook *et al.* 1989: 66)

Initially, the focus of CLISP was on identifying what these alternative conceptions were – but later the project moved on to develop ways that children's ideas could be brought closer to an accepted scientific view. Driver describes the work of CLISP as within the 'general perspective of constructivist epistemology' (Driver 1989), meaning that the project shares the view of many researchers on learning (in a variety of subjects, not just science) that rejects the view of knowledge of a subject as objective and unproblematic. Over the period 1985–88 the project devised, trialled and evaluated constructivist teaching sequences in the science topic areas of energy, the structure of matter and plant nutrition. The project had previously documented problems in children's thinking in these areas (see, e.g., Bell 1985; Brook and Driver 1986). The venture was a collaborative exercise between more than 30 teachers and researchers. First, the teachers taught one of the topics in their own classes using an eclectic range of strategies with children whose ages ranged from 12 to 15. At the same time the students' learning was studied using a number of approaches – including a diagnostic pre and post test, and teacher diaries of progress. Groups of teachers then discussed their views of the ideas being taught, and produced revised teaching schemes that incorporated a structure which explicitly made students aware that learning required them to change their thinking. The published schemes provided teachers with an outline of suggested activities and information about children's thinking (CLISP 1987).

The CLISP view of the role of the teacher in science learning is similar to the one expressed by Driver back in 1983 (p. 84), where she saw teachers ideally 'as mediators between the pupils' experiences and understanding and that of the science community'. The CLISP schemes of work all used children's ideas as a starting point and gave children opportunities to make their ideas explicit and to clarify them. They then undertook a range of activities designed to promote a restructuring of ideas. Finally, the children were given opportunities to consolidate and review their ideas.

As the project's aim was to see how interaction with physical phenomena could help children construct more scientific views of the world, inevitably it relied on children using their science processes and developing them as their understanding progressed.

> The process of bringing present knowledge to bear on new situations and possibly extending or adapting that knowledge in the light of new experiences involves the learner in an active way in the development of his or her understandings. From this perspective the dichotomy between content and process in science does not exist. Learning what is traditionally considered a 'content' in any meaningful way involves the learner in an active process of knowledge construction. Conversely what are conventionally considered to be scientific processes (for example observing, classifying and interpreting) are not carried out in isolation from a neutral perspective . . . they involve the engagement of pupils' prior knowledge. Learning in science is characterised neither by learning 'content' nor by learning 'process' but by a dynamic interaction whereby pupils continually and progressively construct and reconstruct their understanding of the world.
>
> (Brook *et al*. 1989: 76)

Consequently, a project in which children's ideas about concepts was the prime motivator ended up establishing the importance of science processes. The reverse was the case with the research into pupils' investigative skills. The second project we consider went so far as to put both processes and concept in the title.

Although much work has been done in identifying scientific ideas among secondary school pupils, little systematic work had been done with primary pupils until the funding of the Science Processes and Concept Exploration (SPACE) in 1985 by the Nuffield Foundation. The aim of the project, like CLISP, was to investigate the ideas that primary school children have about the world around them, and to encourage the development of ideas closer to the recognised scientific view.

The project focused on the scientific ideas of use and relevance to primary children and researched how these ideas developed. A number of topics were investigated: evaporation and condensation, growth, light, sound, electricity, and materials (SPACE 1990: 1, 2). Even more ambitious was the project's intention that a large number of the range of techniques developed to elicit children's ideas should be readily assimilated into classroom practice. Russell and Harlen (1990) discussed how it might be possible to assess the performance of primary children on science tasks and were dubious about the validity of using paper and pencil tasks alone as CLISP did at first. Consequently, the SPACE project spent much time developing techniques for finding out children's ideas in the context of practical science activities. The techniques found most useful included

open questioning: asking children to draw and annotate their drawings (for younger children the teachers might annotate in discussion with them); encouraging children to write about or talk about their ideas; and listening to children in discussion with each other as well as the teacher.

(cited in Harlen 1992)

Teachers were a key part of the research process. We use the description of the Sound project to describe the methods used and to give a flavour of the results. The way of working did vary from topic to topic, depending on the practical working arrangements for teachers, the stage in the project's history at which the work was undertaken, and the nature of the concepts themselves. Teachers were provided with materials and ideas for exploratory activities which they discussed with children over a period of three or four weeks. They were 'asked to encourage children to interact with them while not teaching the class anything about them' (SPACE 1990: 3).

The children used a diary to record what happened, and were encouraged to make drawings. The research team interviewed a sample of children from each class. After this elicitation phase, the teachers were given a pack of materials which contained descriptions of the activities which they were asked to use with their classes in an 'exploration' phase. After this the team developed a range of intervention strategies based on the ideas expressed by the children. For the intervention phase four strategies were adopted: encouraging children to test their ideas; encouraging children to generalise from one specific context to others through discussion; encouraging children to develop more specific definitions for particular key words; finding ways to make imperceptible change perceptible. The project concluded:

> The implications of the SPACE project research on 'Sound' go beyond informing teachers on the prevalent ideas which children hold about sound. They suggest that the elicitation techniques developed by the project are not only feasible for use but useful for teachers as additions to their repertoire of informal assessment techniques. The development of science process skills is also integral with the approach of children working from their own ideas to lead to conceptual development.
>
> (SPACE 1990: 132)

A special role was given to class discussions in encouraging generalisation:

> It was felt that if the teacher provided opportunities for children to discuss their observations and encouraged them to see areas of communality between classroom experiences then children might develop concepts which were broader and less context-specific.
>
> (SPACE 1990: 85)

A lot was learned about children's ideas about sound. For example, sound and vibration were not immediately seen to be linked by children, but certain experiences could help them to make the link. Junior children often used 'vibrate' and 'echo' to mean repeat. Most children thought sound transmission required an unobstructed path. Many children used different representations of sound in their drawings, some quite like the accepted scientific notation – that is, perpendicular to the direction of travel – some quite idiosyncratic and similar to pictures in children's comics.

Harlen (1992) in a review of the SPACE project's findings concluded that the methods developed for helping children to modify their ideas worked. Essentially these methods were:

> enabling children to test their own ideas (essentially through using and developing process skills); encouraging generalisation from one context to another; discussing the words children use to describe their ideas; extending the range of their ideas; requiring children to communicate their ideas.
>
> (Harlen 1992: 12)

From the above list of intervention tactics you can see a key difference from the approach used in the CLIS project. There is an adherence to methods of helping children to modify their ideas without presenting conflicting or discrepant events. These more gentle methods are used both with right and wrong ideas.

In terms of the specific results that the researchers document, perhaps the most interesting is the content- or situation-specific nature of the children's ideas. This supports Millar and Driver's view that it is the content that influences the links that pupils make between their experiences, not over-arching processes or thinking skills. The current SPACE publications provide the best information available to primary teachers on the ideas that children may have about the topics they wish to introduce. However, although the project expressed an interest in science processes, there has been as yet no attempt to describe the findings of the project in relation to science processes.

FUTURE DIRECTIONS

The research into pupils' thinking and investigative skills has resulted in two quite distinct directions for current research. The evidence that the conceptual demands of tasks are the most significant influence on pupil performance focused concern on the relationship between children's procedural and conceptual understanding. This relationship is now the subject of several research projects.

Shayer and Adey's (1981) earlier research had indicated the possibility of accelerating pupils' cognitive development through certain types of teaching. They conducted a longitudinal study of secondary-aged pupils, which involved an intervention programme of special lessons set in the context of the schemata of Piagetian formal operations. The intervention led to immediate gains in Piagetian measures of cognitive development and to significant improvement in the performance of groups of pupils in the level of achievement attained in GCSE exams taken 2–3 years later in maths, science and English. In Adey and Shayer's (1993) view, their results could be explained by the existence of general cognitive structures which had been positively influenced by the intervention. These general cognitive structures function across domains. This research has added to the speculation about the existence of general versus subject-specific problem-solving strategies and skills, and further research into this issue is planned.

As far as progression in concept development goes, there is evidence in some SPACE documents that there is progression in children's understanding of some concepts, such as sound, growth and energy. McGuigan and Qualter (1993) demonstrate how findings can be mapped on to the National Curriculum key stages. McGuigan, Qualter and Schilling (1993) describe the work of Osborne *et al.* (1992), who suggest that children's criteria for what it means to be alive get more generalised as they get older, older children mention life processes more though mostly growth and movement were the only processes mentioned. But this progression is not the view promoted in curriculum guidelines which assume that new knowledge will simply be accepted, whereas importance of context cannot be over-stressed.

Taylor analysed 13- and 15-year-old pupils' performance on APU tasks looking at types and uses of materials. He found that the statements of attainment in the curriculum guidelines did not 'represent a substantial hierarchy of difficulty and that some statements may well have been misplaced' (Taylor 1990: 36). Furthermore, the APU evidence indicated that pupils were not consistent with their use of idea in questions which were assumed and, widely agreed, to be assessing the same thing. In Taylor's view, a better model of progress is one where a 'pupil may move up and down as learning progresses but over a period of time there is . . . an uphill trend' (1990: 36). Progression is therefore seen as being able to handle 'more difficult and more complex or abstract concepts but also as having experience of a great number of concepts and areas of study' (*loc. cit.*).

The National Curriculum Council, in response to the lack of empirical evidence regarding progression in children's concepts, has commissioned research in this area (McGuigan and Qualter 1993). Driver with others continues to explore the teaching strategies that can best progress pupils' conceptual development. The Conceptual Change in Science project is the most recent attempt to investigate the processes of conceptual change (Driver and Scanlon 1989).

Current research in science education is focused on progression and the development of a better understanding of how pupils learn and act in science. Once this is clearer, the issue of what science education should be like and to what end can be revisited, but from a better informed position particularly with regard to learners and teachers.

REFERENCES

Adey, P. and Shayer, M. (1993) 'An exploration of long term far-transfer effect following an extended intervention programme in the high school science curriculum', *Cognition and Instruction*, 10.

Association for Science Education (1961) *Science and Education*, Hatfield: ASE.

—— (1979) *Alternatives for Science Education*, Hatfield: ASE.

Bell, B. (1985) *The Construction of Meaning and Conceptual Change in Classroom Settings: Case Studies in the Learning of Plant Nutrition*, Children's Learning in Science Project, Centre for Studies in Science and Mathematics Education, University of Leeds.

Bentley, D., Ellington, K. and Stewart, S. (1985) 'An examination of some SSCR philosophies', *The School Review*, 66 (237): 658–67.

Brook, A. and Driver, R. (1986) *The Construction of Meaning and Conceptual Change in Classroom Settings: Case Studies in the Learning of Energy*, Children's Learning in Science Project, Centre for Studies in Science and Mathematics Education, University of Leeds.

Brook, A., Driver, R. and Johnstone, K. (1989) 'Learning processes in science: a classroom perspective', in J. Wellington (ed.) *Skills and Processes in Science Education: a Critical Analysis*, London: Routledge, p.66.

Children's Learning in Science (1987) *CLIS in the Classroom: Approaches to Teaching*, Leeds Centre for Studies in Science and Mathematics Education.

DES (1974) *Educational Disadvantage and the Educational Needs of Immigrants* (Cmnd 5720), London: HMSO.

—— (1985) *Science 5–16: a Statement of Policy*, London: HMSO.

—— (1988a) *Science at Age 11: a Review of APU Survey Findings 1980–1984*, London: HMSO.

—— (1988b) *Science at Age 15: a Review of APU Survey Findings 1980–1984*, London: HMSO.

—— (1988c) *Science for Ages 5–16*, London: HMSO.

—— (1989) *Science at Age 13: a Review of APU Survey Findings 1980–1984*, London: HMSO.

Driver, R. (1983) *The Pupil as Scientist*, Milton Keynes: Open University Press.

—— (1989) 'Changing conceptions', in P. Adey, J. Bliss, J. Head and M. Shayer (eds) *Adolescent Development and School Science*, Lewes: Falmer Press.

Driver, R., Guesne, E. and Tiberghien, A. (eds) (1985) *Children's Ideas in Science*, Milton Keynes: Open University Press.

Driver, R. and Scanlon, E. (1989) 'Conceptual change in science', *Journal of Computer Assisted Learning*, 5(1): 25–36.

Foulds, K., Gott, R. and Feasey, R. (1992) *Investigative Work in Science*, Durham: University of Durham.

Gilbert, J.K., Osborne, R.J. and Fensham, P.J. (1982) 'Children's science and its consequences for teaching', *Science Education*, 66 (4): 623–33.

Gilbert, J. and Watts, D. (1983) 'Concepts, misconceptions and alternative frameworks', *Studies in Science Education*, 10: 61–91.

Glaser, R. (1984) 'Education and thinking: the role of knowledge', *American Psychologist*, 39(2): 93–104.

Gott, R. and Murphy, P. (1987) *Assessing Investigations at Ages 13 and 15*, Science Report for Teachers, 9, Hatfield: ASE.

Gott, R. and Welford, G. (1987) 'The assessment of observation in science', *School Science Review*, 69: 217–27.

Gunstone, R.F. and Watts, D.M. (1985) 'Force and motion', in R. Driver, E. Guesne and A. Tiberghien (eds) *Children's Ideas in Science*, Milton Keynes: Open University Press.

Harlen, W. (1975) *Science 5/13: a Formative Evaluation*, London: Macmillan Education/Schools Council.

—— (1985) 'Does content matter in primary science?', in B. Hodgson and E. Scanlon (eds) *Approaching Primary Science*, London: Paul Chapman Publishing.

—— (1992) 'Research and the development of science in the primary school', *International Journal of Science Education*, 14(5): 491–503.

Hodgson, B. and Scanlon, E. (1985) *Approaching Primary Science*, London: Paul Chapman Publishing.

Hodson, D. (1990) 'A critical look at practical work in science', *School Science Review*, 70: 33–40.

Jenkins, E. (1987) 'Philosophical flaws', *Times Educational Supplement*, 2 Jan.

McGuigan, L. and Qualter, A. (1993) 'What do we mean by progression in primary science?', in P. Murphy and E. Scanlon (eds) *Science*, Primary Module 1 (E880, Postgraduate Certificate in Education, *Teaching in Primary Schools*), Resource Box, Milton Keynes: Open University.

McGuigan, L., Qualter, A. and Schilling, M. (1993), 'Children, science and learning', in P. Murphy and E. Scanlon (eds) *Science*, Primary Module 1 (E880, Postgraduate Certificate in Education, *Teaching in Primary Schools*), Resource Box, Milton Keynes: Open University.

Millar, R. (1990) 'A means to an end: the role of process in science education', in B. Woolnough (ed.) *Practical Science*, Milton Keynes: Open University Press.

Millar, R. and Driver, R. (1987) 'Beyond process', *Studies in Education*, 14: 33–62.

Ministry of Education (1960) Pamphlet no. 38, 'Science in secondary schools', London: HMSO.

Murphy, P. (1988) 'Insights into pupils' responses to practical investigations', from the APU *Physics Education*, 23: 330–6.

—— (1989) 'Observation', in B. Schofield (ed.) *Science at Age 13: a Review of APU Survey Findings 1980–1984*, London: HMSO.

—— (1990) 'National Curriculum Assessment: has anything been learned from the experience of the APU?', *The Curriculum Journal*, 1(2): 185–97.

Murphy, P. and Gott, R. (1984) *Science Assessment Framework Age 13 and 15*, Science Report for Teachers: 2, Hatfield: ASE.

NCC (1991) *Science Explorations*, York: NCC.

Nuffield Primary SPACE Science Course (1993) Teachers Guide, *Theme Guides for Key Stages 1 and 2*; Pupils Booklets, Glasgow: HarperCollins.

Osborne, J., Wadsworth, P. and Black, P. (1992) *Processes of Life*, SPACE Project Report, Liverpool: Liverpool University Press.

Osborne, R. and Freyberg, P. (1985) *Learning in Science: the Implications of Children's Science*, New Zealand: Heinemann.

Russell, T. and Harlen, W. (1990) *Assessing Science in the Primary Classroom: Practical Tasks*, London: Paul Chapman.

Russell, T., Harlen, W. and Watt, D. (1989) 'Children's ideas about evaporation', *International Journal of Science Education*, 11: 566–76.

Screen, P. (1986) *Warwick Process Science*, Southampton: Ashford Press.

SEAC (1990a) *Assessment Matters: No. 1, Measurement in School Science*, London: HMSO.

—— (1990b) *Assessment Matters: No. 2, Measurement in School Science*, London: HMSO.

—— (1991a) *Assessment Matters: No. 5, Profiles and Progression in Science Exploration*, London: HMSO.

—— (1991b) *Assessment Matters: No. 6, Planning and Carrying out Investigations*, London: HMSO.

—— (1991c) *Assessment Matters: No. 7, Patterns and Relationships in School Science*, London: HMSO.

—— (1991d) *Assessment Matters: No. 8, Observation in School Science*, London: HMSO.

Shayer, M. and Adey, P. (1981) *Toward a Science of Science Teaching: Cognitive Development and Curriculum Demand*, London: Heinemann.

SPACE Research Reports *Evaporation and condensation* (1990); *Growth* (1990); *Light* (1990); *Sound* (1990); *Electricity* (1991); *Materials* (1991); *Processes of Life* (1991), London: University of London Press.

SSCR (1983) *Science Education 11–16: Proposals for Action and Consultation*, Schools Council.

Taylor, R.M. (1990) 'The National Curriculum: a study to compare levels of attainment with data from APU science surveys', *School Science Review*, 72: 31–7.

Wellington, J. (ed.) (1989) *Skills and Processes in Science Education: a Critical Analysis*, London: Routledge.

Woolnough, B. and Allsop, T. (1985) *Practical Work in Science*, Cambridge: Cambridge University Press.

Chapter 9

Learning about grammar

Pam Czerniewska

A 6-year-old eating her supper remarked, 'Isn't it funny? We say eat *up* your food but your food goes *down*.' After a little thought she added, 'And we say get *down* from the table but we stand *up*.' This interest in language should not be seen as particularly unusual. After all, children have been surrounded by and learning how to use language since they were very small, so it's not surprising that they should also reflect on its workings. What is surprising is the way we seem to be tying ourselves into all sorts of impossible knots about the teaching of grammar, when exploring language seems such a natural process for children to do.

BECOMING A GRAMMARIAN

Children's familiarity with language forms the basis of new developments in grammar teaching. Any set of curriculum guidelines needs to acknowledge the role played by the learner in language construction. Children are not linguistically empty vessels to be filled with rules and terminology at specific points. They come to school language tasks with a considerable knowledge of speaking, reading and writing developed through their active explorations of the language around them. There are now many descriptions of the child as language-maker, working out the rules of language, often very creatively, fine-tuning them and gradually moving towards the adult language system. Less is known about children's ability to look at and reflect on language structure. But the little that we do know suggests that children's understanding of the way language works is greater than usually assumed and can begin very early. Recent work by Carol Fox (1992), for example, has shown, through her recordings of pre-school children's language, that we may under-estimate their linguistic competence. Her collection of oral language reveals their considerable knowledge of discourse structure, which must reflect the most attentive listening to the language around them. In her samples, she discovered children initiating monologues based on news broadcasts and weather forecasts which included examples like this from a 5-year-old:

Somewhere in Australia a hundred bargains has been cut off by Thatcher.

The use of such language structures – note the passive, *has been cut off*, a grammatical form rarely found in young children's conversation – shows how aware children are of the language around them. Other examples show how children learn, very early, that power is exercised by those who know the right words. Anyone who has listened to children pretending to be parents, teachers, doctors and so on can confirm how these roles are played with exaggerated fierceness. As well as imitating language forms and experimenting with their power, children in Fox's study showed a fascinating ability to re-invent language. Five-year-olds coined words and phrases like:

he had to hobble over the *walking bridges* like this (Sundari, 5:6)

it was *humble* in the sea (Sundari, 5:6)

they were really truly of their home and going to it (Josh, 5:3)

As Fox comments: 'Such inventions and malapropisms show a concern to explore language, to invent and push it beyond its conventional boundaries' (Fox 1992: 9–10).

TALKING ABOUT LANGUAGE

Being able to use the grammatical structures of different registers does not make the child a grammarian in the sense of being able to *identify and talk about* language structures such as passives. But it does show how children enjoy playing with language even when it serves no immediate communicative function, except to amuse. They see language as an object, something worth studying for its own sake. It's very hard to find out what young children can and cannot make explicit about their language. Two- and 3-year-olds may show how clever they are at working out grammatical rules when they produce 'creative errors' like *'breaked, runned, goed'*, but this does not mean that they can make explicit the grammatical rule for past tense markers. However, the emerging evidence suggests that children can reflect on their language at an early age. For example, at a surprisingly young age, children are able to make judgements about how people speak and adjust their own language accordingly. Four-year-olds (and possibly younger children) will adjust their language according to the age of the listener; using simpler constructions for children younger than themselves (Shatz and Gelman 1973). Five-year-olds, and maybe those younger, will talk about the language younger children use and love to talk about their own baby talk. Grieve *et al.* (1983) quote a charming example of a 2½-year-old who clearly appreciates linguistic form:

FATHER: Say, *jump.*
CHILD: Dup.

FATHER: No, *jump*.
CHILD: Dup.
FATHER: No, *jummmp*.
CHILD: Only daddy can say *dup*!

(from Smith 1973)

Bilingual children are good, too, at knowing who can and cannot understand their different languages and from an early age can act as interpreters, a process that involves considerable understanding of language structure.

Around the age of 6, alongside their development as readers, there is often a discernible leap in 'metalinguistic' awareness. Perhaps the most tangible proof of this developing ability is in joke-telling, like these from a 6-year-old:

Q.   What do sheep eat for breakfast?
A.   Barley.

> Knock knock
> Who's there?
> Boo
> Boo who?
> There's no need to cry about it

A 6- or 7-year-old will not only find these funny but explain why they are funny, and prove their understanding by going on to invent equally excruciating humour. Occasionally, we find examples of children in the process of coming to grips with a particular aspect of language workings. A favourite example from the National Writing Project collections is the development of story structure by two Reception children, Fiona and Neil (Czerniewska 1988). They were invited by their teacher, Sheila Hughes, to help each other write, once a week, starting with stories about their favourite colours. Fiona wrote her story herself with some help with spelling; Neil dictated his story for the teacher to write. Each text was accompanied by a drawing. Every week they exchanged books and the teacher wrote their comments underneath. These are some extracts:

Week 1

FIONA WROTE: *I like black because I have a toy black dog and I have always wanted a real life black dog.*

NEIL COMMENTED: *She could have made it better if she'd put legs on the dog.*

NEIL WROTE: *I like yellow wallpaper and I am going to ask my dad if I can have some.*

FIONA COMMENTED: *He should have put wallpaper at the end of his story.*

Week 2

FIONA WROTE:	*Red makes my Mummy happy. She had a red Renault 5 car and there is a lot of room in the boot.*
NEIL COMMENTED:	*She should have put two spokes on the wheels and two lights front and back.*
NEIL WROTE:	*This is a red lorry and I like it.*
FIONA COMMENTED:	*He should have said where the lorry was going and why he liked it.*

Week 6

FIONA WROTE:	*The bear is trying to get some honey out of a tree. He looks very cuddly but really he is dangerous.*
NEIL COMMENTED:	*Drawn a bigger tree. It is a good story.*
NEIL WROTE:	*My teddy bear is sitting by a tree thinking about doing something naughty.*
FIONA COMMENTED:	*Ears and paws on the bear. I would like to know what naughty thing this teddy was going to do.*

Their achievements include the use of complex language in both speech and writing. But more significantly there are acknowledgements of the structures appropriate to the writing task. Fiona, for example, criticises Neil's omission of 'wallpaper'. (Most adults would accept this ellipsis and perhaps Fiona's objection reflects the style of early reading materials.) Fiona, and later Neil, show an ability to reflect on a story's worth, an impressive skill given their very recent experience as authors.

The evidence of children's grammatical awareness is still piecemeal, but it all points in the same direction. From an early age, children are actively exploring how language works, how meanings are made. The parallels with knowledge about reading and writing are clear here. It is now acknowledged that children are not simply taught to read and write; they become literate through an engagement with the processes of reading and writing. Children work out what it means to be a reader/writer and move towards adult literacy through a series of refinements of their constructed system. Similarly, the children in the above examples are trying to find out how meanings are made in their language – which is exactly what grammar is all about. Grammar helps us find out the patterns of language, showing how speakers and writers create different meanings.

NEW GRAMMAR FOR OLD

The evidence of children's interest in and awareness about their own language is a very different starting point from that used in former grammar lessons – the ones so fondly remembered by those bemoaning a lack of grammar and discipline in today's schools. The arguments against traditional grammar teaching have been well rehearsed (e.g. Carter 1990; Hudson 1992). The topics were predetermined with almost no reference to the child's own language use or knowledge about that use. The implication of the curriculum seemed to be that children were missing grammar and needed the gap to be filled. The grammatical structures to fill the gap were fixed, based unquestioningly on written Standard English and with emphasis on 'correct' forms of grammar rather than on ways people actually use grammar. The grammar itself had become outdated, unreplenished by new insights from modern linguistics and out of touch with more child-centred pedagogy. Hudson (1992) suggests that 'school grammar lost its academic roots, and just shrivelled and died'. He goes on to add, however, that when the teaching of grammar stopped, albeit for sound pedagogical reasons, it was a 'clear case of an important baby being thrown out with some rather dirty bathwater'. The 'cleaner bathwater' of a revived grammar curriculum has an important new set of assumptions. It begins with a recognition of children's language learning abilities and their interest in the system itself. Spoken language is as important as written language, and within both the many regional and social varieties are recognised as worth studying. Grammar is seen as a way of describing how language works not as a means of prescribing particular forms. But the description is much more than a naming of parts – it is about understanding the language choices available to us.

MAKING CHOICES

Grammar provides us with methods of description and tools of analysis to look beyond the words on display and to see how they represent a particular way of looking at things. Whenever speakers and writers use language, they make choices about 'how to put it' – choices which can make a message, for example, more formal or informal, more personal or impersonal; can make certain information more or less important and which can make the 'actors' more or less involved. Compare for example:

(a) The wolf arrived. He huffed and puffed outside the door.
(b) There was a huffing and puffing outside the door. It was the wolf.

Grammatically, (a) and (b) have different information at subject, verb and object position, and these determine the effect of the text. In (a) *the wolf/he* is in subject position and the sentences are 'active'. In contrast, in (b) *huffing and puffing* have been nominalised – that is, have been turned into nouns – and the grammatical subject slots have been filled by the 'empty' *there/it*. This has the effect of building up the suspense. The real 'actor' in the scene arrives more dramatically when placed at the very end. At least, that would be my interpretation of the two versions. When I asked a 6-year-old what she thought about the alternatives, she said, after some thought, that (b) was more exciting. But she added that she would prefer to use (a) 'because people who don't know the story might not know who was at the door'.

The central issue for the classroom teacher is how best to develop and formalise children's implicit sense of grammatical choice and thus to give them tools to help them evaluate their own and others' language use. Choices occur at different levels – word, clause, sentence and text level – and at each of these there are different tools that can be used. The main focus for linguists has been the *sentence*, and the methods used to look at sentences provide examples which can transfer well into a classroom. Take a sentence like *The bad fairy waved her wand wickedly*. By playing around with the words we can show what combinations can occur in English and what the relationships are between the words. For example, we can show that the relationships are not equal, some words are dependent on the occurrence of others. You can say: *The fairy waved* but not *The bad wickedly*. By setting up a matrix, we can go on to discover whether there are classes of words that form similar relationships and what other words can be inserted at different points:

the		bad	fairy	waved	her	wand	wickedly
that	very	good	child	sat			quietly
a	fairly	naughty	witch	cast	a	spell	
She				kissed	the	prince	

Slowly, a picture emerges of word classes which might be labelled *nouns, verbs, adjectives*, and so on, and of sub-classes such as verbs that can stand on their own and verbs that need something following them. As this process continues, a profile emerges of the regularly occurring patterns of language. It is purely descriptive, resting on our judgements of what is and what is not acceptable. It can also be used to develop with children the range of options they can draw on in, for example, their own writing. How many times does *very* occur in a piece of writing – what else could be used instead? *Who/what* is at the beginning of the sentence, in subject position? Is it always the chief 'actor'? Could something else act as subject: *The wand was waved wickedly above their heads*?

The grammatical description can be built up by looking at different levels; that is, at units smaller or larger than the sentence. At *word* level, the grammatical analysis could explore markers such as *-s, -ed, -ly, un-* and see when they occur and how they combine with other elements: for example, *they laughed and sang* is acceptable but *they laughed and sing* is not. Another layer can be added to the picture by asking the function that different parts of the sentence serve. Compare, for instance: *Cinderella cooked for the ugly sisters* and *The ugly sisters cooked for Cinderella*. Here the change in position of *Cinderella* from subject to object has dramatically changed the meaning. Word order is central to English grammar, as there are few other markers of case – that is, of who is doing what to whom. Not surprisingly, children rarely make grammatical errors in word order; what they need to explore is the range of potential new meanings that can be created when word order varies.

Above the sentence level, we can look at the effects of different sentence combinations. At a simple level comparison of *She left. They arrived.* and *They arrived. She left.* illustrates how sentence order can affect meaning. Building on such instances, we can start to build up a notion of text grammar – what makes a story a story? What's the difference between a recipe and a science write-up? Each curriculum subject shapes its meaning through the language varieties it uses. Yet often the learning of the appropriate pattern takes place with little conscious attention to the way linguistic structures achieve particular ends. Why, for instance, do we encourage children to use sentences in science like: (a) *The jar was put over the candle and it went out.* rather than (b) *We put a jar over the candle and then we saw the candle go out*? There are good reasons for this preference: for example, the passive form in (a) focuses the reader's attention on the scientifically significant 'actors' of the event. Similarly, how do we know that *'Once upon a time'* signals a particular text structure, and that it would be surprising at the beginning of a maths textbook? A lesson just looking at opening lines of textbooks and of storybooks can provide a wealth of insight into grammatical choice.

WHOSE GRAMMAR?

A highly significant set of grammatical choices that children (and adults) learn about is which variety of English to use. Dialect variation provides one of the most fascinating and yet most controversial aspects of grammar. It is firmly rooted in the National Curriculum – in fact, much of the discussion in the Cox Report (DES 1989) on grammar teaching is subsumed under *Teaching Standard English*. While it is well acknowledged that all dialects are equally complex and grammatical, they are far from equal socially. It seems fair to say that non-standard dialect users are running in a different race from Standard English speakers. This means that discussion of dialect choices is not simply a debate about effectiveness or stylistic preference, it is also about questions of self-identity, and about how others will judge you by your choice.

There seem to be two important dimensions to teaching about dialect choice. The first involves children recognising the great range of variants in English – this is the multi-dialectal approach to language teaching which aims to value each child's language. A starting point is simply to ask children to find out who says what in their community. Questions that can begin a discussion of alternatives people use might include: 'Do you say *up/down/to/over* my friend's house' or 'do you know anyone who says: *they weren't doing nothing/we didn't buy no tickets/she'll no go in there*?' Data from dialect surveys can enrich what children find in their own community. For example, forms of negation found in British dialects include:

Dinna run so fast.
You *shouldna* go in there!
You've *no* to go in there.
My friend broke that, I *never*.
No, I *never* broke that.
Will you not try to mend it – we need an expert.
That *ain't* working.
That *in't* working.
That *ay* working.
He *in arf* stupid.
Not do that John.
Count on me, *I won't* do *nothing* silly.
Anyone mustn't go in there!

(from Cheshire and Edwards, reprinted in Hudson 1992)

The second aspect of dialect teaching is to show the special status of Standard English. Most children learn at an early age that Standard English carries social status – it's 'talking posh'. But it's not only the prestigious form, it is also the one that has been most widely codified in the written language. There are excellent exceptions to this, especially in fiction, but they are still few. As writing and reading play such an important role in learning and assessment, children need to be competent and confident writers in Standard English. Standard English is also the dialect chosen in public contexts such as television and radio, and the one most usually used by teachers. To introduce Standard English on the timetable, as required by the National Curriculum, is not to teach some new area of knowledge. All children will be well familiar with its forms through their reading and the stories read to them, through television and radio, through posters and so on. They may not use Standard English in their day-to-day conversation (and why should they?) but they can most probably produce a close correspondence to, say, a TV news item when asked to. The most important factors in developing children's use of Standard English in appropriate contexts seems to be an awareness of audience and a sense of purpose in what they are writing/talking about. There are many examples of classroom practice (such as the National Writing Project 1989) which show that when children are writing to get something specific done or writing for defined readers, then, with little prompting from the teacher, they make appropriate language choices. When children see that they are expected not simply to 'use their own words' but to use the words others would use – others like newspaper writers, book-writers, poets and so on – then they can begin to explore how to make their messages most effective.

BREAKING INTO LANGUAGE

From these few linguistic explorations, some conclusions about children, grammar and teaching emerge. First, children are highly competent language users and language analysers. Secondly, grammar is not a minefield of potential errors such as where to put the apostrophe. It is an attempt to describe a fascinating, complex, multi-level system, used in slightly different ways by different people, but sharing underlying principles of organisation. Thirdly, those principles can be worked out by all language users by asking what language they use in speech/writing and what effect different choices make to meaning.

As we start to help children explore grammar (instead of telling them about it as in former pedagogies), we will no doubt be surprised at how able young children are to reflect on their language and the language of others. Bruner (1965), after describing a lesson in which children learn about grammar rules through 'discovery' (quoted in the Cox Report, DES (1989), para.5.13–5.15), says:

> Once the children break into an idea in language, once they get a sense of distinction, they quickly 'turn around' on their own usage and make remarkable strides towards linguistic understanding. The only point I would make is that you must wait until *they* are willing reflectively to turn around before you start operating with abstractions.

I like especially Bruner's notion of children breaking into an idea of language. It suggests such a completely different picture from drills on nouns, adjectives and prepositions. Children may find they need linguistic terms but only after they have become aware of what language can do. The overall aim of grammar teaching should be that children learn, as Carter (1990) puts it, to 'see through language', to become aware of its power.

REFERENCES

Bruner, J. (1965) 'Some elements of discovery', in J. Bruner (1974) *The Relevance of Education*, Harmondsworth: Penguin.

Carter, R. (1990) 'The new grammar teaching', in R. Carter (ed.) *Knowledge about Language and the Curriculum*, London: Hodder & Stoughton.

Czerniewska, P. (1988) 'Objectives for language learning', in M. Jones and A. West (eds) *Learning Me Your Language*, London: Mary Glasgow.

DES (1989) *English for Ages 5 to 16* (The Cox Report), London: HMSO.

Fox, C. (1992) '"You sing so merry those tunes", oral storytelling as a window on young children's language learning', in K. Kimberley, M. Meek and J. Miller (eds) *New Readings: Contributions to an Understanding of Literacy*, London: A. & C. Black.

Grieve, R., Tunmer, W.E. and Pratt, C. (1983) 'Language awareness in children', in M. Donaldson, R. Grieve and C. Pratt (eds) *Early Childhood Development and Education*, Oxford: Blackwell.

Hudson, R. (1992) *Teaching Grammar, a Guide for the National Curriculum*, Oxford: Blackwell.

National Writing Project (1989) *Audiences for Writing*, Walton-on-Thames: Thomas Nelson.

Shatz, M. and Gelman, R. (1973) 'The development of communication skills: modifications in the speech of young children as a function of listeners', *Monographs of the Society for Research in Child Development*, 38(5), serial no. 5.

Smith, N.V. (1973) *The Acquisition of Phonology: a Case Study*, Cambridge: Cambridge University Press.

Chapter 10

Issues for curriculum development in primary mathematics

Hilary Shuard

EDUCATION FOR CHANGE

The primary children of today, and of tomorrow, will live out their adult lives in the twenty-first century. It is the hope of all teachers that what children learn at school will sustain them into adult life, in a variety of ways. Teachers hope that experiences encountered at school will open doors in children's minds to interests, activities and challenges that can continue to be pursued as the young people grow older. Teachers also hope that what is done at school will prove to be useful learning, which will equip children to live in the world in which they will find themselves.

Foretelling the future is always a chancy business, especially in a world which is changing as rapidly as that of today. Perhaps the only thing we can be sure of is that today's children will continue to live in a world of change, and that the ability to cope with change is the life skill that will be the most important skill to them.

Primary mathematics has an important place in all children's experience of schooling, and it is therefore important to ask how far it contributes to education for change, to useful life skills, and to abiding interests and challenges in people's lives. The curriculum of primary mathematics needs to change in a number of ways. It does not take sufficient account of how children learn, nor does it take sufficient account of changes in technology. But more importantly, it does not take sufficient account of the need to prepare children to live in a continually changing world, and to face the challenges of change.

A MODEL FOR DESCRIBING PRIMARY MATHEMATICS

The Cockcroft Report calls attention, in paras 240–1, to the fact that effective mathematics teaching needs to attend to a number of different elements of mathematics:

facts;
skills;

conceptual structures;
general strategies for problem solving and investigation;
appreciation of the nature of mathematics;
attitudes towards mathematics.

When a particular mathematics curriculum is described, it is very common for only the first three of these elements – facts, skills and conceptual structures – to be listed. These elements form the *content* of primary mathematics. The other listed elements tend not to be explicitly described in the documentation of a curriculum, except in the most general terms. General strategies for problem-solving and investigation are especially difficult to describe, and it is therefore important to try to describe them as fully as possible, so that they are not overlooked in curriculum building. These strategies form a part of the range of *processes* involved in doing mathematics, and consequently should form an important part of children's mathematical education.

Another important feature of primary mathematics is the fact that, for children, mathematics is set in the context of a variety of situations and experiences, and is built upon these situations and experiences, some of which are found in the children's environment, and some of which are contrived by the teacher. There needs to be a constant interplay between these *situations* and the mathematical ideas the children are learning, if they are to be able to apply their mathematics to everyday situations.

Hence, three important dimensions of the primary mathematics curriculum are the *content, processes* and *situations* of primary mathematics. All three of these dimensions need to be considered in documenting or building a curriculum. So, too, does a fourth dimension concerned with children's *appreciation* of mathematics and their *attitudes* towards it, which need to permeate all the mathematics that is done in school. In Figure 10.1, these four dimensions of the mathematics curriculum are shown as the four faces of a tetrahedron. The front face, which represents *appreciation* and *attitudes*, is cut away to reveal the three faces representing *processes, content* and *situations*.

Thus, any particular mathematical experience which the curriculum provides (such as finding the volume of a small box) can be looked at in terms of the content it embodies (the concept of volume) and the processes which children use (perhaps making a practical experiment by filling it with sand, or creating a mathematical model by first measuring its dimensions) and in terms of the situation from which it came (in this case probably a situation contrived by the teacher to give experience of volume). Finally, the children bring to the experience attitudes such as interest in what they are doing and confidence that they will succeed (or perhaps the opposite).

These four dimensions can be thought of both as inputs to the experience, as suggested above, and as outputs: through the experience, the children will

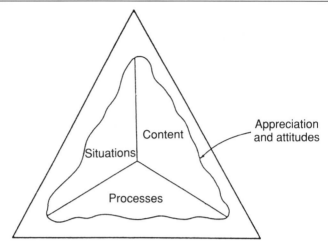

Figure 10.1 The primary mathematics curriculum

strengthen their concept of volume, become more able to create mathematical models, and become more aware of experimental situations embodying volume. Their experience will also strengthen or contribute to changing their attitudes and appreciation of mathematics.

Similarly, the *school* context needs to be considered. If the teaching styles used in mathematics are not consonant with those used in other curriculum areas, or if different teachers have different philosophies, then the pupils will be confused; for example, if one teacher expects pupils to think mathematically for themselves, while the next year another teacher tells those same pupils to learn the rules and not to worry about reasons for them, then the pupils cannot know whether mathematics is concerned with thinking and communication, or whether it is a set of procedures carried out by arbitrary rules. Thus, the context in which it is possible for the curriculum to operate within a particular school must be taken into account in developing a curriculum for that school. Figure 10.2 depicts all these influences on primary mathematics, and can be used as a model for the purpose of curriculum-building.

TEACHING STYLES

It is still the case that the major model of teaching employed in primary mathematics is that of *transmission*. The teacher has mathematical knowledge, and his or her task is to convey it to the pupils. This is sometimes done by exposition followed by practice, or it is sometimes done by practical work, in a 'guided discovery' mode, in which the children carry out activities which should enable them to 'discover' what the teacher has in mind. This model of teaching has two consequences: first, it makes the children depen-

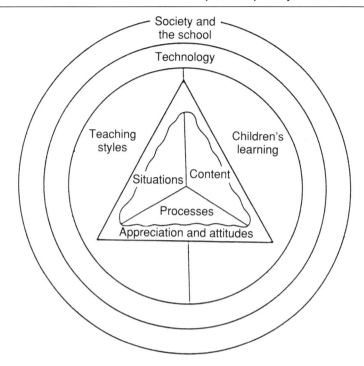

Figure 10.2 A model of primary mathematics for curriculum-building

dent on the teacher – the teacher knows what is right, and the children's work is validated by the teacher's approval. The children's task is more nearly to find out what the teacher is thinking than it is to think out mathematics for themselves. The second consequence is that this model engenders lack of confidence in many teachers, as they privately acknowledge to themselves that their knowledge of mathematics is inadequate for them to be the fount of all wisdom in the subject to their pupils. This often leads to a very narrow teaching style, in which exploratory activity and open questioning by the pupils are not encouraged.

If children are to learn to face challenges with confidence, they need to become independent thinkers, in mathematics as in everything else. The teachers at Kitamaeno School in Japan ask the children to learn to do everything for themselves – including learning how to learn mathematics for themselves. In this country, the 'investigations movement' values children's own mathematical thinking, and does not expect a 'right answer', but rather looks for honest individual thinking at the level of which a pupil or a group is capable. The work which is now being done on discussion as a teaching method in mathematics enables teachers to understand their pupils' thinking much more clearly than they could do in the style of 'exposition by question and answer'. Recent work on the learning of mathematics gives evidence for a *constructivist* view of learning in mathematics – children gradually construct meaning for themselves, by reflection on their experiences. They need to be given opportunities to reflect and to develop their thinking to a more advanced level in discussion with others who hold different views.

A most important challenge, therefore, in curriculum development in primary mathematics, is to develop styles of teaching which give full value to children's mathematical thinking, and which enable them to think independently with enjoyment and energy, and to develop good attitudes to mathematical problem-solving. This is no easy task – teaching styles are much more resistant to change than is mathematical content. Teachers will need to support one another, using their own discussions as a means of learning, during a period of change, and to work together to explore methods of classroom organisation that will enable them to develop their teaching.

A further challenge in the development of teaching styles is provided by the 'seven-year difference'. In a top junior class of mixed ability, some children have a fairly full understanding of most aspects of place-value for whole numbers, some children have had this understanding for several years, and are well advanced in their grasp of the decimal system, and others will not understand place-value, even for whole numbers, for several years to come. Similar differences exist for other age groups, and in other topic areas. All these children need activities which will challenge their thinking at their own level.

PROCESSES

If children are to develop as independent mathematical thinkers, teachers need to know what are the processes of mathematical thinking, and how children learn to use them. Only thus can teachers provide activities and topics for investigation which will help children to become more adept at using these processes. Traditionally, the primary mathematics curriculum has been thought of in terms of mathematical content, rather than in terms of the processes of mathematical thinking. In recent years, many processes have been identified, but little is yet known about the stages at which different children become able to use a process such as classification or generalisation, and in what situations they are spontaneously used. Much work will be needed in this area, involving both research into children's mathematical thinking and the development of activities which embody different processes.

NEW TECHNOLOGY

Another major issue in curriculum development is the impact of new technology on primary mathematics. Calculators have become everyday tools in adult life, and the pencil-and-paper algorithms for the 'four rules' are disappearing fast; people now calculate mentally or use a calculator. In school, the pencil-and-paper algorithms are one of the most important bastions of 'transmission' teaching; children have had to be taught the correct ways of doing these algorithms, even though there is evidence that many children are remarkably resistant to learning them, and prefer their own methods. Now, the algorithms are no longer needed as useful life skills – a calculator is always available for computation which a person cannot do in his or her head. This new context for primary mathematics needs to provoke a complete reassessment of the curriculum in the field of number; at present, calculators are largely being used to support the traditional number curriculum, whose major effort was focused on the pencil-and-paper algorithms.

The removal of the need for children to learn the pencil-and-paper algorithms as tools for use will enable number work to focus on understanding of the number system, and on using it for problem-solving, both within mathematics and wherever else in the curriculum problems occur. In this way, it will become easier for the style of teaching in primary mathematics to move from the 'transmission' model to a 'constructivist' model. However, the pencil-and-paper algorithms for the four rules have been a major, and necessary, element of primary arithmetic for the last hundred years, and it will not be easy for many teachers to grasp that these algorithms are no longer necessary for use, nor that a valid, useful and exciting primary mathematics curriculum is available without them. The new technology of calculation provides the biggest challenge to the content of school mathematics throughout the whole history of compulsory schooling in this country. It is a challenge that must be tackled if the primary mathematics curriculum is not to become 'the sabre-toothed curriculum' – activities that are only done in school, and which have nothing to do with life.

The calculator is a cheap, personal, portable tool which mechanises one type of mathematical skill. The same cannot yet be said of the computer. Outside school, it is still largely a desk-top machine, and within school it is still an expensive resource that has to be shared between many children. However, this may change within the next ten years. Portable computers the size of an A4 file are already available, although the cost is still prohibitive for individual use by most people. It is possible, however, that the next generation of primary children may own portable computers in the way that the present generation own calculators.

Even today's computers have much potential in primary mathematics. Both the Turtle graphics aspects of LOGO, and its potential in control technology, give ways in to independent problem-posing and problem-solving for primary children. Packages now available can mechanise graph drawing and the handling of data, and children can write very short programs of their own to tackle mathematical tasks. Practice activities, when practice is necessary, can also easily be monitored by the computer. All these uses of the computer can only grow in future years, and will open new mathematical doors to children.

Other new developments, such as the digital watch, may change children's environments in such a way as to modify some of their mathematical concepts, giving a different emphasis from that we now take for granted. When a child's first watch is digital, and when it is worn at a very early age, it is dubious how far that child regards the hours as cyclic, in the way that we who were brought up with analogue watches now do. Teaching approaches will need to take account of these continuing developments. Teachers will continue to need to keep up to date with the new technologies that are coming into children's lives, and to adapt their teaching approaches accordingly.

New styles of teaching, and new technology, will also have their impact on content areas other than number. Logic and algebra may become more accessible through computing, both Turtle geometry and the changing environment may change children's perceptions of shape and space, and the increasing sophistication of society, and the increasing ability to handle large amounts of data, bring a new need for understanding of probability and statistics.

Perhaps the chief danger of the impact of new technology on primary mathematics is that it might displace the simple technology of 'practical mathematics', which has developed greatly in the last 30 years. For many years to come, young children will still need to develop their mathematical concepts through counting real things, grouping them into sets, using structural apparatus, measuring, weighing, making shapes, and many other activities. New technology will not provide substitutes for these real experiences, but it does provide supplementary experiences of its own.

OUR CHANGING SOCIETY

Primary mathematics is taught within a society which is itself in a state of rapid change. A new awareness of the sexist nature of much traditional practice, and of the disadvantage suffered by minority groups, needs to be reflected in primary mathematics, as well as in other areas of schooling. Much remains to be done here, as it is still the case that girls and boys seem to perform somewhat differently in mathematics in the primary years, and that mathematics can still seem to children not to be a multi-cultural subject.

It is also now increasingly realised that parents need to be involved in their children's education, in mathematics as elsewhere in the curriculum, and that the school needs to be accountable to the community and to the parents of its children. No longer can curriculum development – especially in mathematics – take place entirely within the school, without reference to the larger community whose children receive their schooling through that curriculum.

And it is this that presents the greatest challenge of all. The attitudes of very many adults to mathematics are extremely negative. They regard it as mysterious, difficult, rule-bound and important. As parents, they are anxious that their children will do well at it, and the only way of doing well at it that many of them know is through the hard grind of learning the rules and practising them. Thus, they think that what they want from their children's schools is pages of sums.

Schools will need to take parents into their confidence and help them to understand the need for new ideas and new methods if their children are to succeed in mathematical thinking. Moreover, parents will themselves need to be involved in mathematical thinking if their attitudes are to change; in a few schools already, parents are working alongside children at investigational mathematics, and calculator games learnt at school are being played at home.

However, this model does not contain all the factors which need to be taken into account in curriculum-building. The curriculum is conveyed to the pupils by the teacher's *style of teaching* and expressed in the resulting organisation of the classroom work. These enable the curriculum to be put into practice, and through them the aims on which the curriculum is based are realised. For instance, only if the teacher is able to present mathematics to the pupils as 'a powerful means of communication' (Cockcroft 1982: para. 3) can the pupils be expected to realise that it is so.

REFERENCE

Cockcroft Report (1982) *Mathematics Counts*, London: HMSO.

Chapter 11

Teaching the arts

The Arts in School Project Team

Outside schools the need to define the arts may seldom arise. Inside schools, where the curriculum has to be planned and agreed, definition of the arts and of their roles in education is essential. Defining the arts is difficult and controversial. Conceptions of the arts have varied through history and in different cultures. In Western/European cultures the arts are usually taken to include music, drama, dance, visual arts and verbal arts. However, many cultures do not distinguish between art forms in these ways. A good deal of work in Western/European arts also challenges these distinctions, including the new forms of artistic practice which have been stimulated by technological developments in film, video, photography, and electronic instruments, computers, and so on. In trying to describe the arts we need to go beyond the art form categories of individual cultures to try to identify the basic characteristics of arts activities in general.

The practice of the arts, in whatever form, involves the creation of objects or events that express and represent ideas and perceptions. The arts emerge from the fundamental human capacity for making sense of experience by representing it in symbolic form. In these terms, the arts are *modes of understanding*. Human experience is of many kinds of qualities and we use a wide variety of ways to make sense of it. Verbal language enables us to formulate some ideas but not others. There are thoughts for which there are literally no words. For these we may use other modes of understanding, such as visual imagery. The painter is not creating pictures of ideas that would be better expressed in words. He or she is formulating visual ideas using an essentially visual mode of understanding. The many different cultural forms of the arts emerge from the following elemental modes of understanding:

- the visual mode – using light, colour and images
- the aural mode – using sounds and rhythm
- the kinaesthetic mode – using bodily movement
- the verbal mode – using spoken or written words
- the enactive mode – using imagined roles

Arts education in schools should provide all pupils with opportunities to work in all of these modes of understanding. This is important in itself, within the accepted aims of education, and also because the arts make an essential contribution to *cultural education*.

The term 'culture' is sometimes used specifically to mean the arts. Increasingly it is used to mean a society's whole way of life including its political and economic structures, its patterns of work and social relations, its religious beliefs, philosophies and values. Each of these various aspects of the social culture interacts with the others to give different societies and cultural groups their distinctive character and dynamic. The arts are not a separate domain of cultural life. The forms they take and the ideas and perceptions they express are woven deeply into the fabric of social culture, stimulating and interacting with developments in all areas of social life. Consequently an effective and coherent programme of arts education is an essential part of *cultural education*, that is, one which

- helps young people to recognise and analyse their own cultural values and assumptions;
- brings them into contact with the attitudes, values and institutions of other cultures;
- enables them to relate contemporary values to the historical forces that moulded them;
- alerts them to the evolutionary nature of culture and the potential for change.

LEARNING IN AND THROUGH THE ARTS

In describing the roles of the arts in the curriculum, a distinction can be made between learning *in* and learning *through* the arts. Although they emerge from innate capacities, mature achievement and understanding in any of the arts call for increasingly sophisticated skills and knowledge. The distinctive roles of arts education are to deepen young people's knowledge of and competence in the arts themselves:

- to develop the concepts and skills which will enable young people to use the processes of the arts;
- to widen their knowledge and understanding of the arts;
- to develop their critical sensibilities.

The working processes of the arts have many applications within teaching and learning in all parts of the curriculum. They bring to life themes, issues and events in history, in social studies, science and personal and social education, and in the teaching of humanities. In learning *through* the arts, the prime focus is likely to be on the theme or subject matter, or on personal and social education; in learning *in* the arts, on the aesthetic or technical qualities of the work. These are complementary roles – in principle, at least. In practice, successful use of the arts in other areas of the curriculum depends on the teachers' and pupils' levels of expertise in the arts: learning *through* requires learning *in* the arts. This balance is not always struck in schools.

TWO WAYS OF ENGAGING IN THE ARTS

There are two general ways of engaging in the arts. Individuals can be involved in producing their own original work, and in responding to existing work. We refer to these two respectively as *making* and *appraising*. Both are of equal and fundamental importance in arts education: each is important in itself and each can stimulate and enrich work in the other. In the practice of the arts young people can be enabled to clarify and communicate their own ideas and values. Through critical engagement with existing work they can be brought into vivid contact with the ideas, values and sensibilities of other people in their own and in other cultural communities. Working in and learning about the arts are essential and mutually enriching elements of cultural education.

Making

Making describes all the processes in which pupils are actively producing their own work. Making may be an individual or a group process. It includes work originated by the individual or group and the performance of other people's material, including scores and scripts. Making is literally what artists do, creating physical objects – paintings, sculptures, prints and so on, and events – music, a dance, a drama. Making in the arts is both a conceptual and a practical process. It is conceptual in the sense that it is concerned with ideas and understanding. It is practical in that artists explore ideas through the manipulation of various media – sounds, words, images, movement, paint, clay, and so on – to create forms which embody their perceptions. Making is not only a way of expressing ideas but also a way of having ideas. Just as a grasp of mathematics can lead to the generation of ideas which are otherwise inconceivable, so the ability to make music or to dance or paint opens up forms of aural, kinaesthetic and visual thinking which are otherwise inaccessible. Arts education should enable young people to get inside these ways of thinking and to generate new insights for themselves.

Appraising

Appraising describes all the processes through which young people engage with existing work. This includes reflecting critically on their own work as well as on other people's work. We use the term 'appraising' to suggest the need for critical judgement and discrimination. Individual response to specific works includes their direct sensory appeal – with music, for example, to its immediate tonal and rhythmic qualities; with photography, painting and sculpture to their direct visual presence. Arts education should deepen young people's sensibilities to actual works by making them more aware of these qualities. A knowledge of artistic concepts and terminology is necessary to facilitate critical perception of other people's work and to articulate personal responses.

Artists work within particular cultural settings and with particular and diverse intentions. Understanding their work requires some knowledge of the context and conventions within which it was made, and of its purposes. One role of arts education is to deepen young people's understanding of the diversity and purposes of the arts in different cultural settings. They should be enabled to understand the different ways in which the arts are produced and used socially and economically, and to develop a critical understanding not just of individual works but of the arts as cultural processes, institutions and, often, commodities.

The following example from a small rural primary school illustrates a project with *making* and *appraising* evolving together. Part of a whole curriculum topic, it involved the pupils engaging with the work of a professional artist through a borrowed exhibition of drawings of trees.

> This project has been stimulated by the loan to us of six of an artist's framed drawings of trees. In preparation the children made their own drawings of trees around the school site. They selected papers, materials and chose lining paper of just the right shade of green to match the chestnut leaves with the sun shining through, to line the walls. Next we brought together their small collection of potted little trees, always available in a school where caring for and growing on is the normal sequel to pips in pots.
>
> Resources were discovered on site. Logs, dead branches, lichens and mosses were investigated. Rubbings of leaves and bark prints were also made. Logs and pieces of bark from the woodyard were brought in. More seedlings came, then a little oak sapling from the potato rows in the farm across the way.
>
> After the arrival of the drawings the children sat down and studied the display, their conversation showing perception and appreciation. We have a custom of using clipboards for notes and drawings during discussions, and I try to build vocabulary by this means.
>
> The infants joined in, and everyone brought along their clipboards to note down good ideas. After discussing and comparing all the drawings, speculating about the artist's reasons for selecting subject and method, we talked about our reasons for selecting a favourite drawing if we could be

allowed to keep one. Conversation turned to reactions evoked by the drawings. Teachers and children shared their reactions and spontaneously searched for fitting phrases to communicate their ideas. We did not say anything about alliteration or comparison but these skills were present. 'You could walk through the wood like getting lost in the mist.' 'The crispy leaves crunch and crackle under my feet.'

The children discussed the techniques of drawing: 'I think that's clever the way he's left little bits of white between the shadows. It makes it look like sunshine.' 'The squares are a good idea. I had a problem fitting mine onto the page. Is that why he uses squares?' We remembered the phrases and jotted them down for future use.

The children's exploration of trees is balanced with the critical processes of examining an artist's interpretation of trees. This is an example of how children's creative work can be enhanced by reference to equivalent work by an 'expert'. Through the discussion of the drawings conceptual language was beginning to emerge which would support further development in both making and appraising.

Exploring another culture provided the stimulus for a term-long project with a Year 6 class in another rural primary school, involving work in visual arts, drama and music.

A secondary visual arts specialist led a session exploring the theme of symbols through various media: printing with polystyrene blocks, cut-out paper work and symmetrical pattern design, later extended into Islamic patterns. In preparation I had led a discussion on language and the problems of communicating with people who do not speak the same language as we do, leading into consideration of signs and symbols. We also talked about different alphabets, dialects and accents.

These language ideas were extended into music, with groups working on question-and-answer phrases on the xylophone, glockenspiel and chime bars. We then listened to some African drumming music and the children paired up with a drum and tambour to compose their own pieces of drumming. This highlighted the complexities of trying to create variety on a drum without using sticks, and we agreed that their compositions were very dull in comparison with those we had listened to.

Sign language was extended into drama, with two sessions conducted in virtual silence. Speech was only resorted to when communication had broken down or when clarification beyond all our signing abilities was needed. Having begun with miming games, each child endeavoured to communicate to a partner something that they wanted him or her to do. In the second session the ideas were developed in groups of three or four and, by signing, the children worked out a short story and enacted it for the rest of the class. These were set to music with groups coming in and miming at different points.

I had been fortunate enough to obtain a tape-recording of some Berber wedding music, and during the next few days the children listened to it in groups. We then had a class discussion about it, which was quite difficult for me as I found the music very hard to appreciate. Their write-ups, however, showed them far more catholic in their taste: another reason for early exposure to other cultures.

THE PROCESSES OF THE ARTS

Making and appraising involve a number of related processes, including exploring, forming, performing, presenting, responding and evaluating.

Exploring

The arts are ways of exploring ideas. In improvised drama, for example, a group looking at the social issues of poverty may experiment with a variety of situations and roles to explore their different perceptions of these issues. The processes of dramatisation are used to formulate and share ideas around the theme. Equally, individuals or groups may use the forms and media of visual arts, dance, music or writing in the same speculative ways to open up areas of interest and to begin to shape their ideas about them. This exploratory work need not lead to a finished piece for others to see: it may be tentative and its outcomes immediate and self-fulfilling. Exploratory work is also important in the media of the arts in developing new forms and techniques of expression. This includes experimenting with new materials, movements, colours and sounds to test their range and potential.

Forming

Making involves the forming of objects or events which embody and present artists' perceptions. These perceptions are not simply translated into dramatic, visual or musical forms. They are conceived as dramatic, visual or musical ideas whose meanings and nuances are only fully available in that form. The initial idea for a new work may be vague and the first form very approximate: some jotted notes, a sketch, a tentative phrase of movements, a first model or maquette. The process of making is one of working on the form itself, and bringing ideas into clearer focus. Ideas are often reassessed, reworked, refined and clarified through shaping the form.

Performing

In the performing arts there are two related and dependent processes of making: those of the choreographer, dramatist or composer who originates the work, and those of the performers who bring it to life. Performing is a process of re-making. Working on a role in a play or interpreting a dance or music composition can be as creative as the original act of composition, as the performer evolves a personal interpretation of the work.

Presenting

Presenting is any process of sharing work with another person and ranges from sharing ideas, notes and preparatory studies in the classroom to participation in public performances and exhibitions. Sometimes this may be to other members of the class, the rest of the school and sometimes more publicly. Aspects of this process are a natural and informal part of any arts lesson, for example, in the discussions which take place about work in progress between pupils and with the teacher. Presenting involves an audience, however informal. The experience of sharing work with other people, of hearing their responses and testing their perceptions, can be positive and beneficial for all pupils. The sense of audience can also be a powerful and valuable influence in sharpening the focus of individual work and its powers of communication. Presenting requires pupils to pay careful attention to detail and to how their work is displayed or performed to best effect. Pupils should be encouraged to experiment with different ways of presenting their own work. The appraisals of others can greatly increase their sense of ownership and pride in their work and can be a significant stimulus to further work and development.

Responding

The arts have to be experienced at first hand. The nature of our response is influenced as much by the personal and cultural values and attitudes which we bring to the works as by what they offer to us in themselves. That is, aesthetic response is influenced by artistic understanding. Arts education is concerned with deepening young people's sensibilities to the arts, and the range and depth of their aesthetic experience and understanding.

Evaluating

To make an artistic judgement we need to know about the themes, content and conventions of the work. There are no absolute criteria or rules which can be applied automatically to works of art. Judgement develops from experience and acquaintance. It is important to be able to justify appraisals by giving reasons for them. This includes citing details and offering descriptions of work to support these evaluations.

The different processes of making and appraising may be intimately related. A piece of work may provide the opportunity for pupils to engage in several and even all of these aspects of the arts. Their responses to the work of other people will stimulate new work of their own, and their experience of making will deepen their understanding and enrich their perceptions of existing work.

There is a logical distinction between the various processes. Pupils need to have acquired certain concepts and skills before they can begin making. Something must have been made before it can be presented, and presented before it can be appraised. At each stage the pupils need to have learnt certain ideas and information in order to proceed and they acquire new skills and information as the work progresses.

THE ROLES OF THE ARTS TEACHER

Teaching the arts demands a flexibility of style and requires the teacher to take on a variety of roles: facilitator, mediator, assessor, partner, questioner, instructor and artist.

Facilitator

In this role the teacher enables pupils to participate in all aspects of arts education by providing source materials, appropriate tools, media and equipment, and a stimulating environment for learning. Skills, concepts and methods of working are taught which enable pupils to work in a confident, informed and creative way. Relevant information and resources are provided from within and beyond the school. These resources – including professional artists, visits to galleries, theatres or concerts – enable pupils to experience the wider world of the arts.

Sometimes facilitating means standing back and letting pupils experiment freely, intervening occasionally to help a pupil who is stuck or to challenge a pupil who is complacent. The teacher is enabling pupils to direct their own learning and to take responsibility for their own art-making.

Mediator

The teacher helps the pupils to make connections between their own experience and the wider context of the world of the arts. Different ideas or values may need explaining and reconciling in order to help pupils to understand and contextualise their own thoughts and feelings. This can be uncomfortable for pupils, and the teacher will need to mediate when pupils are asked to respond to work which does not suit their personal preference or is beyond their comprehension. The teacher can help to make connections between the ways in which artists communicate their ideas and perceptions and the ways in which the pupils can do so.

Assessor

Assessing pupils' progress and achievements is an integral part of everyday teaching. Within each lesson the teacher is checking pupils' progress and is ready to give advice or support. The development of a conceptual language enables teacher and pupil to discuss work together, and through this process of negotiated assessment the teacher is building the pupils' powers of self-assessment, which are fundamental to the process of art-making.

It is important to have criteria for success in any art-making and pupils and teachers should negotiate these, particularly where there is room for a variety of responses. The kinds of criteria which might be agreed are:

- applying certain skills
- communicating ideas appropriately
- understanding particular concepts
- sustaining work from initial idea to realised form

If basic criteria like these are understood from the outset by the pupils and discussed as work progresses, assessment becomes an integrated process within teaching and learning.

Partner

In the *making* mode the arts lesson is a laboratory for the transformation of ideas and requires an open-ended, negotiated and supportive teaching style where the pupil and teacher are in partnership, both expecting the unexpected. Artistic solutions are not predetermined. Success and failure are moments in a process of experimentation as the pupil tries to achieve a satisfactory resolution to an artistic task. The teacher should encourage pupils to be adventurous.

Questioner

Sometimes the teacher will play a more provocative role in raising issues and discussing ideas. For example, a performance by a visiting theatre-in-education or dance company, a visit to an exhibition, or a class improvisation with teacher and pupils in role, can provide a safe environment for confronting ideas. After the arts experience, the teacher can question and challenge attitudes and assumptions through discussing the ways in which ideas were introduced and developed. The questions posed need to be open-ended and designed to move forward the pupils' thinking. Alternative points of view should be generated, encouraged and tolerated.

Instructor

There will be moments in any lesson, and at different stages in pupils' development in the arts, when it is appropriate to teach in a more instructional manner, for example, in the development of technical skills or where all pupils need certain factual or conceptual information. These sessions will need to be balanced with those which foster pupils' independent self-directed learning.

Artist

Some teachers have considerable personal skills in the arts. There will be times when it is appropriate for the teacher to demonstrate his or her own art-making skills as a teaching strategy. For pupils to see their own teacher as a painter, musician, dancer, actor or poet can be a source of inspiration to them and provide valuable exemplars for their own work.

The greatest challenge in arts teaching is sustaining the parallel development of *making* and *appraising*. The teacher needs to balance activities between those which require spontaneous and unrestricted exploration of arts media, ideas and intuitions, those which require careful application of skills and those which require observation, reflection, critical analysis and discussion. To have teaching programmes solely concerned with making or appraising would be to lose sight of the interdependence of the two modes.

Chapter 12

History and geography in the primary curriculum

Alan Blyth

HUMANITIES AS AN AREA OF KNOWLEDGE AND UNDERSTANDING

History and geography are often grouped together in the school curriculum as humanities. So, before considering the place of history and geography in the primary curriculum, it is important to think about the whole area of knowledge and understanding within which they are often assumed to fall.

Humanities can be generally taken to cover the various fields of study that are concerned with human beings. That is how I shall use the term in this chapter, meaning the study of humankind, past and present, in its physical environment (Blyth 1990). It includes not only history and geography, but also the various social sciences.

Not everyone would agree. Some would group history together with literature and the arts, philosophy and religion, as embodying the essence of human culture, while linking geography with the social sciences and the natural sciences as a quite different kind of study. The terminology used in higher education reflects this ambiguity. Faculties carry labels in which the terms 'arts' and 'humanities' figure in different ways and with different meanings. So, to use the term to cover history, geography and the social sciences is to adopt a point of view that is open to challenge, but one that also has wide support and is often built into the way in which schools and other institutions are organised.

Inevitably, much of the subject matter of humanities is located within more than one academic 'discipline'. For example, the story of a town is a piece of unique history; it happens in a unique place; yet it also exemplifies some general economic, sociological and religious phenomena, and perhaps aspects of human biology. It may also give rise to literature, poetry, art and music. A useful way of expressing this interrelation of the disciplines of the human intellect (Blyth *et al.* 1976) is to think of each as providing its own *perspective*. Each such perspective is built upon particular ways of learning and thinking, investigating and reasoning, feeling and action: all of them have their part to play in a full understanding of a human phenomenon, such as the growth of a town.

Within humanities, history and geography provide two of the major perspectives. They are much older than the others, for the social sciences have really only emerged during the past two centuries. It is important to consider them more closely.

A CLOSER LOOK AT HISTORY AND GEOGRAPHY

History as a perspective

History, in the broadest sense, is everything that has happened in the world. More helpfully, it is what survives as a record of all that has happened to people in the world. In practice, as a discipline, it is the discovery, analysis, synthesis and interpretation of that record. Time is its currency, chronology its notation, and change through time one of its principal concerns. In most people's experience, history is still further limited to what happened to people in some parts of the world at some particular times, including recent times. When all of these limitations are taken into account, what is left is still immense, so that people who consider themselves relatively well educated in history find themselves caught out by their comparative ignorance of the background of urgent events whether in Bosnia, Iraq or Cambodia. Yet, as this example shows, all history does matter to all of us; and some history matters a great deal to some of us, as the Irish and the South Africans know; and as the Russians know, it is never possible to abolish the past.

In practice, what we know as history tends to be what historians have said that it is. They have not spoken with one voice. Some have interpreted the past with grand theories. Others have stayed as close as they could to precise research studies, eschewing anything more ambitious as dangerous. Some have omitted great tracts of human experience as not 'proper' history. Others have concentrated on what they consider has been, perhaps unjustly and deliberately, omitted by others: the stories of vanquished peoples and subordinated social groups, including the female half of humankind.

All do, however, share, at least to some extent, particular ways of finding history out, from documents and letters, portraits and stories, archaeological remains and imprints on landscapes and, for more recent times, visual and aural records and the recollections of living people. Some of these records are now developed into databases to be analysed through information technology. Historians also have particular books and journals within which to express their ideas about history in general or about the particular part of history that interests them most. Others have made it their task to render the work of professional historians accessible and intelligible to the general public, including, of course, teachers.

Geography as a perspective

Like history, geography covers a potentially vast field of knowledge. As with history, geography can be seen first as all that happens on the earth's surface; then, more specifically, all that has been and can be recorded about what happens where people interact with their physical environment; and finally the systematisation and interpretation of those data. Unlike history, however, much of geography is in the present and thus open to direct investigation.

There are disputes about the essence of geography, just as there are about the nature and scope of history. It is quite widely agreed that the perspective of geography is about places and distributions and environments and the relation between people and their physical surroundings. Without that minimum it lacks any distinctiveness. But beyond that there is room for much disagreement. For example, is geography basically a natural science, as physical geographers in particular would emphasise, or is it primarily a social science? Is it about regions, or about general principles? Does it appear to assume that physical conditions determine human responses, or does it start from the belief that people in similar circumstances, can act in many different ways? Should it concentrate on describing the interrelations of things as they are, or should it be more concerned with constructing ideal 'models' of landscapes and settlement patterns and transport systems and then seeing how helpful these are in interpreting actual examples? Finally, should geography try to interpret the world as it is, or should it go further and, by illuminating social problems, suggest what the world ought to be like?

As with history, despite disagreement about the nature of geography there is a measure of consensus among geographers about the many tools of their trade. Some are indeed the same tools as historians use, but geographers use more kinds of maps than historians do, and in addition there are the data derived from field observations and measurements and considerably more mathematical techniques as well as those of information technology. One big difference between historians and geographers is that the latter are more likely to be working outdoors. However, when results and interpretations are to be made, they too have their books and journals, and their back-up team of writers who make their findings available to the general public, sometimes in the guise of travel and adventure but often as geography itself.

A comment on other humanities

To complete this brief survey of the perspectives that comprise humanities, it is necessary to mention briefly that economics, sociology, social psychology, anthropology and political science all have their own distinctive contribution to make to a complete view of human societies, one which they often exaggerate while historians and geographers sometimes look askance at what they do. They also have their internal disputes, often very conspicuous, but also their own methods of study, which for the most part involve more testing of hypotheses and more statistical analysis than historians and geographers use. Finally, they have their own, often highly technical, publications that are in turn translated for others to try to understand.

HUMANITIES IN THE PRIMARY CURRICULUM

A case must now be made for including humanities, in some shape, in the education of younger children. It has sometimes been maintained that any study of human society is necessarily beyond the comprehension of preadolescent children. A more usual view is that of Jerome Bruner (1966) who considered that humanities is an essential component of the education of growing human beings. Indeed, it is difficult to see how any kind of education committed to the preparation of future adults and citizens could omit some kind of study of children's own society and preferably others' (Campbell and Little 1989), though that study might not necessarily figure in the core of the curriculum. In England and Wales today, for example, it does not.

In deciding how young children should learn and understand the perspectives of humanities, it is necessary to consider how they actually do so. The perspectives of history and geography will now be considered from the standpoint of young children's growth and learning and how the curriculum can stimulate that growth and learning.

Young children and the geographical perspective

Very young children soon begin to structure their immediate surroundings and the people in them. They start as geographers before they start as historians. In doing so, they construct mental maps, that differ according to their general abilities but also according to the communities and cultures in which they live (Bale 1987; Wiegand 1992). Some of them devise their own ways of depicting their perceptions in real maps, but most need to be introduced to the practice of map-making and then to the reading of standard maps made by other people (Catling 1988). So one of the basic skills of the geographical perspective can be developed from children's experience, beginning quite early but always extending. By the use of models and aerial photographs, map interpretation can be extended and the representation of relief introduced.

Mapping is only one element in the geographical perspective; a tool, though a very important one. Other and richer aspects of that perspective also arise initially through children's experience but need to be developed and articulated as they acquire further experience. One of these is about events that happen in their environment, and in particular, how people behave there; how and why they move about; and how they respond to physical conditions such as the weather (another experience that can be recorded) and the landscape. From all of this experience there emerges some sense of people in places, which is one of the basic considerations in geography and probably its most important notion in the primary curriculum. Indeed, Michael Storm (1989) has gained considerable support for his suggestion that the whole geographical perspective can be introduced to young children through these questions:

> What is this place like?
> Why is this place as it is?
> How is this place connected to other places?
> How is this place changing?
> What would it feel like to be in this place?

> (Storm 1989)

These and similar questions can be asked about children's own place; but the geographical perspective is severely limited if it does not then extend to other places nearby, and to distant and very different places too. The further away those places are, the less likely it is that the children will have been there, and the more necessary it becomes to depend on experience derived from television, film, video and other resources, including some purposely designed for primary geography.

Experience in learning about more distant places also makes it increasingly possible for the idea of the whole world and its diversity to take shape in children's minds. This in turn implies some understanding of the globe, of the conventions of latitude and longitude, of the atlas and large-scale maps, and of the elements of general geography (for example, river, rainfall, volcano, route, pollution).

It also requires, in practice, some knowledge of where the continents and oceans are, and of the location of some countries and places, knowledge that is more readily gained in this way than through rote learning.

Alongside the acquisition of these skills and ideas, two other important aspects of the geographical perspective will necessarily be encountered. The first is relatively uncontroversial: namely, that learning about the world and places in it can and ought to be enjoyable – to be fun. But the other aspect is not so easy to handle. Attitudes and controversies are involved. They are inescapable in humanities. One growing need during the primary years is to be able to handle such matters with increasing intelligence and maturity. Another, linked to this, is the need to combat stereotyped ideas about other people (e.g. Wiegand 1992; the literature is quite extensive). Yet a third, related, issue is the need to realise that there are not always simple, right answers to questions, especially where there is not enough information to be quite sure about the whole truth. This is dangerous ground; but children need to learn how to handle such matters in a compassionate but realistic manner.

So that is a demanding agenda for the introduction of primary-age children to the importance of the geographical perspective. It clashes with another way of learning geography – namely, by trying to cover the world piecemeal. But something must always be missed out, and experience (HMI 1989) indicates that knowledge and understanding gained with due attention to how the children, as individuals, learn, is more soundly based than knowledge based on the shape of geography in higher education, or in the memory of lay adults.

Young children and the historical perspective

It usually takes children a little longer to sort themselves out in time than to sort themselves out in space. Indeed, there has been a widespread notion, based on research some years ago as well as on some teachers' experience, to the effect that although young children can master mathematical time (clocks and so on), they do not and cannot have any idea of historical time. More recently, authors such as Smith and Tomlinson (1977) and West (1982) have confirmed that children do progressively acquire an idea of *sequence* (this must have happened before that) and that this, when related through time-lines and time-charts to family and local and then to wider history, can lead at least to a comprehension of conventional chronology, if not to a fuller understanding of time.

Such development in the historical perspective can be aided by introducing children to the various ways in which the evidence of the past is seen in the present: artefacts, buildings, legends and stories, and the memories of older people (Joan Blyth 1989). One important and related matter explored by Knight (1989) is the extent to which young children understand that past times were inhabited by real adult people who thought and felt much as adults do today, and not by comic-strip legionaries and peasants. But the most important steps in the introduction to the historical perspective are two: the formation and mastery of historical and social concepts (medieval, king, society, trade, Victorian); and the acquisition of the skills of reasoning and deduction about the changing past, together with the capacity to make evaluative judgements without succumbing to bias or prejudice. For the historical perspective, even more than the geographical, is riddled with controversy. There is some evidence (e.g. Cooper 1992) that children display increasing sophistication in handling these matters as they grow older, and that direct teaching, related to their experience, helps this development. It is even more true of history than of geography that reasoning must often be based on inadequate information that cannot be supplemented, and that children have to 'tolerate ambiguity', to face the reality that the historical perspective often yields no simple, right/wrong answers.

All of these observations about children's acquisition of a historical perspective emphasise that this is a gradual, developmental process. But it is often assumed that the learning of history is something quite different: Egypt, then Greece, then Rome; Tudors, then Stuarts; and so on. For the historical perspective is incomplete unless it provides some sort of grand backcloth to the human story. Somehow, through time-charts relating one episode to another, that backcloth has to be developed too, just as some broad idea of continents and oceans has to appear in the geographical perspective; but as with geography, this is most effectively done when it is related to topics that really engage children's attention. The basic problem in primary history is of course how to combine development in children's thinking with the sweep of history itself. Inevitably there must be selection of content and, as with geography, that selection involves bias of some kind, for neither timetables nor children's minds are infinite in capacity.

To summarise: a possible set of guidelines for development of the historical perspective in the primary curriculum might be:

- that young children should have an idea of the major epochs of Western history combined with a firm recognition that there are other histories too, of other continents;
- that they should realise that real adult people with great achievements lived in the past;
- that there can be great stimulus and pleasure in learning about the past;
- that there are no simple, right/wrong answers about the past;
- that the historical perspective should always be considered when looking at problems in the present.

PRIMARY HUMANITIES AND CURRICULUM PLANNING

The task facing any school is that of weaving the development of the historical and geographical perspectives, and of a few ideas from the economic and social-science perspectives too, into a coherent and progressive programme. Since individual children have different modes and paces of learning, there has to be a common policy that allows of some compromise. The National Curriculum in England and Wales, and its counterparts elsewhere in the British Isles, attempt to embody such a policy, and at Key Stage 1, where pressures are less, it achieves a great deal. At Key Stage 2, especially in England, its virtues tend to be obscured by the amount of content required, and by the rigid initial separation of history from geography as subjects (rather than perspectives), which is only partly compensated by reminders about where they might be jointly considered. Yet the structure of the National Curriculum does allow for, even where it does not encourage, an approach based on how most children learn. Some of that learning requires joint consideration of perspectives; some concentrates on one of them.

The *locality*, where the interplay of different perspectives is most readily evident, must play a major part in this process. Here, history and geography are closely knit together, but so are the wider aspects of humanities implied in the cross-curricular themes and dimensions of the National Curriculum as defined in England (Hall 1992) and somewhat differently in Wales and Northern Ireland. Throughout primary education, understanding of the locality can be strenuously widened and deepened and used as a springboard for systematic and sustained learning historically and geographically about the home country (not over-emphasising England), and thence to comparison with what is more distant in place and time. All this is practicable within the confines of what the National Curriculum prescribes for subjects, themes and dimensions.

Yet local studies, and national studies, manifest two dangers. One is that they can lack – and have often lacked – the very progression and development that is their main potential. In some topic work, repetitiveness has sapped the virtue of thoroughness. The other danger is that they can be inward-looking as well as repetitive. So, as the National Curriculum encourages, there must be a wider context too. Stories and episodes from the past are essential to an interpretation of the present, and so are vignettes of life in contrasted parts of the country and of the world today, all with the help of increasing mastery of skills and against the background of a growing awareness of the major shape of the centuries and the continents. There is a case, especially with older juniors, for looking at topics with a historical or a geographical, or occasionally an economic or other focus, while bearing in mind that any worthwhile topic that taps the whole range of children's learning cannot be confined to a single subject. It is then necessary to weld together a series of topics, within and beyond humanities, in such as way as to promote children's development, as the attainment targets in history and, less clearly, in geography aim to do, and at the same time to fit in with the programmes of study across the curriculum.

All of this takes much time and thought. It involves co-operation within and between schools, and with other sources of information and materials. It also requires confidence in the potential content of primary humanities, which does not occur automatically even to graduates in the relevant disciplines, but which does arise through experience and reflection on experience. So does confidence in organising the relevant work inside, and still more outside, the classroom. There is another whole dimension of endeavour in deciding how to assess the children's development, by observation, by commenting on their written and other work, by focused questioning, and through the judicious use of optional test material. So humanities is one of the most demanding elements in the primary curriculum. It is also one of the most rewarding.

REFERENCES

Bale, J. (1987) *Geography in the Primary School*, London: Routledge & Kegan Paul.

Blyth, A. (1990) *Making the Grade for Primary Humanities*, Buckingham: Open University Press.

Blyth, A. *et al.* (1976) (for the Schools Council) *Place, Time and Society 8–13: Curriculum Planning in History, Geography and Social Science*, Glasgow and Bristol: Collins/ESL Bristol. This project, conducted by the present author and his colleagues, generated some of the terminology used in certain of the current statutory and other documents.

Blyth, J. (1989) *History in Primary Schools*, 2nd edn, Buckingham: Open University Press.

Bruner, J.S. (1966) *Towards a Theory of Instruction*, Cambridge, MA: Belknap Press.

Campbell, R.J. and Little, V. (eds) (1989) *Humanities in the Primary School*, Lewes: Falmer Press.

Catling, S. (1988) 'Using maps and aerial photographs', in D. Mills (ed.) *Geographical Work in Primary and Middle Schools*, Sheffield: Geographical Association, pp. 168–88.

Cooper, H. (1992) *The Teaching of History*, London: David Fulton.

Hall, G. (ed.) (1992) *Themes and Dimensions of the National Curriculum*, London: Kogan Page.

HMI (1989) *Aspects of Primary Education: the Teaching and Learning of History and Geography*, London: HMSO.

Knight, P. (1989) 'A study of children's understanding of people in the past', *Educational Review*, 41(3): 207–19.

Smith, R.N. and Tomlinson, P. (1977) 'The development of children's construction of historical duration: a new approach and some findings', *Educational Research*, 19(3): 163–70.

Storm, M.J. (1989) 'The five basic questions for primary geography', *Primary Geographer*, 2 (Autumn): 4.

West, J. (1982) 'Time charts', *Education 3–13*, 10(1): 48–50.

Wiegand, P. (1992) *Places in the Primary School: Knowledge and Understanding of Places at Key Stages 1 and 2*, Lewes: Falmer Press.

Chapter 13

Learning design and technology in primary schools

A. Anning

I have a long-established interest in enhancing the status of 'the intelligent hand', and it was this aspect of technology education that appealed to me. I set about monitoring the first year of technology in 12 primary schools in two local education authorities (LEAs). Gill Kicks, a researcher with a teaching and town-planning background, collected most of the data, and this is a first attempt to make some sense of what we found. In the autumn term we visited the 12 schools to talk to the headteachers, technology co-ordinators and teachers of Years 1 and 3. They were still reeling under the stress of the requirements to teach to the English, mathematics and science Orders. A sense of 'overload' was a recurrent complaint. As one teacher succinctly put it, 'It's getting ridiculous.'

We returned to four classrooms, two Year 1 and two Year 3 age groups, to observe children working on activities defined by their teachers as design and technology. We wanted to explore how the teachers translated their strategic models of design and technology into operational models. We also wanted to collect empirical evidence of young children's capability to set against levels of attainment for Key Stages 1 and 2. We used a mixture of field notes, tape-recordings, photographs, photocopies of children's work and stimulus material, and videorecordings, to collect detailed data.

Time and time again teachers ask for research findings to be presented in a way that relates to their language and everyday classroom concerns. I have chosen to illustrate some of the many general issues arising from our analysis of the data through the specifics of four classroom incidents. The four exemplars have been selected to illustrate particular features of capability and related implications for teaching and learning: young children's thinking through modelling, investigating the properties of materials, learner-directed activities and teacher-directed tasks.

YOUNG CHILDREN'S THINKING THROUGH MODELLING

Exemplar 1, Key Stage 1, designing an exercise area for the school hamster (James 5.5 and Stephen 5.4)

The task was in response to a real need. The hamster, constipated and unhappy, had been taken to the vet and declared to be in need of exercise. The vet's diagnosis was discussed at the start of the day class session.

The two boys were encouraged to draw their ideas first. The researcher's suggestion that they might 'scribble' down a few preliminary ideas met with looks of astonishment and disbelief. Instead, the two boys embarked on an elaborate, detailed and highly imaginative drawing. They drew a table and chairs with (no doubt healthy!) breakfast cereals, a bed with pillows and duvet, a jacuzzi for the hamster to relax in, a pool for it to drink from and a train set for it to play with. Their only concession to hamster need was to define his colour preferences as pink and yellow.

Finally they began to draw in cage-like elements on the design – horizontal bars for the sides 'so that he can poke his little head out' and a door 'because he does need to go out for exercise'. When it was suggested that they might write labels for parts of the design to help them when they made the model – the rudiments of an annotated drawing – they politely declined 'because we're not very good writers'. It became increasingly clear that they intended their drawing for the hamster, 'He's only a little baby hamster and he can't write . . .'. At this point the children were making no links at all between their detailed 2D drawing and the possibility of translating their ideas into a 3D model. 'We don't want to make a model, do we?' was the dominant child, James's, firm response.

The next day the teacher re-focused the boys' attention on making a 3D model. She helped them to identify and draw up a list of materials they would need – coloured paper (they chose gold, silver and black – a concession to the concept of a metal cage?), coloured chalk (James had been waiting for his opportunity to get hold of these!), a box, carpet and wallpaper pieces, mirror, special paper to look through (for windows), string, wood, paint and brushes, a hole punch (for air holes), and a knife to cut window shapes (to be controlled by the teacher). It was clear from their talk and gestures that the boys were now imaging with materials clearly in mind.

On task they began by cutting the flaps off the top of a large box and carefully painting the outside, pausing only to stick small squares of gold and silver paper on the surface. Did these represent windows or were they a reference to metal? James then set Stephen the task of measuring and cutting a piece of string which they attempted to glue across the top of the box on to the still wet surface. The researcher suggested they cut slits in the box to fix the string. They explained that the string was for the hamster to run along.

Had James seen the television advertisement where the squirrel runs the gauntlet of the washing line to reach the nuts? James painted the string, but then began to worry that 'I've made it a bit slippy'. He sent Stephen off to find something soft for the hamster to land on in the event of a fall. Instead Stephen returned with some wood offcuts and the boys began to make a diving board. When they could not attach it to the top of the box, they simply converted it into a bed. James then turned his attention to cutting some steps out of card for the hamster to climb up to the string. Card steps proved to be too difficult to make. Ever the pragmatist, James decided that the hamster could use 'his sharp little claws' instead. However, by chance he discovered some thin strips of balsa amongst the wood offcuts and immediately began to concentrate on sticking them with wood glue up the inside of the box to make a ladder.

This long session of designing as they made occupied the boys for several hours. They returned sporadically to the task of mechanically re-painting the surface of the box, as if this gave them time for reflection.

Discussion

One of the issues illustrated within this exemplar is the use of drawing in promoting young children's designerly thinking. Many of the teachers we interviewed spoke of misgivings about the appropriateness of requiring children at Key Stage 1 to draw out a design. An infant teacher said,

> I don't think they need to draw and plan it at five. I think they want to make it first and possibly record and draw about it afterwards. They don't know what it looks like before they make it. To see it before you've done it, that's hard.

Even at Key Stage 2, teachers spoke about the difficulties of getting children to produce realistic design drawings.

> The designs they make at the beginning, however fantastic they look, very often the end product isn't like that at all. I think that what actually happens is that they are re-designing as they go along all the time, as they are making things. . . . They are always over-ambitious in the drawings.

The intellectual demands we are making of children in asking them to represent a 3D model in 2D form would tax many adults. The ability to visualise objects in diagrammatic form and translate these images into line drawings, with all the attendant complexities of perspective, scale and overlap, is a particularly sophisticated, taught convention.

We need to *teach* children a range of drawing conventions, the equivalent of teaching them a range of writing registers. This can start at Key Stage 1 by sharing talk about different kinds of diagrams and their appropriateness for different purposes – cross-sectional drawings, architects' plans, exploded diagrams, botanical drawings, annotated drawings, rough sketches. These are simply the equivalent resources in graphic terms to the range of reading material – fiction, non-fiction, reference, catalogues, comics, and so on – provided in many classrooms.

Children should be encouraged to draw in different ways for different purposes. James and Stephen were imbued with the notion of a drawing as a finished product, in this case a gift for the hamster, not as a tool for thinking. They had no experience, within school conventions, of the way designers use sketches to clarify their emergent ideas. We saw other examples of confusion about the purpose of design drawings. A group of Key Stage 2 children had drawn designs for decorating pump bags. When they actually began to cut out the shapes they had drawn in felt, they had great technical difficulties. They realised that they needed to simplify their designs drastically but, concerned that their original drawings should be seen as 'wrong', they surreptitiously rubbed out sections to produce 'correct' versions for the teacher.

The exemplar also illustrates the dilemma of children 'imaging' without information. The children had no obvious resources to support their imaging of a design for a hamster exercise area – no access to a real cage or commercially produced hamster exercise aid, nor even catalogues with photographs of equipment for pets. Their thinking was therefore constrained by images of artefacts from their own world.

In other instances, the 'over-ambitious' design drawings we saw children produce at Key Stage 2 had no underpinning of (1) a conceptual knowledge base of the properties of materials to be used, or (2) the production techniques required to translate images into outcomes. In most cases, teachers did not focus children's attention on the need to plan with these constraints in mind. Here the teacher-directed listing of materials, identified by the children as what they needed to make their model, served the useful functions of (1) getting the children to image with materials in mind, and (2) training them to use advance organisers in translating design intentions into achievable outcomes.

A further issue is a general lack of clarity we found about design intentions. In this example, the hamster was never given the opportunity to try out his gymnasium. It was not clear if the boys ever believed that this was a real possibility or if it mattered to them whether they were making a model, a prototype or an artefact with a real purpose. Both the drawing and making tasks were productive in all kinds of ways for the children's learning. We observed many excellent examples of children working in kinaesthetic mode in what appeared to be an *ad hoc* way but which provided systematic opportunities for them to practise and refine techniques of handling materials and tools while 'designing as they did'. However, lack of clarity about the purpose of tasks, both in the teachers' and the children's minds, could result in aimless and unproductive model-making sessions. As one teacher said,

> It's making children aware of their design capability that is important. Whilst children are simply making 'houses' out of cornflake packets, there is little sense of purpose in that. It isn't to investigate the properties of a house (or the properties of card) or anything of that nature. It's to produce a house that can stand on a shelf and look nice in front of some written work or something.

INVESTIGATING THE PROPERTIES OF MATERIALS

Exemplar 2, Key Stage 1, experimenting with paper structures (Sarah, Tracey, John, Martin, Sean, 5-year-olds)

The teacher introduced the task to the group of children by demonstrating ways of strengthening paper – rolling, folding, layering, and so on. The instructions were to build upwards by experimenting with paper. Resources provided were scissors, Sellotape, strips of paper ready cut, approximately 9 in by 1 in.

Left to their own devices, initially all five children started to make paper chains. They tested for 'strength' by blowing the chains and judged the strongest to be the one that moved least! The teacher intervened to refocus them by demonstrating coiling and folding paper again and reminded them that they were supposed to be building upwards with the paper. The children began to work independently on a range of interesting structures (Figure 13.1).

Sarah built a series of platforms using coiled paper for columns and flat strips of paper as cross-pieces. Tracey, working alongside, began with a similar structure as a base and tried to build up looped paper strips on top of her base. When it toppled sideways, she ingeniously used a circle of card Sellotaped to the base platform to stabilise the whole structure.

John worked with great concentration on rings of paper with doubled-over strips inserted inside like a lantern. His was the tallest and sturdiest structure. But an indication that he was in fact drawing on a mental model of paper lanterns for his construction was that he added a 'handle' to the top ring. Sean continued to experiment with paper chains. Using the kind of lateral thinking typical of streetwise 5-year-olds, he taped the final ring of his chain to the back of his chair so that it dangled to the floor and announced that he had made his stand and it was the tallest! Martin made an elaborate device of coiled paper and strips, but soon became frustrated when he could not attach side supports to make it stand up. The researcher demonstrated to him the concept of triangular support frames using folded paper strips, but he did not have the manipulative skills to use the ruler and scoring technique she showed him, and he abandoned the task.

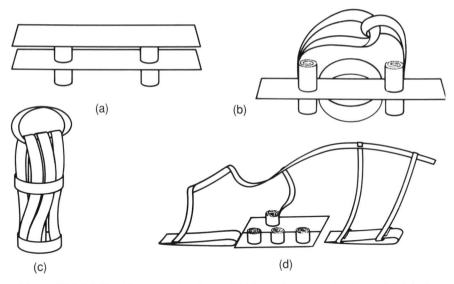

Figure 13.1 (a) Sarah's paper structures; (b) Tracey's paper structures; (c) John's paper structures; (d) Martin's paper structures

Discussion

It seems essential for children to have opportunities to explore the qualities of materials and techniques for fixing and joining them. In the NCC document *Issues in Design and Technology* (NCC 1991: 10), a distinction is made between *resource tasks* (designed to help pupils acquire the knowledge, understanding and skills necessary for design and technology capability) and *capability tasks* (designed to provide pupils with opportunities to demonstrate capability). Here investigation of the properties of paper and ways of using it to build structures (resource tasks) underpinned a subsequent set of activities designed to build and test the weight-carrying strength of 'bridges' made of paper (capability tasks). In the other Key Stage 1 class, we observed children moving on from freely experimenting with ways of fixing card together – with hole punchers, paper clips, staples, butterfly fasteners, plant wire – to the task of making Christmas cards with moving parts. This task was resourced by examples of books and cards with moving parts provided by the teacher. The combination of the experience of experimenting with materials and skills for fixing and joining them, and teacher-led discussions about real cards and pop-up books, led to successful and innovative designs. Analysing the component parts of tasks and planning systematically to build up a knowledge base and set of practical skills over a half-term would ensure progression in children's learning.

One way of managing exploratory work would be to set up a workshop area where the resources would be structured over a period of weeks to focus on strands within the Programmes of Study – for example, joining materials and components in a simple way. If activities involving making vehicles were planned, the workshop area would be set up with construction kits, and box modelling materials with containers of wheels and axles sorted and categorised into shapes and sizes. Adjacent pinboards would (1) have outlines to indicate where tools should be stored when not in use, thus training children to keep the working surfaces tidy and safe, and (2) skill cards and prompts to demonstrate different methods of making wheels and axles, fixing chassis, and so on. Children can be given the freedom to experiment without the pressure of a task which requires an end product. Class or group discussions can be used to draw attention to interesting experiments. Children can be encouraged to keep their own records of what they have achieved over a half-term in notebook form – much like a designer's pad. Exploratory work then becomes much more purposeful for children.

LEARNER-DIRECTED ACTIVITIES

Exemplar 3, Key Stage 2, making a model of a traction engine (Susan, Shelley, Ruth, 7-year-olds)

The girls had come across instructions to make a traction engine model in a library book: 'I'd been wanting to make it for ages 'cos it looked right good.' They asked their teacher if they could make the model. She encouraged them to list the materials and equipment they needed. In a workshop area set up in a corner of the classroom, they assembled boxes, corrugated card, PVA glue, a glue stick, a large pair of scissors, pea-sticks, string and Sellotape.

They began by casting around for containers to draw round to make four large and four small circles for the wheels. Following the diagrams in the instructions, they made tyres by cutting strips of corrugated card, measuring the length by eye, gluing them to the circles and chopping off any overlap. They completely missed a crucial strengthening device of cotton reel inserts for the wheels. Prompted by the sight of an eggbox and card tube in a container nearby, Susan turned her attention to another section of the instructions, scheduled for much later, and began to make the smokestack: 'Don't know what it's for. Might be for the smoke, but it's got that thing on top.'

Returning to the task that afternoon, the children decided to use a block of wood for the main body of the engine. They took turns to struggle, without a bench hook or clamp, to saw the block to size, again gauged by eye. They attached the smokestack using the technique, learned from a sculptor (recently artist in residence in the school), of a set of card struts folded at angles of 90 degrees and glued to the body of the engine and the upright chimney.

Their choice of the wooden block caused a series of technical difficulties.

The steering and axle mechanisms of the illustrated model involved making holes in the main body through which to feed the pea-sticks. LEA policy restricted the use of a drill in school until a drill-stand had been delivered. The children resorted to drilling holes with the sharp end of a large pair of scissors and a small screwdriver to attach the front axle! In the end, they attached the surface paraphernalia of a steering mechanism – a cotton reel and length of string attached to the front axle – but never got it operating. They fixed a smart little card canopy, as illustrated in the instructions, with pea-sticks attached to the wooden block by copious lengths of Sellotape. They coated the finished model with white emulsion paint – again a technique learned from the sculptor – and decorated it with powder paint using unsuitably large brushes.

In all the girls had spent sessions spread over five days on the model and were proud of it. 'We worked hard, didn't we?' When asked about possible improvements, they acknowledged that they knew how they could make the steering wheel work. 'We've got to put a pencil through there, but we can't be bothered. We *can* make a hole in it, but it takes too long.'

Discussion

The children made a laudable attempt at following quite complicated diagrammatic instructions but, without a teacher on tap to guide them at decision points, they were frustrated by difficulties which could have been avoided. We observed that children often selected materials because of their outside dimensions rather than their workable properties, and were seduced by the novelty of unfamiliar or exotic materials. For these children a brand new block of wood looked enticing. If an adult had drawn the children's attention to the internal workings of the model as represented in the diagram, which showed a hollow box for this component, they might have been dissuaded from using the wooden block. But in this classroom, as in many, the teacher was managing a whole class of lively Year 3 children on a range of curriculum activities, and was able to pay only sporadic attention to the workshop area.

The teachers we interviewed had adopted a range of strategies to make time to teach and monitor technology. Some teachers timetabled sessions when they targeted the technology activity for their 'quality time'. Some set up whole days when all the children did practical activities. Many of these were 'holding' activities in which the children were well trained to operate independently – role play, construction, sand – while the teacher focused her attention on small groups. Others involved parent helpers.

The teachers were perplexed by the difficulty of getting children to *evaluate* their work, particularly when the outcome was the result of personal choice and commitment. These girls were quite open and confident about evaluating their product, but in general teachers commented that they found children reluctant to make negative comments about their work. 'We ask the child when they've finished a model or a piece of work, are you pleased with it or would you like to change it, but they usually say "Well, I like it as it is".' Teachers felt that it was unrealistic to expect a young child to re-do work – 'it might put them off' – and negative feedback from the teacher at the end of a task was seen as potentially unproductive. We observed that sensitive ongoing evaluations fed back into the task as it evolved, provided insights which improved the quality of subsequent work. But in order to do this, teachers had to pay regular and careful attention to what was happening while the children were on task. Since practical work has traditionally been regarded as something the children can be left to get on with, this requires a major shift of attitude for primary teachers.

TEACHER-DIRECTED TASKS

Exemplar 4, Key Stage 2, making a wooden noughts and crosses game (groups of 6 Year 3 children)

The task was for each child to mark out a standard grid pattern on squared paper, transfer the grid design by pressing drawing pins through the paper Sellotaped on to a ready-cut square of wood, to drill holes for wooden pegs, to sand the surface of the wood, and thus to make a simple board game. The objectives of the task were to give the children practice in copying diagrams, to teach them how to operate a drill, and for them to make a Christmas gift to take home.

With these specific objectives in mind, the sessions were characterised by the tight control of a well-trained parent helper. She insisted on high standards. The children were expected to work methodically through the stages and help each other where one of a pair was struggling. The drills were small with pistol-grip handles, attractive to look at, but quite awkward for small children to grip at table height, and no concession was made to left-handers – they had to turn the handle towards them. In each pair one child held the block steady while the other drilled. The incidental talk was productive – about the number of turns required and the amount of pressure they needed to exert on the drill, the heat of the friction, the age rings and smell of the newly cut wood. Though the pace was brisk, the children enjoyed the sessions, and the quality of the completed board games was uniformly high.

Discussion

Training and supervising children in the use of unfamiliar tools was a constant source of anxiety for the teachers. 'If they have an accident with paint or something on their clothing, parents expect that, but if they go home with a cut from a saw I think you'd have a lot of justifying to do if you weren't there.' Teachers also worried about the classroom furniture! 'It's not only inflicting injuries on themselves or other people, but . . . the furniture, tables and chairs and the floor, you know. You might find yourself ending up with a pile of firewood.' The kind of supervision illustrated by this exemplar may seem regimental. It certainly goes against the grain for many primary teachers who would argue for the benefits of an informal teaching and learning style such as that illustrated in Exemplar 3. But the objectives of the task were achieved. Everybody learned how to use a hand drill safely.

We observed recurrent problems with equipment. We tend to forget how difficult some of the manipulative skills implicit in design and technology activities are. Often children have ambitions to make things which the limitations of their hand/eye skills simply cannot match. We saw many children actually getting tied up in knots of Sellotape – masking-tape seemed a lot easier to handle. We also found that small bench hooks, particularly when they were not clamped to surfaces, were very difficult for children to use. Pushing against the hook with one hand, while sawing with the other, left pieces of wood flailing about wildly. Saws were equally tricky, as were a range of drills we saw children operating. Snips were useful, but most of the younger children needed two hands to cut with them. We saw collections of tools on smart display boards in primary classrooms which simply did not function properly in children's hands. We need research which monitors accurately the development of hand/eye manipulative skills in young children so that tools can be designed to be more user-friendly for young children.

CONCLUSION

Despite the inauspicious context into which Key Stages 1 and 2 technology was introduced in 1990, we were impressed by the capability children were already displaying and by the commitment of their teachers to experiment with new areas of knowledge and skills.

Difficult though it was for the teachers to absorb the model of design and technology outlined in the Order (the iterative nature of designing and doing), our observations of children confirmed that this was the way in which they worked most productively. They shifted from talking, to manipulating materials, to drawing, to copying others, to seeking help from more knowledgeable peers or adults, to trying things out, to modifying and evaluating as they worked through a task.

The teachers were also learning as they went along. They recognised the need to resource children's thinking by providing opportunities for them to build up a knowledge base in order to underpin their design decisions. They were beginning to understand when and how they should demonstrate practical skills to children, and to rethink the management of their time to allow for this. They recognised that the organisation of workshop space, storage of tools, ways of working collaboratively, and generating a climate of 'critical friendship' for evaluation, all needed to be 'taught' rather than 'caught'.

We could see the potential in design and technology for children to demonstrate 'creative and practical capabilities'. Technology offers opportunities to pay real rather than rhetorical attention to practical work in primary classrooms.

ACKNOWLEDGEMENTS

My thanks to Gill Kicks and David Layton for comments on an earlier draft.

REFERENCE

National Curriculum Council (1991) *Issues in Design and Technology, Key Stages 1 to 4, Teachers' Notes*, York: National Curriculum Council.

Chapter 14

Chances of a lifetime
Exceptional educational events

Peter Woods

Teachers in primary schools have recently been criticised for alleged blind adherence to outmoded 'dogmas' (Alexander *et al*. 1992) and 'sacred cows and shibboleths', among which 'thematic work, topics, enquiry methods and group work' figure prominently (Alexander 1992: 194). Certainly, it has for long been accepted that not all projects and topics are clearly educationally worthy. Some merely relay second- or third-hand knowledge. Some are badly structured, with ill-defined aims and uncertain outcomes, and insufficiently articulated with children's development. On the other hand, these activities can be among the most exciting and rewarding educational activities, and this is certainly true of some of those I witnessed in some recent research (reported in full in Woods 1993). They stood out from normal practice. They had won wide acclaim. Some had won an award. They included creative use of the school's immediate environment in the teaching of science; on-site history, after the discovery of ancient remains beneath the playground; the use of field studies and film in the teaching of children with special needs together with mainstream children; global education through electronic mail. I came to realise that some of these activities had a number of common properties, which led me to the concept of 'critical events'.

They were 'critical' in the sense of being crucial and momentous for both pupil and teacher learning and development. They were 'events' in that they all had a similar, clearly demarcated structure. I studied three such events in detail: (1) the making of a noted children's book, *Rushavenn Time*, at Brixworth Primary School, Northamptonshire; (2) the making of a film about their village by pupils of Laxfield Primary School, Suffolk; and (3) 'The Chippindale Venture', involving the planning and design of a heritage centre on a real site in Winchester by pupils from Western Primary and All Saints Community Primary School. In addition, because I suspected that such events were not limited to primary schools, I studied an outstanding drama production (*Godspell*) at Roade Secondary School, Northamptonshire, which seemed to have similar properties.

PUPIL LEARNING AND DEVELOPMENT

In what ways were they critical? First, students have received a considerable boost to their personal development. This is especially marked in relation to attitude to learning. There is enhanced disposition and skill in listening to others, and being listened to. Increased, or new-found, confidence in oneself is frequently mentioned, as is motivation for learning. Sarah, for example, found the Rushavenn project gave her 'a lot of confidence, speaking in a group and telling people my ideas. . . . It made me feel that my pieces of paper weren't inferior to anybody else's. It made me feel that it was worthwhile trying to do my best.'

Secondly, there are several reports of self-discovery, a realisation of abilities and interests, and a 'coming-out' of a new-found self which might coincide with a 'blending-in' to the culture of a group hitherto impenetrable. Such was the case with a boy in the Chippindale Venture, who was a 'very worried child' yet 'loved this project and thrived on it and produced exceptional work. . . . It was lovely to see him shine.' In Rushavenn, Theresa Whistler, the author, was told by others that Stephen 'didn't think he could write . . . he has very good ideas, but he draws them'. After a while, however, Stephen 'produced a story about a magic paintbox, and it was full of inventiveness and imagination'. Several of the Laxfield children proved to be surprisingly good interviewers, and with groups ranging from toddlers to the over-60s. Sara, in *Godspell*, had had a difficult time at school, doing her 'A' levels that year, and not knowing many people, having arrived late at the school. She tried to back out of it at the beginning, but was persuaded to stay: 'And if I hadn't have stayed there I don't know what sort of a person I would be now. I feel I've gained so much from this.'

Emotional development, seen by some as essential to 'imaginative learn-ing', was also prominent. There was much aesthetic appreciation involved in these activities, and central to that was the catalyst of trauma – emotional disturbance which brought about a powerful concentration of attention and led to a sense of discovery of a new, powerful truth. The quality of these revelations, an amazing contrast to normal or routine experiences, is such that they assume a magical, almost mystical character. *Godspell* provided the best example of this. At times, 'we were absolutely in floods of tears the whole day, and it was very, very difficult to control'. The realisation of the exquisite opportunities on offer had to be worked for, but by the end of the production period, the participants had 'created a kind of truth in the play' (Sara). They had found a new depth of emotional engagement and a subtlety of expression that achieved a new level of belief and sophistication.

Thirdly, there has been refinement of the 'art of learning'. Imagination and creativity have been stimulated, but within a disciplined framework. They have learned skills of communicating in a variety of media. They have learned how to research, how to find things out, how to conceive, develop and express ideas. They have learned the ability to self-evaluate, and to reflect critically on their own work and that of others. They have been challenged, stretched, fulfilled.

There are many expressions of this in the events. Sarah spoke of a special quality of childhood brought out by the Rushavenn project and preserved in the book. Stephen was 'able to write more creatively and honestly'. They learned through their own experience what it was like for a real author to conceive, plan, create and write a real book. The Laxfield children developed artistic appreciation in the composition of a camera shot, in using their ears for the phrase that 'speaks volumes', and in compiling the film as an entity, which involved skills of discriminating, selecting and organising. This enabled them to capture what villagers recognised and applauded as the essence of village life. The Chippindale pupils found a new language and means of communicating. They had discovered 'designerly' ways of knowing. The architects were impressed with their use of the three-dimensional, and with their 'lovely ideas'. Some of their designs were 'extraordinary for 10–11 year olds'. Learning about oneself was matched by learning about others, including teachers, other professionals, and members of the community. Barriers of sex, age, social class, status, role and structure were transcended to some degree. They learned the nature and benefits of working co-operatively in a group, democratic procedures, decision-making. They realised they could both enhance the group and be enhanced by it; that their own worth was valued, and that they could value the work of others – surprisingly so in some cases. There was respect and dignity for both self and others.

Thus Sarah and Stephen reported how, in Rushavenn, to their astonishment, 'boys and girls worked together'. Stephen said the boys in the group all surprised one another with what they could do. In the classroom normally 'you would probably be ridiculed if, where everybody's talking about playing football, you suddenly mention "this wonderful poem I've written"'. In the project you had the great resource of both interests, and that was new to him. Theresa noticed the youngest and oldest in this group 'having a lovely respect for each other'. The same applied to students and teachers. You usually expect 'to see the headmaster strolling around being officious . . . so to see him coming in jeans and being human was great'. Theresa felt there was 'a sort of spontaneous family party feeling about it', while Dawn saw her 'as a friend', and Stephen, reiterating the family point, 'as a kind of great-aunt'. *Godspell* was felt to be remarkable by participants chiefly for the spirit, enthusiasm and selfless camaraderie generated by the group. Kevin said there was 'so much contact and closeness'; to Sara, 'You've all got this big thing in common that outsiders just don't really know about.' The group developed a special culture which many of them had not experienced before. It was accompanied by strong affective ties, forged, released almost, by the discovery of a new truth and sincerity through the requirements of the play. It was totally non-hierarchical, though composed of those with clearly differentiated statuses in ordinary life. It led to, frequently surprising, discoveries about oneself and about others. Barriers were broken down. It was invigorating, for all came to stimulate and refine one another's creativity; and it was empowering, for all could rely on spontaneous and mutual support.

The character of the learning has thus been something special. It gains the highest rating in their educational careers from the students. Stephen still looks for his name in *Rushavenn Time* in the public library. Ian can look back on *Godspell* and feel that 'he helped to please so many people'. For Jo, 'It's something you never forget . . . a once-in-a-lifetime chance.' For Matthew, as an experience in his school career to date, 'Emotionally it comes top. Mentally, it comes joint top along with my GCSE results' (he achieved nine As in these). For Claire, 'the last fourteen months have been the best months of my life'. Two-and-a-half years after the event, the Laxfield pupils, now at secondary school, had lost none of their enthusiasm. They had a feeling they 'had done something worthwhile . . . that you will keep for years'. Louise said 'it was definitely more interesting [than more formal work] and it's a very good way of learning'. Comparing some of their other experiences, they pointed out they were 'more in charge' of the video project. They 'made up the ideas', with 'the teacher there to help us along'. Those people who wanted more traditional teaching 'should come and find out for themselves'. For Ben, the Chippindale Venture was 'much more exciting' than normal school. 'It was very enjoyable', but it was not just fun because 'it did make you feel as if you could do things better'.

THE LEARNING AND DEVELOPMENT OF OTHERS

These events are also critical for teachers and the other participants. They allow for creative expression of the self and the practical realisation of their finest ideas. This yields the most profound satisfaction, fulfilment, exhilaration even. It is the high point of teaching, the 'great moment of teachability' (McLaren 1986: 235). It is a moment, then, for them of profound truth. In contrast to being deskilled and demoralised – a not uncommon feeling among teachers – these teachers through these experiences are enskilled and re-moralised.

For Sally, the producer of *Godspell*, the experience had 'changed her life'. She would not be the 'same person' again. It had made her 'happier' and 'more positive', given 'meaning to life', made 'everything worthwhile', given her 'confidence', 'hope' and 'insight'. It had been 'the ultimate production' for her, the 'most satisfactory', and she had developed it 'as fully as possible within the job that we do'. For Peter, the originator and co-ordinator of Rushavenn, it was an apogee, an experience that 'brought everything together'. Everything prior to that had been leading up to it. As the project unfolded, things began to 'fall into place'; it provided 'the key to a whole range of earlier experiences', and showed how things could be changed and improved to the advantage of everyone. He had felt marginal up to then, occupying an uncomfortable position between traditional, formal schooling on the one hand (the bane of his childhood) and a vision of an alternative, child-centred, free and flexible education on the other. For a period at least, the vision became reality. As the project works out, therefore, so does confirmation of one's beliefs and instincts.

Melanie (Laxfield) puts this well:

> You do it for the state of mind that you are in when you're doing it, when you're making something, so you feel you're putting out energies and you're testing what you're doing against your own standards, your own intuition of quality, whatever it is you believe in. You know, every mark you make goes up against what you think. It's something to do with being in touch with yourself.

Melanie also refined her pedagogical and technical skills, much of this development being self-motivated and -acquired. She took books out of the library, consulted a friend who runs a film company, another who teaches media studies in an art school, and drew on some parents who offered related expertise. With hands-on experience, Melanie and her pupils advanced beyond the book and found better and more efficient ways of doing things. Melanie saw this direct involvement as far more effective than what was available to her in courses. It was an adventure for her as well as the children, and she found the intricacies of filming and editing 'absolutely fascinating'. Melanie has become regarded as something of an expert in the production of educational videos, and has been asked by her LEA to talk to other teachers about her experiences.

Other participants also benefited. Theresa 'loved every minute' of doing *Rushavenn Time*. The book was based on a farmhouse which had 'meant so much to me in my own childhood'. She had a

> very, very strong passion for the place. . . . It wasn't quite like setting out to do a project. It was much more like writing the thing I really wanted to write, with the extra stimulus of these wholly sympathetic and delightfully alive companions.

In the Laxfield project, other beneficiaries were members of the community. Some spoke of the binding and integrating function of the film. The delight of people was not simply at a project well done, but one of unique properties that carried elements of excellence and surprise. As well as educational, it had historical and archival worth. It roused a sense of pride in people. It was a 'very, very valuable thing to do, and a very nice record for us later'. One governor thought that it was 'absolutely brilliant. . . . They covered literally everything and showed it as it is.' There was so much in it that 'the beauty of it would come out over the years'. Mr High, retired mole-, rat- and rabbit-catcher and agricultural worker, and now a leading light of the Horticultural Society, was similarly impressed. A lot of people told him he was a 'star' in the film, but he didn't know if he was. He was certainly enthusiastic about it – the girl who interviewed him, the coverage of the show, general information – 'they didn't miss much out in the village'.

In the Chippindale Venture, many of the architects and planners were having their first taste of teaching, and relating to, primary school children. They had been detailed by their firms, and were 'very, very worried about what they were expected to do' and their ability to communicate with the children. As one commented, 'we had to learn a new art'. They succeeded valiantly. The children had been delighted with *their* architects, and the architects in turn had learned a range of new skills and broadened their perspectives on educational architecture. Planners had found the experience 'absolutely amazing'. They had no idea that children were capable of tackling some of these challenges; and it was refreshing for them to get a whole range of perceptions different from those they would usually receive, 'uncontaminated by bureaucratic thought systems', and which would often cause them to think differently about an approach to planning and design.

THE STRUCTURE OF CRITICAL EVENTS

All these events had a similar structure, running through fairly well-defined stages:

1 *Conceptualisation*. The beginning of the process is the inspired thought that conceives and gestates the idea. It might be a single person's idea or dream (for example, Rushavenn), or the product of discussion among several (such as Chippindale).
2 *Preparation and planning*, entailing the clarification of aims, the assembling of resources, briefing and enskilling.
3 *Divergence*. This is an 'explosion' stage, when pupils are encouraged to be innovative and creative, explore opportunities, test and stretch their abilities, experiment with different media and forms of expression, capitalise on working with others. Space is left for the unexpected, for you cannot predict what will arise and develop from creative activity.
4 *Convergence*. This is an integrating stage, where the products of the previous stage are examined to find those that best serve the collective enterprise.
5 *Consolidation*. The work is refined in the writing-up, editing, picture-mounting, performance or whatever medium is being used. The full artistic merits of the piece in its separate parts and in their relationship with each, becomes clear.
6 *Celebration*. This marks the end of the event. It may be an exhibition, a performance of a play, the launch of a book, a concert, the public

showing of a film or a full public planning committee meeting. It is an acknowledgement of achievement, and there is an air of excitement and something special about it. It also marks the end of the event, and constitutes a rite of passage out of 'criticality' and back into 'normality'.

Learning proceeds through these stages with a certain rhythm and flow. Periods of equilibrium alternate with sudden disequilibrium, and learning spirals and accumulates and becomes more complex as the event unfolds. This process corresponds with a fine balance that is struck between structure and chaos, planning and freedom. Jennifer Nias (1990), commenting on the research underpinning her book *Primary Teachers Talking*, 'emphasises the value of chaos as a seed bed for creativity'. The same holds for teaching and learning. But it is accompanied by a more sober discipline, which anchors ideas, gives them shape and brings them together in relation to the aims of the task in hand. As the project proceeds, therefore, creativity is founded on an increasingly solid basis, which in turn promotes creativity of a higher order.

CONDITIONS FOR CRITICAL EVENTS

Context was of crucial significance for all the events. 'Regular patterns bring a regular pattern of response from the children,' said Peter (Rushavenn). Though this may be necessary at times, at others it inhibited an 'honest and in-depth response'. The base for Rushavenn was the staffroom, the time Saturdays (over the period of a year), the basic organisation a circle, 'where no one occupied a position which was more important than anyone else'. All the events used a great deal of extra-curricular time and space. This aided the sense of holistic and real learning, and counteracted any bureaucratic tendencies of the institutional structure. The more general context of the school was also important. Institutional values were empathetic, school organisation facilitated, resources were made available, and heads and others lent support.

The context had to be chosen or designed to serve the principles of co-operation, collaboration and negotiation. Shades of the competitive spirit hung on in all the events, but subsided as the benefits of co-operation took hold. Thus at Laxfield, they 'wanted to be best' and saw it as a competition, but finally settled for working to do their best design and appreciating the best in others. As for Rushavenn and *Godspell*, they both won prestigious competitions, but neither had set out with that aim in view, and indeed were only entered after excellence had been established.

The collaboration took a number of forms. Students had to work together in teams; then the teams had to relate together in the interests of a greater whole. Teachers, while maintaining a co-ordinating role, were part of these teams. They also developed a special relationship with students, characterised by mutual respect and warmth. The projects also benefited from the quality of team-work among the teachers and other professionals. Their roles interlocked, with the teachers accepting general responsibility and the professionals providing specialist expertise. This proved a highly productive compound role. This team-work took place against a background of a 'culture of collaboration' within the school as a whole.

Content was another key factor. The book, film design, or play was relevant to students' concerns and needs. It was meaningful to them, and it caught their imaginations, elevating them above the conventional and offering a new perspective. It provided a range of opportunities and challenges in a stimulating framework. Thus Sally's inspired interpretation of *Godspell*, while remaining faithful to the basic text, embraced many more students than the original production, provided for the generation of unity among them, capitalised on the qualities of youth, and, above all, provided its own impetus for further multiple individual and sub-group interpretations with the overall plot.

At the centre of operations is the 'critical agent', the teacher. These teachers have high levels of 'planning genius'. Their readiness to tackle new initiatives has them and others 'bubbling like a hot spring' (Nias 1989). All the critical agents here secured additional resource, recruited skilled and technical assistance, initiated enthusiasm, managed the tempo of the event, and created time where none was thought to exist. Critical others – the other professionals – also played a key role. They lent an authenticity to the proceedings, raised the activity to a new level, injected novelty as well as expertise. They helped forge the link between school and the outside world. They provided a new kind of role-model for students, extending their horizons and making bridges between professional and person. Students learned to appreciate these others as human beings, and were encouraged to exercise part of the professional's role.

The use of multi-methods was evident in all the events, variety and flexibility being the keynote. There was a basic fitness-for-purpose behind their use, but all the teachers subscribed to a student-centred philosophy which emphasises students' control of their own learning to some degree and ownership of knowledge. This produces 'real learning'. Real learning builds on pupils' relevancies, and their existing cognitive and affective structures. There is a strong emphasis on reality, on a real problem or issue of importance or value, on real rather than contrived emotions, on an authentic situation, on using experts for the task in hand, on collecting first-hand evidence and materials, on doing things oneself, on having a realistic aim. As Debbie said with regard to the Chippindale Venture, 'It was a real site, a real need, with real people involved. It had a real context for them, and that did, I think, give it some meaning.' Similarly, *Godspell* provided opportunities for a range and depth of emotional expression that has a relevance for real life. It offered experience in searching for truth, and for what is real, for the discovery of genuine, rather than theatrical, emotion. Rushavenn produced a real book, and Laxfield a film of genuine community and archive work.

For such events to be possible, there must be scope within the curriculum structure. All of these activities took place before the National Curriculum took effect. What, therefore, is the current situation? The teachers here certainly feel things have changed. Melanie, for example, 'didn't feel as open and as ready to take the risks of that kind of long-term commitment. . . . I don't feel I have the freedom of scope to do such a project.' Peter felt a confusion in the headteacher's role, with pressure on him to take more part in financial management. His current aim is not to go on to more experiments in creative teaching, but to defend what he has achieved while attempting to overcome the problems brought to the school in the wake of the Reform Act.

Certainly, at least for the moment, there is less scope for experimentation. Research shows that some teachers at least, under pressure of required demands, are moving away from work designed to stimulate children's interest in imagination. For some, there is 'less fun and joy' in teaching, and much less time for 'preparation and planning' (Campbell *et al.* 1991). Teacher morale is also at a low ebb. On the other hand, a reading of attainment targets and programmes of study suggests the National Curriculum *requires* critical events. They also promise to promote the cross-curricular elements, such as skills of 'communication, of studying, of problem solving, and personal and social skills'. It might be argued that the current concern with primary teaching is not with projects or 'child-centredness' *per se*, but with an excess of freedom over structure, divergence over convergence – that is, a lack of balance among the various phases of the rhythm of learning. Some commentators feel that the opportunity is there for diversity and spontaneity within a rigorous and systematic framework; and after initial nervousness, many teachers appear more optimistic about creative work. It is not difficult to find creative and constructivist principles in the National Curriculum, even if other parts, notably the assessment, are heavily behaviourist.

Exceptional events, in short, seem legitimated in principle but obstructed in practice, though some pathways are beginning to be found. If these are closed off, students and teachers will be deprived of opportunities for creative excellence of the highest order. They will not have sight of that ultimate standard by which all else might be judged. They will not feel the thrill of motivation, nor experience the breakthrough of ability, driving them to summits of achievement, hitherto unforeseen and perhaps undreamt of. They will not be able to avail themselves of those rare moments when golden opportunities are presented and all goes right – the chance of a lifetime. Back in 1947, A.N. Whitehead was cautioning, 'Unless we are careful, we shall organize genius right out of existence' (p. 96). Rushavenn, Laxfield, Chippindale, and *Godspell* show what we would be missing.

REFERENCES

Alexander, R.J. (1992) *Policy and Practice in Primary Education*, London: Routledge.

Alexander, R.J., Rose, J. and Woodhead, C. (1992) *Curriculum Organisation and Classroom Practice in Primary Schools: a Discussion Paper*, London: Department of Education and Science, HMSO.

Campbell, R.J., Evans, L., St J. Neill, S.R. and Packwood, A. (1991) *Workloads, Achievements and Stress: Two Follow-up Studies of Teacher Time in Key Stage 1*, Policy Analysis Unit, Department of Education, University of Warwick.

McLaren, P. (1986) *Schooling as a Ritual Performance*, London: Routledge & Kegan Paul.

Nias, J. (1989) *Primary Teachers Talking: a Study of Teaching as Work*, London: Routledge.

—— (1990) 'Primary teachers talking: a reflexive account of longitudinal research', in G. Walford (ed.) *Doing Educational Research*, London: Routledge.

Whitehead, A.N. (1947) *Essays in Science and Philosophy*, New York: Philosophical Library.

Woods, P. (1993) *Critical Events in Teaching and Learning*, London: Falmer Press.

Part IV

Critical approaches to assessment

Chapter 15

Another way of looking

Michael Armstrong

This chapter takes up some of the issues which emerged in Chapter 14, calling for assessment procedures which recognise and acknowledge children's achievements which go beyond programmes of study. The author provides a strong and at times polemical critique of National Curriculum assessment methods, with special reference to English. In the light of his chapter, readers may want to consider whether and how far national assessment should become involved in the assessment of 'meaning' or be based upon interpretative readings of children's understanding. Some might argue that interpretation should form the basis of formative and diagnostic assessment, but should not be central to standardised assessments. Others might feel that if Armstrong's arguments are not heeded, the narrower features of learning focused on by the tests will come to dominate the curriculum. The chapter points up some fundamental issues relating to the disjuncture between the goals of teachers and their use of formative assessment, and a national system of monitoring pupil attainment against certain standardised criteria.

The National Curriculum betrays the children whose intellectual interests it is supposed to serve.

I say this despite the well-intentioned efforts of liberal teachers to play the National Curriculum game in the hope of subverting its rules. It seems to me that any attempt to gentle the National Curriculum is necessarily futile because that curriculum is framed in terms which misconstrue the nature of learning and of teaching. The narrow specification of the curriculum by subject ignores the way in which the course of learning proceeds in imaginative classrooms. The language of targets and levels of attainment reduced achievement to a false hierarchy of technical accomplishments. The unacknowledged metaphor of 'delivery' deprives children of their constructive and reconstructive role in the acquisition of knowledge.

For me, the moment of truth had a very particular location – paragraph 10.19 of the first report of the National Curriculum English Working Group, *English for Ages 5 to 11*. This first report is the most progressive to have emerged so far. Over and over again the report insists on the importance of attending to the significance of what children have to say rather than to its apparent form. Teachers are urged to show 'respect for and interest in the learner's language, culture, thought and intentions'. It is suggested that teachers 'provide the greatest encouragement for children to communicate in writing when they respond more to the content of what is written than to [errors of letter formation, spelling and composition]'. 'Meaning', we are told, 'should always be in the foreground'.

Until, that is, we reach paragraph 10.19. For there we read:

> The best writing is vigorous, committed, honest and interesting. We have not included these qualities in our attainment targets because they cannot be mapped on to levels. Even so, all good classroom practice will be geared to encouraging and for fostering these vital qualities.

That last sentence reads as a desperate attempt to avoid the implication of what has just been said. For this paragraph can only mean that meaning itself, its quality, its value, is not to be assessed within the National Curriculum and finds no legitimate place among its 'clear objectives'. Look through the attainment targets carefully. You will find among the Working Group's slender descriptions not a single trace of meaning. It is true that attainment target no. 3 is defined as 'a growing ability to construct and convey meaning in written language'. But nowhere does the character or quality of a child's meanings feature among the statements of attainment, level on level, that follow this opening definition. Meaning is central but meaning is not to be assessed. Children may be 'makers of meanings in their own texts' but the meanings they make are unexaminable.

It says a good deal for the honesty of the English Working Group that it has so frankly acknowledged the irrelevance of meaning to the language of attainment targets, the language that has determined the National Curriculum. In this, as in much else, it has the advantage over the National Curriculum Council. Indeed, it is worth pausing a moment to notice the National Curriculum Council's way with paragraph 10.19. Acknowledging the alarm of many teachers at the implications of the paragraph, the Council claims to have 'undertaken the task of mapping such qualities (as vigour, independence and commitment) on to levels in its recommended statements of attainment'. This specious claim is a choice example of the Council's piecemeal and extempore methods.

It was not until the publication of the English Working Group's *second* report – by which time paragraph 10.19 had become paragraph 17.31 – that the National Curriculum Council took any notice of the notorious paragraph. By that time levels 1 to 3 of the attainment targets for English had already been determined by statutory order, following the recommendations of the Council itself. They could not be revised again. So levels 1 to 3 still contain no reference to qualities of meaning. It is charitable to attribute this to the Council's oversight. Or is it that the Council considers children below level 4 to be incapable of significant utterance?

In the end it hardly matters, for when at level 4 the National Curriculum Council at last proceeds to revise the Working Group's statements of attainment to take account of meaning it does so in a manner that is entirely frivolous. The Working Group had described level 4 as the level at which children are able to 'write stories which have an opening, a setting, characters, a series of events and a resolution'. To this admittedly banal definition of an average 11-year-old's literary artistry the Council adds the words 'and which engage the sympathy and interest of the reader'. Just that – no more. Now it's important, who can doubt it, to engage a reader's interest, especially if that reader happens to be your teacher. But to suppose that this is enough to dispense with the problem of paragraph 10.19 – that reader response is the unique key to meaning – is at best careless.

There is no evidence in either of the National Curriculum Council's Consultation Documents on English in the National Curriculum to suggest that the Council has in any way understood the dilemma recognised by the Working Group. This is scarcely surprising. For what 10.19 shows us is that the language of the National Curriculum is impervious to the significance of children's thought and affords no access to an understanding of children's understanding, either of how to describe it or of how to promote it.

So what are we to do? How is it possible to rewrite the National Curriculum in language that restores meaning to its place at the centre of learning and teaching? I don't know the answer to this question but I think I know how to begin to find out. I would begin with interpretation. What does it mean to ascribe significance to children's thought and action, and to see that significance as the clue to learning and to teaching – the clue also to content and method in the curriculum? I want to approach this question through one particular instance. The English Working Group has once again provided the opportunity.

Appendix 6 of *English for Ages 5 to 11* presents a series of illustrative examples of 'children's developing writing with reference to our attainment targets', as the Report puts it. Here is the fourth example, 'an unaided first draft by a middle infant girl' (see Figure 15.1).

Here is how the English Working Group describes this wonderful tale, which is said to 'illustrate several Level 2 features of writing':

> This is a simple chronological account with a clear story structure, including a conventional beginning, narrative middle and end. The sentences are almost all demarcated, though via the graphic, comic-strip layout and not via capital letters and punctuation. The spelling is almost entirely meaningful and recognisable. In several cases, it shows that the author has correctly grasped the patterns involved, even though the individual spellings are wrong (e.g. trooth, eny, owt, sumthing, cubad).

When I was naughty

It wasa ferw weex Past my birthday wen me and my sister went to the kitchen

I went to the cubad and Clare opnd the cubad and we tuck the crips and we went up seris my

dad cort me and Clare so he said have you tuck sum thing from the cubad no we said

then my dad said have you, noI lid are you teling lis no no no I lid again In the end my dad mad me tell the trooth

then he said you naughty gils and sent me and clare to bed with owt eny supa and Clare blamd it on me .

Figure 15.1 'When I was naughty'

The handwriting occasionally mixes upper and lower case letters, though only at beginnings and ends of words, not at random.

That is all the Working Group has to say about 'When I was naughty'. It's all that the National Curriculum requires it to say. Is that really all a 6-year-old writer can do? Is that all her knowledge, skill and understanding amount to? Is that all that's worth saying about this story? Is it, at any rate, all we need to record, all we need to know, as parents, teachers, storytellers ourselves? Can this really be how to talk about children and their work? For myself, I can't imagine a thinner description of a young child's narrative achievement. At no point is there the smallest recognition of the story's significance, of the relationship between its meaning and its form, of the quality of narrative thought which is seeking expression here. Any teacher who attempted no more than this would have little chance of understanding this child's understanding, let alone of promoting it. If this is really how we are expected to evaluate our pupils we're surely in the wrong trade.

So let's take a closer look at the story.

'When I was naughty' examines the moral order and its relation to experience, as seen from the perspective of 6 years old. It deals with questions of truth and lying, mutuality and recrimination, guilt and blame. It addresses, at least implicitly, the conflict between a child's and an adult's view of these matters. One of the most striking aspects of the story is the way the narrative dramatises the interlocking conflicts which make up its subject matter. And the drawings play as important a part in this drama as the writing.

'It was a few weeks past my birthday when me and my sister went to the kitchen.' There's a feeling of a formula about this opening, and yet, compared with 'Once upon a time' it's strikingly precise. It marks out what is to come as a reminiscence – fact – rather than a fairy tale. Might it be more than a formula, though? 'A few weeks past my birthday . . .': might that birthday signify the coming of a new age, the age of moral awareness, a new maturity? Part of the business of interpretation is to persuade ourselves that such speculations are appropriate, even to a 6-year-old's story.

The second frame is all uninhibited action: 'I went to the cupboard and Clare opened the cupboard and we took the crisps and we went upstairs.' The tiny, canonical sentences hurry by, each with its active verb in a simple past tense – 'went', 'opened', 'took', 'went' – each linked to the next by an indispensable 'and'. How beautifully the first three drawings express the impulse of this action. In the first drawing one child is already in the kitchen, approaching the cupboard, while the other crosses the living room with its large, round, central light. By the second drawing both children have reached the kitchen and Clare is already at the cupboard, stretching up to remove the crisps. The living room is empty. What a way for a 6-year-old to picture movement! The third drawing, which really belongs with the second frame, shows the two children striding upstairs, the leading one in the act of stepping from one stair to the other, caught in the act, as she is just about to be.

So far in the story there's been no trace of the moral order, unless we choose to read the words 'the cupboard' as suggestive of a guarded space, or the words 'the crisps' as hinting at the fatefulness of the object taken. The two children seem to be acting without constraint. Nothing yet has been forbidden them. It's fascinating to see how subtly the storyteller emphasises the mutuality of the sisters at this point in their adventures. *'Me and my sister* went' . . . *'I* went' . . . *'Clare* opened' . . . *'We* took' . . . *'We* went upstairs', and now a sudden eruption: dad, lies, punishment, recrimination, the world of moral order.

The author is remarkably particular about this shift. At the end of frame two the flow of action is brought sharply to a stop. Could it be significant that the break comes with the last word of frame two rather than with the first word of frame three? Every other frame closes on a full stop. Not this one, though. Is the writer trying to highlight the interruption of the action in full flow? In a complementary move the drawing that follows in frame three is still bound up with the interrupted action, as if the momentum of the previous frame has overflown, so to speak, its own arrest.

'My dad caught me and Clare . . .' 'Caught': this one word transforms everything that has gone before, turning the children's freedom of action into a transgression, a flouting of the rules. 'Caught' not 'met' or 'saw' or 'came across'. At once the guilty deed is exposed. 'So he said.' That 'so' is significant too. The *OED* tells us that the particle 'so' denotes both sequence and consequence, sometimes both at once. So it is here. The 'so' of the story – and I think it could be argued that the lack of punctuation here is an advantage, heightening the double significance of 'so' – implies, surely, that dad has already guessed the truth. From here on all that will count is the acknowledgement of what is already recognised as guilt.

See how the drawing to frame four captures the moment of truth. Dad has appeared in a doorway at the foot of the stairs on which the two sisters are suddenly frozen. The leading sister's striding foot has dropped back a step. It's a beautifully observed detail.

I love the confessional scene, the way it escalates. 'So he said, have you took something from the cupboard? No, we said. Then my dad said, have you? No, I lied. Are you telling lies? No, no, no, I lied again.' The rhetoric of this passage is wonderfully artful. It has all the storyteller's flair. But the artfulness is surely born of a certain familiarity, and with more than the single event which the story tells, assuming it's a true story. Observation, memory and art are almost inseparable here, though I suppose we might wonder about that 'have you took'.

This is the moment at which the mutuality of the sisters begins to break down. It is the narrator alone, in the end, who is made to tell the truth. 'No *we* said. . . . no *I* lied . . . no no no *I* lied again . . . in the end my dad made *me* tell the truth.' Divide and rule; it's as if our 6-year-old storyteller has seen it all.

'In the end my dad made me tell the truth.' Young writers sometimes have an enviable knack of cutting a long story short. We do not need to know the how of it. The point is that it's impossible to get away with it. A father's authority is sufficient to get at the truth. Or perhaps it's his trickiness, his deviousness. I think it's worth observing that the storyteller offers no comment, either as to the rightness or wrongness of the father's forcing the truth or indeed of the sisters' taking of the crisps in the first place. We may interpret the morality as we will. We are presented only with the outcome. It's characteristic of young children's stories to be open in this way.

Finally, then, retribution. 'Then he said, you naughty girls, and sent me and Clare to bed without any supper and Clare blamed it on me.' In frame two the sisters appeared to be in control of their own destiny – 'we took the crisps and we went upstairs'. Now the tables are turned. Instead of 'went' we find 'sent' – 'sent to bed without any supper'. The girls after all are subject to their father's will. In the final drawing the stairs have grown steeper, almost mountainous. They are no longer the quick, easy passage from kitchen cupboard to children's room. Now they mark the sad, slow ascent to the place of punishment. Clare has disappeared, appropriately enough since the father's intervention has destroyed the sisters' mutuality. 'And Clare blamed it on me.' The narrator, who in acknowledging her guilt gave the game away, is left to face her father's anger alone as he stands at the foot of the stairs, enforcing his order.

So what are we to make of one tiny story, however charming?

The English Working Group chose it to illustrate the meagre account of attainment set out in their statutory targets and levels. It is more appropriately read, first as an indictment of that account, and second as a clue to an alternative account. For there *is* another way of looking.

'When I was naughty' allows us to glimpse a young child's thought in all its imaginative richness. The artistry of its 6-year-old author is apparent in every aspect of her story. In her exploitation of narrative style, with its formulas, its suspense, its various concealments and revelations, its openness to interpretation. In her acceptance of constraint and her turning of constraint into opportunity; think of her virtuoso treatment of the limited sentence structure available to her at this point in her narrative development, the way she makes use of the conjunction 'and' and the particle 'so'. In her critical judgement, so apparent in her choice of vocabulary. In her concern to express her own sense of life in the ordered medium of written and drawn narrative. In short, in her appropriation of form.

For me the history of learning is the history of the appropriation of form, in this way and in countless other ways, while the history of teaching begins and ends in the *interpretation* of appropriated form. By 'interpretation' I mean the critical scrutiny of children's intellectual enterprise, from moment to moment and from subject matter to subject matter, over the course of children's school careers. The description which I've just attempted of 'When I was naughty' is an example of interpretation, as applied to one particular product of one particular child's intellectual enterprise at one particular moment in time. Multiplied across the curriculum and sustained over the years, a set of descriptions of this kind, accompanied by their objects – the works described and the evidence of the manner of their composition – would amount to an intellectual biography, a kind of documentary history of individual, and therefore incommensurate, achievement. This is what I mean by another way of looking and it is equally another way of speaking, as distant from the language of attainment targets as it is possible to imagine.

The focus of interpretation is a child's thought and action at its most significant. Our interest, in interpretation, is not in simulations of thought – exercises, tests, prescribed tasks, standard procedures – but in the work which is most expressive of each child's struggle with meaning. As far as the study of English is concerned that includes children's stories and poems, diaries and notebooks, arguments and conversations, play-acting and make-believe, reflections and speculations on language and literature.

One of the most important tasks in interpreting children's work is to describe its patterns of intention: the interests, motifs, orientations, forms of meditation that govern a child's thought and seek expression in her practice. The concerns expressed in a story like 'When I was naughty' are clear enough, some of them at any rate: concerns, for example, with family relationships, with issues of loyalty, deceit and authority, concerns which further examples of the author's work would help us to evaluate more precisely.

A second task is to examine the interplay between form and content in a child's thought, and between technique and expression. The relationship of word to picture in 'When I was naughty' is an example of this kind of interplay, as is the author's manipulation of a limited range of sentence types to maximum effect.

A third task for interpretation is to trace the circulation of a child's ideas through all the various aspects of the curriculum. See how literature, art, moral thought, personal and social education, are all implicated in our 6-year-old's one story.

A single text has served me as an example of how to interpret children's thought; but this is in a way misleading, for it's characteristic of interpretation to be concerned with the development of a child's ideas from work to work over time – a week, month, year, career.

This is the moment at which it becomes necessary to talk about intervention as the natural complement of interpretation. Interpretation and intervention are the two faces of teaching, assuming that teaching is seen as a way of sustaining children's critical engagement with thought in all its forms. To interpret a 6-year-old's story is to begin to understand her own understanding, and that in turn is to begin to understand how to promote further understanding. Interpretation sets the agenda for intervention. It suggests to us, in the case of 'When I was naughty', the stories the writer might read to aid her own writing or to develop her sense of literature. It shows us how to help her to address the moral concerns which dominate her narrative. It clarifies for us the interplay of words and pictures in her thought. It helps us to see how we might raise with her, however tentatively, the questions of narrative voice and narrative identity. It illustrates the significance which at this point in her development she attaches to punctuation; we notice the simple, large full stop decisively placed at the end of her tale and wonder, maybe, how significant the matter of punctuation might seem to her just now.

It would be nice to imagine that the division of the National Curriculum's statutory orders into attainment targets and programmes of study reflected this distinction between interpretation and intervention. Nice but fanciful. The attainment targets have nothing to do with interpretation and for this reason they afford no purchase on intervention. It is the fatal weakness of the entire enterprise.

Many of the Working Groups, it is true, have sought to use the programmes of study to emphasise the wealth of learning and teaching that resists the language of targeting, and none more so than the English Working Group. Its two reports are quite adventurous about intervention. They describe the 'diverse roles teachers will have to play in the development of young writers: they will be observers, facilitators, modellers, readers and supporters'. They insist that the 'teacher's response to written work should aim to foster a child's confidence in the exploration of ideas'. They ask teachers to write alongside their pupils in the classroom. They demand well-equipped classrooms full of books, notepads, post boxes, word-processors, play-houses. They suggest that 'opportunities should be provided . . . to read and write lists, labels, letters, invitations, leaflets, pamphlets, plans and diagrams', not to mention 'diaries, stories and accounts of things'. They tell us to encourage children 'to share their writing with others, to discuss what they have written and to publish stories, newspapers, magazines, games and guides'.

Useful as these various statements are, they remain incoherent because of the failure to relate them to the interpretative outlook in which they gain their educational justification. It is not possible, for example, to make sense of the demand that teachers write alongside their pupils unless education is perceived as common and collaborative struggle for meaning in which both teachers and taught have much to share and much to learn from each other, whether the pupils be 5-, or 15-, or 50-years-old.

Inasmuch as it depends on the recognition and promotion of significant utterance, education thrives on conversation. Unfortunately conversation is at odds with the ideology that has inspired the National Curriculum. Laid down from above, expressed in the language of law, obsessed with standardisation, committed to a hierarchical model of achievement, the National Curriculum can only get in the way of the conversation that thrives in resourceful classrooms and sustains the course and the cause of learning. To rewrite that curriculum in a way which supports conversation will take a long time, and great political determination. I have suggested that a promising way to begin is to look at how we interpret children's thought. There are plenty of other ways too. Let the exploration begin.

Chapter 16

Assessment and gender

Patricia Murphy

The question of bias in assessment processes is the subject of this chapter. Many of the problems related to gender in assessment are also relevant to other issues such as race, language background and class. The author shows how different experiences, learnt ways of experiencing and styles of expression can influence the responses of boys and girls to assessment tasks, and alter the assessors' perceptions of their achievements. She argues for open-ended assessment tasks which will allow all children to express their interests and understandings.

The problem of bias in teaching and assessment is widely recognised but, unfortunately, not well understood. This is evident in the National Curriculum guidelines. Paradoxically, teachers are cautioned about the problems of bias, yet no account of it is taken in the selection and organisation of curriculum content. It is commonly assumed that a National Curriculum ensures equality of access, but pupils will not have equal access to knowledge if the curriculum provision they receive fails to validate their experiences and ways of 'making sense' of the world.

The national assessment system introduced in association with the National Curriculum has been justified, to an extent, on the grounds that it will facilitate more efficient curriculum planning which in turn will lead to an improvement in children's learning (TGAT 1987). However, bias in assessment means that many pupils' positive achievements go unrecognised. Hence the information gathered could be misleading. The intention to use the assessment results to monitor and evaluate pupils, teachers and schools makes it imperative that the sources and effects of bias are understood. The Task Group on Assessment and Testing recommends the removal of biased items – which presupposes that we can detect and isolate the sources of bias in assessment items – and that information from such items does not illuminate curriculum planning. I would take issue with both of these assumptions.

In this chapter I will consider the implications of bias largely from a gender perspective, referring to research into gender differences and the results of the Assessment of Performance Unit's Science project (Murphy and Gott 1984). This project monitored the performance of populations of 11-, 13- and 15-year-old pupils in all types of schools from 1980 to 1984 and carried out research into assessment until recently. I will use the results to make general points about the nature and effects of bias in assessment procedures and some of the implications for teaching.

BACKGROUND EXPERIENCES

A central assumption in assessment is that the results can be interpreted in terms of what was intended to be assessed. There is an increasing amount of evidence that difference in pupils' performance is related to their different experiences both in and out of school. For example, in the APU science surveys, boys and girls at ages 11 and 13 perform at the same level on assessments of the use of apparatus and measuring instruments. However, on certain individual instruments – for example, microscopes or stopwatches – girls as a group do significantly less well than boys. The number of instruments to show this effect increases as children go through school until at 15 boys are performing at a higher level overall. Pupils in the surveys were asked what experience they had, out of school, of the various measuring instruments used. Boys' performance was found to be better than girls' on precisely those instruments of which they claim to have more experience. If the results of assessments are to be interpreted correctly, it is important to collect this additional information. Without it one could assume that such results reflect innate differences between pupils. Consequently, the decisions about where to go next in the curriculum and, more importantly, how to get there would be misinformed.

The different experiences of pupils does not just affect the skills they develop but also their understanding of the situations and problems where their skills can be used appropriately. To interpret assessment results and to plan effective classroom strategies it is necessary to focus on both the nature of the differential experiences as well as their consequences. For example, boys across the ages are better able to use ammeters and voltmeters yet they do not use these outside of school. They do, however, play more with electrical toys and gadgets than girls. Such play allows boys to develop a 'feel' for the effects of electricity and how it can be controlled and manipulated. This is a prerequisite for understanding how to measure it. Another example of this relates to girls' inexperience of modelling activities. To overcome this many teachers provide Lego for young children to play with, but are often discouraged by girls' apparent failure to engage with it. When boys play with Lego they do so in a purposeful way. Their play allows them to establish the link between their purposes and the potential of Lego to match them. It is this relationship that girls need a chance to explore. To facilitate this teachers need to identify tasks and problems that girls find motivating where Lego could serve a useful function.

DIFFERENCES IN WAYS OF EXPERIENCING

Research into gender differences has related the different patterns of nurturing that many girls and boys receive to the different values and views of relevance they develop (Chodorow 1978; Harding 1985). These lead them to look at the world in different ways. As a result, children come to school with learning styles already developed and with an understanding of what is and is not appropriate for them. What they judge to be appropriate they tackle with confidence; what they consider alien they tend to avoid. The consequences of this are evident in assessment.

The results of the science surveys show that irrespective of what criterion is being assessed, questions which involve such content as health, reproduction, nutrition and domestic situations are generally attempted by more girls than boys. The girls also tend to achieve higher scores on these questions. In situations with a more overtly 'masculine' content – for example, building sites, racing tracks, or anything with an electrical content – the converse is true. For example, girls and boys at ages 11 and 13 are equally competent at using tables and graphs. Yet if the graph is about a day in the life of a secretary then some boys do not respond, whereas girls will tackle the item with confidence and so overall obtain a higher score. If, on the other hand, the graph is about traffic flow through a town, the reverse happens. For some pupils then, the items are not about graphs but about their experience of the content. Yet assessors assume that the content is largely irrelevant.

These findings occur for the full ability range of pupils, across profile components and attainment targets. The dilemma for assessors is that such questions are sources of assessment invalidity which need to be eradicated for the summative purposes of reporting and evaluating. On the other hand, they provide the teacher with invaluable formative insights to aid curriculum planning. This latter point is of particular significance. Without information about the nature of gender differences teachers cannot develop effective strategies for overcoming them. Consequently, the effects of pupils' alienation are not addressed. Alienation ultimately leads to under-achievement as girls and boys fail to engage with certain learning opportunities. The APU survey results show at age 11 one test difference in favour of boys but by age 15 this has increased to four out of a possible eight (Johnson and Murphy 1986). It is important to consider pupils' performance on features of tasks other than subject-specific criteria to provide the information needed to understand gender differences.

Teachers are also susceptible to seeing areas of the curriculum as gender-appropriate. The study of Goddard-Spear (1983) showed that the same pieces of science writing when attributed to girls received lower marks from teachers than when they were attributed to boys. The introduction of teacher assessment in the national system is to be applauded, but at the same time efforts must be made to enable teachers to understand the nature of bias. Without this understanding many pupils will continue to receive inappropriate curriculum provision.

STYLES OF EXPRESSION

An outcome of children's different images of the world and their places in it is that the problems that girls and boys perceive in set tasks are often very different given the same circumstances. How pupils express what they have learnt will also reflect these differences. Typically, girls tend to value the circumstances in which activities are presented and consider that they give meaning to the task. They do not abstract issues from their context. Boys as a group conversely do consider the issues in isolation and judge the content and context to be irrelevant. This latter approach is generally assumed in assessment practice. Research that shows that boys do better than girls on multiple-choice items relates to these differences (Murphy 1982; Harding 1985). Girls, in taking account of features of items that the assessor regards as 'noise' or padding, see ambiguity in the responses offered, and commonly either do not respond as no one answer 'fits', or give more than one response. Another example of this effect occurred when pupils designed model boats to go round the world and were investigating how much load they would support. Some of the girls were observed collecting watering cans, spoons and hair dryers. The teachers assumed that they had not 'understood' the problem. However, as the girls explained, if you are going round the world you need to consider the boat's stability in monsoons, whirlpools and gales – conditions they attempted to re-create. In another situation pupils were investigating which material would keep them warmer when stranded on a mountainside. They were expected to compare how well the materials kept cans of hot water warm. Again girls were seen to be doing things 'off task'. For example, they cut out prototype coats, dipped the materials in water and blew cold air through them. These girls took seriously the human dilemma presented. It therefore mattered how porous the material was to wind, how waterproof it was and whether indeed it was suitable for making a coat.

These examples of 'girls' solutions' are judged as failures either because their problems are not recognised or because they are not valued by assessors. There are two issues to consider here. First, on what grounds are girls', and other groups of pupils', views of relevance accorded low status in assessments? Secondly, if pupils' views are to be denied, then interpretations of assessment results should indicate that pupils address alternative tasks rather than failing to provide 'correct' responses to meaningless tasks.

Another potential source of assessment bias arises from the different interests that girls and boys typically develop. Girls enjoy reading a wide range of books; boys, on the other hand, tend to read non-fiction, particularly technical and hobby manuals. These preferences affect the styles of writing children adopt. Girls choose to communicate their feelings about phenomena in extended and reflective composition; boys provide episodic, factual, commentative detail (Gorman *et al.* 1988). The significance for assessment is that differences in style alter assessors' perceptions of the content of pupils' responses and thus become equated with differences in achievement. This is dependent on the subject being assessed. For example, in science, a boy's typical style will be favoured, whereas in, say, a humanities assessment, a girl's is more likely to be favoured.

DISCUSSION

How might we tackle the idea of gender-fair assessment? One strategy is to eradicate the effects of bias by using items on which girls and boys achieve equivalent scores. However, gender bias arises from a complex interaction of effects related to the features of assessment tasks; for example, a question involving a particular biological content focusing on distinctions between colours with girls and boys as groups achieving equal scores. However, some boys will fail to respond because the content alienates them, while others may have difficulties because they typically do not consider colours as relevant data (Murphy 1990; Murphy and Moon 1990). On the other hand, some girls will not have responded because they cannot see the one 'right' answer. If results are not interpreted at this level of detail, the information they provide will misinform curriculum planning as all pupils who fail to provide the 'answer' are assumed not to have the knowledge being assessed. A further problem with attempting to eradicate bias is that not enough is known about the features of tasks which affect pupils' ability to construct meaning from them.

An alternative approach would be to provide tasks that allow all pupils to express their interests and understandings in a manner that suits them. However, in tasks of this kind it follows that pupils will see different problems and different solutions. For example, in a recent study pupils were given the task of designing a learning activity for young children. Overwhelmingly, boys' designs were of adventure or assault courses exclusively communicated in drawings. Other designs were largely for games about numbers or shapes, often computerised. The girls focused on games, usually letter games associated with animals and colour. The girls communicated their ideas in writing or by making prototypes. No girls referred to computer games. The problem for assessment is that one cannot compare such responses – they are just different. Nor can one assume that a task of this kind will provide information that 'fits' a subject yet alone an attainment target or a level within it. Yet these naturalistic assessments provide teachers with the information they need about an individual's understanding. They also provide a rich array of alternative views of the world which pupils can share. These experiences enable pupils to develop an awareness of the potential for choice in the selection and use of their knowledge.

I would recommend the use of tasks that allow pupils to show what they know and how they know it. In making this recommendation I have accepted that information will not readily be forthcoming to fit children neatly into levels in any one attainment target in any one subject. My argument is that to attempt to do the latter is to impose assessors' tasks on pupils who then have to make sense of them. Research shows that many pupils either fail at this or their alternative perceptions of the tasks go unnoticed and their achievements unrecognised. For these reasons assessment should start with establishing the pupils' tasks. Finally I would interpret a gender-fair assessment as one that allowed children to demonstrate what they have learnt and how they understand it, rather than one where overall scores for girls and boys were equal.

REFERENCES

Chodorow, N. (1978) *The Reproduction of Mothering*, Berkeley, CA: University of California Press.

Goddard-Spear, M. (1983) 'Sex bias in science teachers' ratings of work', in *Contributions to the Second GASAT Conference*, Oslo, Norway.

Gorman, T. *et al.* (1988) *Language Performance in Schools*, London: HMSO.

Harding, J. (1979) 'Sex differences in performance in examinations at 16+', *Physics Education*, 14(5): 280–4.

—— (1985) 'Values, cognitive styles and the curriculum', *Contributions to the Third GASAT Conference*, London.

Johnson, S. and Murphy, P. (1986) *Girls and Physics: Reflections on APU Survey Findings*, London: DES.

Murphy, P. (1990) *Gender and Assessment in Science*, Milton Keynes: Open University Press.

Murphy, P. and Gott, R. (1984) *Science Assessment Framework Age 13–15. Science Report for Teachers No. 2*, Association for Science Education.

Murphy, P. and Moon, R. (eds) (1990) *Developments in Learning and Assessment*, Milton Keynes: Open University Press.

Murphy, R. (1982) 'Sex differences in objective test performance', *British Journal of Educational Psychology*, 52: 213–19.

TGAT (1987) *DES Task Group on Assessment and Testing: a Report*, London: DES.

Chapter 17

Bilingualism and assessment

Eve Gregory and Clare Kelly

Of all the issues relating to standardised assessment in the primary school, one which has caused much anxiety among teachers has been the assessment of bilingual pupils in the early stages of learning English. It is important to be clear that there is no reason why a bilingual child should not achieve as highly as a monolingual child across the curriculum. Indeed, the authors refer to a growing body of research which suggests that living with two languages can offer children a number of cognitive advantages if schools are sensitive to the children's own skills and own ways of understanding. However, where a child has entered school, either at age 5 or later on in their schooling, with little experience of using English at home and in their daily life, the authors show how they are disadvantaged if an early assessment is made of their cross-curricular achievements in English. They are also disadvantaged if assessed in their home language where that has not been supported within the classroom and within the particular curriculum area being assessed. Their first language skills and cross-linguistic skills of interpreting and translating are not included in National Curriculum assessment. They do not know less than their peers, but sometimes know different things. Similarly, older children newly arriving in UK schools often bring with them highly developed understandings and skills from their previous school experience which can go unnoticed in their new school. In this chapter, the authors raise the same question put by Patricia Murphy in Chapter 16 of how assessment processes might value different ways of learning and the different knowledge and skills pupils show in relation to assessment tasks.

The setting is an inner-city classroom of 5- to 6-year-olds. Husna and Naseema are reading *Each, Peach, Pear, Plum*, by Janet and Allen Ahlberg, together. Despite the attractions of the illustrations, their eyes are drawn to the print and they read quickly and fluently. Husna points carefully to each word to help Naseema, who is more hesitant. 'Each, Peach, Pear, Plum, I spy Tom Thumb. Tom Thumb in the cupboard, I spy Mother Hubbard. Mother Hubbard down the cellar, I spy Cinderella. Cinderella on the stairs, I spy the Three Bears . . .' Husna breaks off with 'I can count to ten in

Bengali: Ek, dui, teen, chaar, panch, chhoy, shaat, aat, noy, dosh.' 'Gosh?' asks the teacher. 'Mmm. But this is ten/dosh, not like gosh in "Oh, my gosh, my golly." ' The teacher laughs, knowing she is referring to one of the 'Story-chest Big Books' with which she is very familiar. The children continue with the text glancing only occasionally at the illustrations which complement this nursery-rhyme world. As they reach the page featuring a magnificent plum pie, the teacher interrupts and asks, 'Can you show me the plum pie in that picture?' The children stare blankly at the teacher and the page. Eventually, Husna points quickly to something nondescript in the back-ground. The teacher shows them the pie and allows the children to get back to their reading. They finish the text and are impatient to change the book for another.

Like many of their classmates, Husna and Naseema entered school speaking very little English. In just over a year, they will be examined on the same tests as their monolingual peers. Unlike children at school in Wales, who will be tested in spoken Welsh and receive teacher assessment only in their English reading skills, the Education Reform Act (1988) stipulates that all bilingual children in England must have equal access to the attainment targets and programmes of study of the National Curriculum and should be subject to the same tests. Annexe E of the Act allows exemption only for children who have been in Britain for less than six months.

The above interaction between two bilingual children and their teacher highlights a number of questions. What are the strengths and weaknesses of bilingual children after two or three years of school learning in a second language? Can these strengths and weaknesses be revealed adequately in tests designed for monolingual English 7-year-olds? What might be the dangers inherent in standardised tests? Should bilingual children be examined differently? Should the tests be in the children's first language? How far can monolingual teachers and testers be competent in assessing and testing bilinguals? Using the example of Husna, Naseema and their teacher as a springboard, this chapter aims to give the reader access to current research findings enabling informed answers to be made to the above questions. Although the focus is on bilingual children, a number of issues are discussed which relate equally to the testing of all children whose cultural practices are not those of the white middle-class mainstream in British schools. Finally, if standardised tests were to be abandoned, what alternative approaches to assessing the progress of bilinguals might be developed for classroom use?

THE STRENGTHS AND WEAKNESSES OF BILINGUAL CHILDREN IN ENGLISH CLASSROOMS

As our above vignette shows Husna and Naseema reading, let us start by examining their likely performance on the SAT should it be administered to the children now. The attainments to be tested appear clear enough:

Level 1:   Begin to recognise individual words or letters, such as shop signs or 'bus stop'; talk in simple terms about story content.
Level 2:   Use pictures, context and phonic cues in reading; read something without help from the teacher and talk with confidence about it.
Level 3:   Read familiar stories aloud with expression.

Testing Husna and Naseema, however, presents us with a dilemma. If we start at level 1, we find the children well able to recognise individual words and letters but often unable to talk about the story content, especially if it is new. However, if we jump to level 3, Husna, Naseema and their classmates will have no difficulty in reading familiar stories out loud. But they will have considerable problems if presented with formal content-based questions to answer on them. The complexities involved in testing Husna and Naseema are already becoming apparent.

It is obvious that talking about the content of a story is going to be a much harsher test for children learning a second language than for their mono-lingual peers. If we take on board Sapir's claim that language 'does not . . . stand apart from or run parallel to direct experience but completely inter-penetrates with it' (1970: 121) then we must recognise that bilingual chil-dren's performance will depend upon whether they can identify with the experience in English and consequently call upon appropriate lexis and structures with which to express it. During this learning process there is a considerable gap between what can be understood and what can be actively produced. Understanding cannot be examined by testing talk. Yet discussion and explanation are important attainment targets in all the core curriculum areas and have been picked out to be tested.

Level 2 gets to the heart of the reading process by testing how the children are progressing in making sense of print. It draws on recent research telling us that getting meaning from print means learning to utilise different cueing or 'clueing' systems to help predict the text (Goodman 1973; Holdaway 1979): semantic or meaning cues, where the reader has sufficient conceptual background and experience in the culture to make sense of what is being read; syntactic cues, where the reader is able to draw upon a knowledge of the grammatical structure of the language being read to predict correct parts of speech; and graphophonic cues, where a knowledge of sound/symbol associations helps accurate word prediction.

Most standardised reading tests for young children try to measure how competently these cueing systems are being used. Children are asked to complete sentences such as 'The p - - has run out of ink'. In the early stages help is often given in the form of a picture and/or choice of words; for example, plant, pen, elephant. Comprehension tests are also used to examine how far a child has understood a text. However, strict rules for ascertaining whether an answer is correct or wrong must be adhered to in order for an

SAT to be standardised and summative. Any freedom of interpretation necessarily invalidates a test.

Husna and Naseema present us with a paradox. Strictly speaking, they are still unable efficiently to use any of these cues. Semantically, they do not yet have sufficient experience with English culture and language to predict likely objects or events. Syntactically, they often rely on repeating well-known 'formulae' (Hatch et al. 1979) or whole chunks of speech or text as in 'Oh my gosh, my golly!'. Phonically, they are still sometimes unable to notice fine distinctions in sounds when meeting English words, for example 'dosh' and 'gosh'. Nor, of course, is their teacher, as she encounters Bengali words. Sometimes it is difficult for the children to know what a sound actually refers to. Is a 'p' an object or a sound?

Yet their reading shows that Husna and Naseema are obviously taking meaning from print, which is the very first attainment target of Key Stage 1. But their way of coming to grips with a text is undoubtedly different from that of their monolingual peers. With time, they will be equally at home with all the cueing systems, but in this transitional stage other cues seem to be used in the quest for meaning. If bilingual children are showing evidence of learning differently from their monolingual peers, might we need a different way of measuring their progress and skills? But first, we need to be aware of what special linguistic, cognitive and social skills bilingual children bring with them in approaching the task of making sense of school learning.

Husna and Naseema's reading already provides evidence of a number of linguistic skills. They have completely separated their two languages and are able to use appropriate linguistic sets in different situations. They know the names of their two languages and refer to them. Moreover, they are learning to read not just in two languages, but using two totally different scripts. They have an interest and an excitement in the words themselves, shown by wanting to pick out individual words and compare them. They realise the arbitrary nature of language; that is, they know that words are not tied to their referents and that 'dosh' or 'gosh' can mean different things in different languages. This realisation made possible an early mastery of one-to-one correspondence which we see now as they carefully point out separate words. The children show an awareness of the importance of syntax. They know that 'dosh' in Bengali is not just semantically different from the English, but is a different part of speech and must be used differently in sentences. From this, they realise that the syntax of a language is arbitrary too and can be different in different languages.

The awareness that language is arbitrary, together with a lack of knowledge of the conventional word, often enables the children to play with words and experiment with them. Teachers of bilingual children can provide lists of imaginative experiments with words such as 'a necklace man' (a mayor), 'a kissing lady' (a bride), 'Happy Wu Year' and 'a ghonster' (ghost monster). Lacking the conventional word used unconsciously by their monolingual peers forces these children into a conscious search for the real meaning behind a concept in order to find an appropriate synonym. These experiments show the children to be aware of what they do not know and to be active in devising various strategies to find out, such as asking 'What's the opposite of "up"?' In other words, they are using language to find out more about language itself.

The above examples all show the children to have what is called a highly developed metalinguistic awareness. This means that they are able to get outside language and be aware of its forms and properties (Baker 1988) or to make language forms opaque and attend to them (Cazden 1984). This type of knowledge found a strong place in *English from 5–16* (DES 1984), Kingman (DES 1988b) and *English for Ages 5–11* (DES 1988c). It is also in Key Stage 1 of the final Orders. However, it does not feature in the attainment targets for SAT assessment.

Evidence for the linguistic strengths of bilingual children can be found in a number of studies. Vygotsky (1962: 110) claimed that bilingualism enabled a child 'to see his language as one particular system among many, to view its phenomena under more general categories . . . [which] leads to awareness of his linguistic operations'. Later work by Feldman and Shen (1971), Ianco-Worrall (1972), Ben-Zeev (1977), Swain and Cummins (1979), Bain and Yu (1980), Arnberg (1987) and Hakuta (1986), among others, has investigated different aspects of bilingual children's raised language consciousness and advanced metalinguistic skills. Some of this reflects closely strengths shown by Husna and Naseema and deserves further description.

Working with 4- to 9-year-old monolingual English and bilingual Afrikaans/English children, Ianco-Worrall (1972) found that the bilinguals excelled in ability to state the principle that names are arbitrarily assigned to things. For example, they understood symbol substitution games, such as the following, two to three years earlier than their monolingual peers:

RESEARCHER: This is named 'plane', right?
Well, in the game it's called turtle.
Can the turtle fly?

Cummins (1978a) extended this in a test of 53 monolingual English and an equal number of bilingual English/Irish 8- to 9-year-olds, matched on verbal IQ, socio-economic group, sex and age. Here, children were not only asked whether words could be interchanged, but to justify their answers. A significantly higher number of bilingual children gave answers such as 'You could change the names because it doesn't matter what they are called', whereas a large majority of monolinguals replied, 'They are their right names, so you can't change them'. Similar tests led the authors to conclude that bilingual children were better able to detect contradictions, ambiguities and tautologies and generally possess more flexibility and emancipation in separating words and their meanings.

Other studies have found evidence of a greater analytic ability of bilingual children. Ben-Zeev (1977) found that bilingual Hebrew/English children between 5 and 8 were able not only to substitute nouns but also to analyse linguistic stems by ignoring both word meaning and sentence framing, for example:

RESEARCHER: If 'they' means 'spaghetti', how do we say 'They are good children'?

In being able simultaneously to reply 'spaghetti are good children', the children had grasped the basic idea that the structure of language is different from the phonological representations and meaningful words in which it is embodied.

In a series of studies, Bialystok (1987) attempted to pinpoint exact linguistic operations in which bilingual children were more advanced than monolinguals. Advantage occurred when the children were (1) required to separate individual words from meaningful sentences, (2) focus on only the form or meaning of a word under highly distracting conditions, (3) reassign a familiar name to a new object. Each of these tasks requires selective attention to words or their features and the performance of some operation on an isolated component. The children's strength, therefore, may be to attend selectively to words and their boundaries. This is precisely what we see Husna and Naseema doing. Other studies have suggested that it may be the potential interference between the two languages as well as the incipient contrastive linguistics undertaken which force the child to make more processing effort (Baker 1988). Such studies are important, as the supposed negative effects of interference have long been a strong argument for denying a child access to contrastive linguistics through bilingual education in the school setting.

These linguistic strengths stand in stark contrast with young bilingual children's performance in traditional language tests designed for monolingual children. When asked to re-tell a story, bilingual 5-year-olds were found to make a far greater number of grammatical mistakes than their monolingual peers and were very inferior in the Peabody Picture Vocabulary Test in both their languages (Ben-Zeev 1977). In other words, although their consciousness of language and their analytic skills were more advanced, they had less experience in each of their languages than their monolingual peers. The above studies begin to indicate both the untapped strengths of bilingual children and the biased nature of the SATs.

A number of studies argue that bilingual children have cognitive advantages over their monolingual peers. Husna and Naseema's ability to jump over semantic and syntactic boundaries with Husna's use of 'g/dosh' may be characteristic of what Ben-Zeev refers to as the 'liberated thought' of bilinguals. Their developing knowledge of different word and concept boundaries in different languages, for example the knowledge that 'cousin' is a broad-based concept in English, covering a number of different words and concepts in Bengali, may be an example of a 'cognitive flexibility' (Lambert 1977). Through their developing bilingualism, the children are learning a double set of rules. These comprise not just the lexis and structure of a language but the boundaries of concepts and culture. Plum pies are not just words but a way of life.

Other studies have found bilingual children to be ahead in concept formation. This may take the form of an earlier ability to conserve measurement (Liedtke and Nelson 1968), classify according to shape, colour or size (Ben-Zeev 1977), or mentally manipulate and reorganise visual patterns (Peal and Lambert 1962). From a number of tests, Peal and Lambert went on to conclude, 'there is no question about the fact that he (the bilingual child) is superior intellectually. In contrast, the monolingual appears to have a more unitary structure of intelligence, which he must use for all types of tasks' (p. 20).

The linguistic and cognitive advantages of bilingual children have often been attributed to their greater responsiveness to perceptual hints and clues than their monolingual peers. Ianco-Worrall (1972) and Ben-Zeev (1977) suggest that bilingual children have a greater social sensitivity. Their fear of falling into the wrong language makes them extra aware of the importance of appropriateness and they are constantly scanning to see if their language is correct. Other studies show bilingual children better able to adapt instructions to blindfolded children (Genesee *et al.* 1978) and more sensitive to facial expressions or other non-verbal communication (Bain and Yu 1978; Skutnabb-Kangas 1984). It was obvious to Husna and Naseema that the teacher did not share their language and they were keen to initiate her into it. Had she been more alert, she could have pointed out the difference in the sound of 'dosh' and 'gosh'. As it was, the children gave her their own feedback on the different use of the word.

The above studies end this section with a paradox: if bilingual children are linguistically, cognitively and socially advantaged, why do many fall behind in school? We read that Bangladeshi children particularly suffer 'severe educational underachievement' (Home Affairs Committee 1986–87). Two main explanations have been offered in research studies. First, bilingualism must be additive, not subtractive, in order for the advantages outlined above to ensue. This means that a second language and culture must be added to the first and not replace them (Cummins 1978b; Swain and Cummins 1979). Secondly, the child's first language must be of high and not low prestige (Skutnabb-Kangas 1984). Both of these factors demand that a child's existing linguistic competence be recognised. If bilingual children are being examined on tests written by monolinguals for monolinguals using material which only monocultural children can identify with, none of these potential strengths will be revealed. To understand more fully the dangers of such tests, we need to examine past experiences.

STANDARDISED TESTS AND BILINGUAL CHILDREN

> . . . the number of aliens deported because of feeble-mindedness . . . increased approximately 350% in 1913 and 570% in 1914. This was due to the untiring efforts of the physicians who were inspired by the belief that mental tests could be used for the detection of feeble-minded aliens.
>
> (Goddard 1917)

It is easy now to react with incredulity at such a belief. Official prejudice based on this level of naivety appears unthinkable today. However, a moment's pause forces us to ask how far the belief has really disappeared or whether it is simply expressed in a more subtle form. With this question in mind, the section which follows investigates tests which have been given to young children who are still 'strangers' to the language and culture of the classroom by examining briefly the nature of bias in standardised tests and ways in which this reflects in minority group children's test results. Finally, we relate these experiences to the situation in British infant schools and consider what questions remain unanswered. Such terms as 'feeble-minded' may no longer be used, but will children's bilingualism mean they are still seen as 'slow learners'? Is it possible to test a young bilingual's real ability in school?

Nearly a century later, it appears obvious that the real issue behind the 'feeble-minded aliens' in the quotation above was socio-political. The aim was to restrict entry to foreigners who could not speak English while at the same time maintaining they were being given a 'fair' test. Cummins (1984) argues that school tests today serve similar socio-political aims which militate against the success of minority-group children. He illustrates how standardised tests, especially verbal ones, must inevitably be biased against minority groups. By definition, the standardisation of a test on a representative sample means that the bulk of the sample will come from the dominant group. Individual minority groups will only be represented to a minor extent. Thus, in the pilot stage of item development, the majority of items selected for try-out will reflect the prior learning experiences of the majority Anglo group.

For Husna and Naseema in our last section, this means that even if items reflecting their unique learning experiences were to be included in the try-out phase, they would be quickly screened out in the final item analysis. The very nature of 'standardisation' means the inclusion only of items which are neither too easy nor too difficult for the majority of children. Husna and Naseema's linguistic skills would be too advanced for the majority of the test norming sample and would, therefore, not correlate well with the total test. In this way, standardised tests are 'culture loaded' (Kaufman 1979) to reflect both the language and values of the dominant group. They are norm-referenced in spite of every claim that they should be criterion-referenced.

The 'culture loading' of standardised tests needs further explanation. How can, for example, describing a scientific process, discussing a story or working with two- and three-dimensional shapes (all attainment targets to be covered by the SATs) reflect anything but what the child has learned in school?

Ethnographic studies which follow the child from home into school provide a number of examples showing how the socialisation or learning experiences of minority groups may differ in many respects from those of the dominant Anglo group. Heath's study (1983) of two working-class communities living only a few miles apart in the Appalachians shows how each group differs greatly in ways of socialising children. From data collected over ten years, Heath argues that even what counts as an acceptable 'story' is culturally determined. The religious demands of the white community cause their children to find difficulty in responding to any story which is not 'true'. The other group has equal difficulty in keeping within the boundaries of 'truth' for news-time presentations.

The actual way events are narrated also differs according to cultural background. In a study of infant children's 'news retellings' in the United States, Michaels (1986) shows how Anglo-American children have very different discourse styles from the Afro-American minority group. The majority children use what she refers to as a 'topic-centred' approach where talk focuses on one particular topic, whereas the minority children's talk is 'topic-associating' where a number of topics radiate from an initial theme. In a standardised test, only one approach – namely, that of the majority group – could score as logical.

Michaels argues that if children's contributions are treated differentially, they may well refuse to answer the teacher at all. Her conclusions are backed up by ethnographic evidence indicating that a child's willingness to respond at all to a test is strongly influenced by whether cultural norms from home correspond or clash with those in school.

Children's response to words themselves will differ according to the frequency with which they have been encountered. The cross-cultural psychologist Michael Cole (1975: 51–2) points out that

> children from different sub-cultural groups are exposed to different vocabulary. How children (or adults) respond to a problem (even one so simple as saying what comes to mind when we say 'peach') depends in large measure on their familiarity with the content of the problem and this familiarity varies in unknown ways with the child's home culture.

Finally: is it adequate to test a child in his or her first language? A return to Sapir and the body of research mentioned in the last section arguing for an intimate link between language and experience reveals the complexity of this question. If a curriculum is being taught only in English, it is highly unlikely that the appropriate specialist vocabulary will be accessible to a child in the first language. The story language of plum pies, the scientific lexis involved in describing the workings of a water pump or even talking about odd and even numbers may well not be within a child's first language experience. Only children following a parallel syllabus in the first language at home or at an evening or Saturday class would benefit from first language testing. The conclusion, therefore, that it would be fairer to examine a bilingual child in the first language is potentially a very dangerous one. We cannot suppose that a complex and specialist vocabulary will be available in a young child's first language simply because it is lacking in the second. Results from first language tests are likely to strengthen the belief that bilinguals may be 'slow learners' or, to return to the quotation opening this section, 'feeble-minded'.

ISSUES OF PEDAGOGY AND TEACHER ASSESSMENT – THE WAY FORWARD?

> All pupils share the same statutory entitlement to a broad and balanced curriculum, including access to the National Curriculum.
>
> (DES 1989: para. 8:1)

The above statement may at first appear uncontentious, but the question is, does it go far enough for children like Husna and Naseema whom we met at the beginning of this chapter? They should be offered not merely equality of entitlement to participate in the National Curriculum but an equal opportunity to succeed, to achieve. This section addresses issues of pedagogy and assessment and focuses on how linguistic and cultural differences can be viewed in positive terms both cognitively and socially within a teacher-led assessment framework which recognises and encourages the creative nature of second-language learning.

Significant developments have been made in recognising and meeting the needs of second-language learners since the Bullock Report declared, 'no child should be expected to cast off the language and culture of the home as he crosses the school threshold' (DES 1975: 543).

Clearly, teacher assessment is the tool which should be used to provide 'rounded qualitative judgements' (DES 1989: para. 6:5) and offers the opportunity for the personal and intellectual growth of all learners to be recognised and recorded. The Education Reform Act (1988) assures us that teachers are free to employ their own methods of formative assessment, yet there is a disturbing tendency for teachers to use the summative measures (attainment targets) as a yardstick for formative assessment and recording (Barrs 1990), thereby losing their valuable opportunities to use their skills and professional judgement in a way that will be of great benefit to children and their families, particularly those from bilingual communities.

It would seem that there is a place for a philosophy of bilingual education to be debated publicly among the teaching profession, a debate that would consider total educational experience, and which would not only continue to explore the place of bilingualism in children's intellectual, social and cultural development but more crucially would address the issue of how teachers can move forward effectively in assessing the achievements of second-language learners and documenting their progress.

Since the assessment process 'needs to be incorporated systematically into teaching strategies and practices at all levels' (DES 1988a: para. 4), it is appropriate here to focus on the extent to which pedagogy can alleviate the cultural mismatch experienced by many minority children and the consequent effect upon their intellectual and personal development. Research (McDermott 1978; Mohatt and Erickson 1981) has shown the extent to which children are unable to participate in classroom life when the interactional style demanded by a teacher from the dominant group differs significantly from that of the minority culture.

In 1971, the KEEP project (Kamehameha Early Education Program) in America demonstrated clearly how academic achievement is directly related to the experiences to which children are exposed. The project was set up to improve the low performance of native Creole-speaking Hawaiian children who were inattentive, uninvolved and often aggressive in class. Ethnographic studies showed that in their communities, the same children were used to little adult supervision and worked co-operatively, and their learning was based on observing other children. When the restrictive culturally specific participant structures (Phillips 1972) were uncovered and classroom communication and management structures were revised in line with the children's familiar cultural practices, they experienced an increase in motivation and consequent rise in academic achievements. It must be said, however, that ethnographic researchers in the KEEP project worked for many years to uncover the exact patterns of communication that were impeding children's development; nevertheless this project and others (Phillips 1972; Fillmore 1983; Heath 1983) show clearly that under-achievement is caused by the inadequacy of classroom practices to meet the child's needs rather than by the incompetence of the child.

As educationists we need to examine our practice and reassess the linguistic and cultural assumptions on which it is based, and move forward to accommodate what Heath (1983) characterises as different ways of talking and knowing which will benefit all students. It becomes very important therefore to gain insights into the learning experiences of the minority child within his or her community. At the same time we must recognise the huge demands this will make upon a teacher whose class members represent a variety of groups and sub-groups. Parents and other members of the community who are willing to allow their language skills to be used as a resource have a major role to play in acquainting staff with the linguistic and cultural background of the children in their care.

Any system of assessment that recognises and attempts to build upon the metalinguistic awareness of young second-language learners and their ability to understand the symbolic and abstract nature of language would need to be grounded in what Marie Clay refers to as 'systematic observation of learning' (Clay 1979). Such observation would necessarily be based upon the teacher's clear understanding of the development of linguistic skills and knowledge of the wider context in which children learn, and would be formalised in a record-keeping system that adopted a broad view of achievement similar to that embodied in the Primary Learning Record (CLPE 1990). In this way the considerable capabilities of children like Husna and Naseema would be acknowledged.

Children who come to this country with a well-developed conceptual framework but need time (more than the six months allowed under the National Curriculum) to develop the linguistic proficiency necessary to explain complex ideas successfully, require a system of teaching and assessment that will both help them to attain that proficiency and allow them to show what they really know. Cummins (1984) suggests that providing second-language learners at all levels with tasks that are both cognitively demanding and yet firmly embedded in context, ensures a more successful communication of ideas, since learners will be able to rely on a wide range of situational cues in order to negotiate meaning. Although good early years' practice recognises the importance of meaningful contexts for all learning, it must be acknowledged, too, that there are particular benefits for second-language learners.

The provision of context-embedded, cognitively demanding tasks will ensure a higher degree of success in facilitating and assessing children's learning (Donaldson 1978). Such tasks should enable children to develop a more positive self-image when faced with the challenging task of becoming proficient in a second language, whilst building on the cognitive gains achieved in the first.

Any assessment of language acquisition would need to take account of the notion that language learning is an untidy process and as such presents many problems for formulating evaluative procedures.

Fillmore (1976) has suggested that a child in a natural environment will go through three stages in acquiring a second language. First, she or he will establish social relationships with speakers of the second language and in doing so will rely heavily on both non-verbal communication and fixed verbal formulas. Moving on to the second stage, she or he will begin to generate meaning by using new combinations of the formulaic words, and finally will concentrate on the correctness of language form itself. Fillmore has identified five cognitive strategies employed during these stages. Such strategies could form the basis of a system for both assessing progress in each area and also evaluating the performance of teachers in scaffolding children's achievement in language.

The first of these strategies is to assume that what people are saying is directly relevant to the situation at hand or to what they or you are experiencing – their metastrategy being to guess. Teachers would need to evaluate how far what they are saying is relevant to context and, as discussed earlier, ensure situational, non-verbal cues to support communication.

The second strategy is to get some expressions that are understood and start talking; the third is to look for recurring parts in formulas. Teachers would need to be aware of which formulas are available to children and examine ways in which to facilitate children's language development by encouraging them to talk, thereby using and building upon the fixed formulas.

The fourth strategy is to make the most of what is available; and the fifth to work on 'big things', saving the details for later. Teachers would need to ensure that children were operating in a context that enabled them both to use formulas with which they were familiar and at the same time take the risks necessary to work on the 'big things' and in doing so arrive at a clearer understanding of how language works.

Fillmore further suggests that second-language learners employ three social strategies in order to support their own learning:

1 Join a group and act as if you understand what is going on, even if you don't.
2 Give the impression with a few well-chosen words that you can speak the language.
3 Count on your friends for help.

Teachers would need to examine the extent to which second-language learners are given the opportunities to develop social relationships and operate within an environment where they are enabled through their own motivation to employ such strategies in an uninhibited way.

This section, which has focused on teacher-led assessment, has shown that in order for young, minority-group learners to be assessed fairly, teachers need first to understand the principles of language development and second to be aware of the social and educational factors that shape it. Above all, we must not lose sight of the importance of what Vygotsky (1978) has termed the 'zone of proximal development' and the key role played by teachers and others in helping the child's 'ripening structures' to develop and the significance of such practice in any teacher-led assessment procedure.

REFERENCES

Arnberg, L. (1987) *Raising Children Bilingually: the Pre-school Years*, Clevedon, Avon: Multilingual Matters Ltd.
Bain, B. and Yu, A. (1978) 'Toward an integration of Piaget and Vygotsky: a cross-cultural replication (France, Germany, Canada) concerning cognitive conse-

quences of bilinguality', in M. Paradis (ed.) *Aspects of Bilingualism*, Columbia, SC: Hornbeam Press.

—— (1980) 'Cognitive consequences of raising children bilingually: one parent, one language', *Canadian Journal of Psychology*, 34: 304–13.

Baker, C. (1988) *Key Issues in Bilingualism and Bilingual Children*, Clevedon, Avon: Multilingual Matters Ltd.

Barrs, M. (1990) *Words NOT Numbers: Assessment in English*, London: NAAE/NATE.

Ben-Zeev, S. (1977) 'The influence of bilingualism on cognitive strategy and cognitive development', *Child Development*, 48: 1009–18.

Bialystok, E. (1987) 'Words as things: development of word concept by bilingual children', *Studies in Second Language Acquisition*, 9: 133–40.

Cazden, C. (1984) 'Play with language and metalinguistic awareness: one dimension of language experience', in M. Donaldson, R. Grieve and C. Pratt (eds) *Early Childhood Development and Education*, Oxford: Blackwell.

Centre for Language in Primary Education (1990) *The Primary Learning Record*, London: CLPE.

Clay, M.M. (1979) *The Early Detection of Reading Difficulties*, Auckland, NZ: Heinemann.

Cole, M. (1975) 'Culture, cognition and IQ testing', *National Elementary Principle*, 54: 49–52.

Cummins, J. (1978a) 'Immersion programs: the Irish experience', *International Review of Education*, 24: 273–82.

—— (1978b) 'Educational implications of mother-tongue maintenance in minority language groups', *Canadian Modern Language Review*, 34: 855–83.

—— (1984) *Bilingualism and Special Education: Issues in Assessment and Pedagogy*, Clevedon, Avon: Multilingual Matters Ltd.

Department of Education and Science (1975) *A Language for Life* (The Bullock Report), London: HMSO.

—— (1984) *English from 5–16*, London: HMSO.

—— (1988a) *National Curriculum: Task Group on Assessment and Testing: a Report*, London: HMSO.

—— (1988b) *Report of the Committee of Inquiry into the Teaching of English Language* (The Kingman Report), London: HMSO.

—— (1988c) *English for Ages 5–11. Proposals of the Secretaries of State* (The Cox Report), London: NCC/HMSO.

—— (1989) *ERA: a Bulletin for School Teachers and Governors*, Issue 4, Autumn, London: HMSO.

Donaldson, M. (1978) *Children's Minds*, Glasgow: Fontana.

Feldman, C. and Shen, M. (1971) 'Some language-related cognitive advantages of bilingual five year olds', *Journal of Genetic Psychology*, 118: 235–44.

Fillmore, L. (1976) 'The Second Time Around: Cognitive and Social Strategies in Second Language Acquisition', PhD dissertation, Stanford University.

—— (1983) 'The language learner as an individual: implications of research on individual differences for the ESL teacher', in M.A. Clarke and J. Handscombe (eds) *On TESOL '82 Pacific Perspectives on Language Learning and Teaching*, Washington, DC: TESOL.

Genesee, F., Tucker, G.R. and Lambert, W.E. (1978) 'The development of ethnic identity and ethnic role taking skills in children from different school settings', *International Journal of Psychology*, 13: 39–57.

Goddard, H.H. (1917) 'Mental tests and the immigrant', *Journal of Delinquency*, 2: 271.

Goodman, K. (ed.) (1973) *Miscue Analysis: Applications to Reading Instruction*, Urbana, IL: ERIC/NCTE.

Hakuta, K. (1986) *Mirror of Language: the Debate on Bilingualism*, New York: Basic Books.

Hatch, E., Peck, S. and Wagner-Gough, J. (1979) 'A look at process in child second language acquisition', in E. Ochs and B. Schieffelin (eds) *Developmental Pragmatics*, New York: Academic Press.

Heath, S.B. (1983) *Ways with Words: Language, Life, and Work in Communities and Classrooms*, Cambridge: Cambridge University Press.

Holdaway, D. (1979) *The Foundations of Literacy*, Sydney: Ashton Scholastic.

Home Affairs Committee (1986–87) *Bangladeshis in Britain*, Vol. 1, London: HMSO.

Ianco-Worrall, A. (1972) 'Bilingualism and cognitive development', *Child Development*, 43: 1390–1400.

Kaufman, A.S. (1979) *Intelligent Testing with the WISC-R*, New York: Wiley.

Lambert, W.E. (1977) 'The effect of bilingualism on the individual: cognitive and sociocultural', in P.A. Hornby (ed.) *Bilingualism: Psychological, Social and Educational Implications*, New York: Academic Press.

Liedtke, W.W. and Nelson, L.D. (1968) 'Concept formation and bilingualism', *Alberta Journal of Education Research*, 14: 225–32.

McDermott, R.P. (1978) 'Relating and learning: an analysis of two classroom reading groups', in R. Snuy (ed.) *Linguistics and Reading*, Rowley, MA: Newbury House.

Michaels, S. (1986) 'Narrative presentations: an oral preparation for literacy with 1st graders', in J. Cook-Gumperz (ed.) *The Social Construction of Literacy*, Cambridge: Cambridge University Press.

Mohatt, G. and Erickson, F. (1981) 'Cultural differences in teaching styles in an Odawa school: a sociolinguistic approach', in H.T. Trueba, G.P. Guthrie and K.H. Au (eds) *Culture and the Bilingual Classroom: Studies in Classroom Ethnography*, Rowley, MA: Newbury House.

Peal, E. and Lambert, W.E. (1962) 'The relation of bilingualism and intelligence', *Psychological Monographs: General and Applied*, 76(546): 1–23.

Phillips, S. (1972) 'Participant structures and communicative competence: Warm Springs children in community and classroom', in C. Cazden, D. Hymes and V.J. John (eds) *Functions of Language in the Classroom*, New York: Teachers' College Press.

Sapir, E. (1970) *Culture, Language and Personality*, Berkeley, CA: University of California Press.

Skutnabb-Kangas, T. (1984) *Bilingualism or Not – the Education of Minorities*, Clevedon, Avon: Multilingual Matters Ltd.

Swain, M. and Cummins, J. (1979) 'Bilingualism, cognitive functioning and education', *Language Teaching and Linguistics Abstracts*, 12(1): 4–18.

Vygotsky, L.S. (1962) *Thought and Language*, Cambridge, MA: MIT Press.

—— (1978) *Mind in Society: the Development of Higher Psychological Processes*, Cambridge, MA: Harvard University Press.

Chapter 18

A question of ability

Jill Bourne

This chapter suggests that assessment is as crucial and controversial as it is because, rather than focusing on attainment in relation to teaching, it still calls up long-held myths about the human mind which suggest that assessment is about discovering an individual's 'potential', some underlying 'ability' or 'intelligence'. As long as these beliefs hold, any form of ranking of attainment runs the danger of being used to limit some children's future educational opportunities.

Talk in pubs:

'She's got a talent for it.'

'Got the right brains for it.'

'In the family.'

(from Howe 1990)

Talk in schools:

In this school we try to meet each child's needs according to their age and ability.

(School booklet)

I teach in a mixed-ability classroom.

(Class teacher)

I want every child to develop their abilities to the full.

(Headmaster)

In this chapter, I want to raise questions about the 'common-sense' concept of 'ability', to trace its origins, and to look at the implications for primary teachers today. What do we mean when we talk about a child's 'ability'? My dictionary defines ability as cleverness, talent or mental power. When we speak of a child's 'ability', are we describing some kind of in-born 'intelligence', a genetic inheritance? How do teachers know how to assess a child's 'ability'? Can one label a child 'bright' or 'slow'? Why is it that the newer models of assessment avoid the term 'ability' and choose instead to focus on 'attainment'?

Despite decades of research, there is no clear evidence of any single underlying 'intelligence' or generalised 'ability'. Research on people who have been brain-damaged suggests the contrary; while some areas of activity are impaired, others are not. Gardner (1983), therefore, has proposed that there are multiple 'intelligences'. Sternberg (1984) defines intelligence as 'consisting of purposive selection and shaping of and adaptation to real-world environments relevant to one's life'. The problem with a definition like this is that it leaves one to work out what each individual perceives to be the most relevant to their lives. As Salmon and Bannister (1974) have argued: 'People rarely just fail to learn; they leave us with the problem of finding out what it was they were learning while they were not learning what we expected them to learn.'

Of course, the fact that we have such words as 'intelligence' or 'ability', as with the unicorn, does not mean that such things have to exist. But although the terms may not be real,

> they can, and do, create barriers to ordinary people's capabilities. That is because they encourage us to believe that we cannot realistically aspire to many accomplishments which we are actually capable of achieving.
>
> (Howe 1990)

As with most 'common-sense' concepts, there is a history behind this concept which has come to be such a natural way to talk about children in the United Kingdom. Yet the concept is historically and culturally specific. Not long ago children and their achievements were looked at very differently, as they are in other places in the world today.

When mass schooling was first introduced in the last century, 'ignorance' seems to have been conceived of in moral terms as the result of 'sloth' or laziness (Birchenough 1914). However, education was not equally open to everyone. There was a different form of differentiation among children, one based not on in-born mental characteristics, but in terms of social hierarchy. Children were educated to take up 'their' place in society. Jacqueline Rose (1984) has shown how, in the nineteenth century, a different form of language education was marked out for different social groups: classics for the wealthy, English literature for the middle classes, basic literacy and 'clear expression' for the poor. Crabbe wrote of the way education was becoming a social device to mark out social groups and to control the new industrialised society:

> 'For every class we have a school assigned,
> Rules for all ranks and food for every mind.'
>
> (cited in Birchenough 1914: 5)

Over this century, however, explicit control over different types of 'knowledges' for different classes, and indeed, gender groups, was gradually relaxed, as intellectual 'ability' or 'intelligence' became naturalised as a biological construct. The influence of Darwin's evolutionary theory, in the context of the heyday of British imperialism, brought about the popularity of 'eugenic' theories of genetically superior types, providing 'scientific' explanations for the dominance of men over women, of the upper and middle classes over the poor, of white over black groups. Poverty was taken as a sign of inferiority, wealth a sign of strength.

I have written these opening paragraphs polemically, and certainly have dealt with this historical period superficially, but what I am trying to bring out is the point that theoretical advances are not divorced from history, but carry with them shadows of old, unstated assumptions, and retain some unsavoury foundations, which can be traced through to the present day.

A SCIENCE FOR SELECTION AND THE START OF 'STREAMING'

In the elementary schools earlier this century, children worked through each 'standard', the majority moving up to the next 'standard' as they passed the annual examinations, others repeating the year (a familiar system today in many parts of the world). But the schools were also given the function of discovering 'individual children who show promise of exceptional capacity', to send them on scholarships to fee-paying 'secondary schools', previously used only by children of the middle class. The concept of 'bright' and 'slow' children seemed an unquestioned assumption, with psychological theories suggesting the direct dependence of attainment on mental abilities.

The Hadow Reports on secondary (1926) and primary (1931) education enshrined psychometric intelligence testing into the education system, recommending separate schools after the age of 11 years for different groups of pupils identified by the tests. The technology of IQ testing made the new system of selective schools feel 'fair'. There were, after all, only a limited number of places at universities and in higher education, yet compulsory, free education was for all. By the 1950s nearly all schools which were big enough were streamed. Children went to secondary schools that matched their innate 'abilities' and were not only differentiated between schools, but also within them, segregated into different 'streams'. The system spread down into the junior and infant schools. A survey of those junior schools large enough to be able to stream was carried out by Brian Jackson (1964). It showed that 96 per cent were streamed, and that 74 per cent streamed the children by 7 years old. So, children's life chances were usually fixed by the age of 7, as there was very little transfer between streams (Plowden 1967). Brian Simon (1971) concluded: 'the school system appeared to be (as indeed it was) run on the assumption that no child could ever rise above himself, that his level of achievement was fatally determined by an IQ'.

EFFECTS OF STREAMING

Brian Jackson's study identifies some of the effects of streaming. Taking the quantifiable evidence first, he found that pupils were disadvantaged by streaming on three main counts:

1 *Social background*. Children whose fathers were in unskilled jobs had a far greater chance of being placed in a C stream than those with similar IQ scores from the professional classes. Streaming seemed to work as a covert, albeit unconscious, form of social selection. The choice of questions, the design of the test and the process of setting norms and standardising the tests are all ways of differentiating between social groups, by validating the knowledge and experience of some and denying those of the others. Apart from IQ test bias, both Jackson and Barker-Lunn (1970) found a tendency among teachers to under-estimate the 'ability' of working-class children, often leading to placement in the lower streams.

2 *Date of birth*. There were also less easily foreseen consequences of streaming. Children with an autumn birthday, and thus both older and with more experience of school, were found to have a far better chance of entering an 'A' stream.

3 *Teachers*. Streaming had led to a concentration of more experienced and qualified teachers in the 'A' streams, with younger and less experienced teachers given the low-status 'C' streams.

Ethnographic studies showed an increase in low expectations for 'B' and 'C' stream children, while the 'A' stream elites appeared to suffer in their turn from dull and repetitive coaching for secondary entrance exams. Brian Jackson describes how, when he began teaching, streaming was so entrenched as a 'common-sense' strategy that he just took for granted that 'A' streams were 'eager, apt and docile' while the 'C's contained 'the rebellious, the apathetic and the weak'. Such case studies remain salutary reading on the self-fulfilling prophecy of selection.

Finally, there seemed to be no research evidence suggesting that standards of achievement were significantly better in streamed schools. Barker-Lunn concluded that streaming was less critical to children's achievement than underlying differences in teachers' attitudes and practice.

After visiting newly de-streamed schools, though, Brian Jackson wrote: 'I suspect that there had been no change of values or teaching technique in these schools.' Although heads 'de-streamed', the change in organisation rarely seemed preceded or followed up with a focus on new teaching strategies to replace old routines. And the underlying concept of innate differences in ability remained stronger than superficial organisational changes, as I shall try to show in the next section.

ABILITY AS 'READINESS'

Susan Isaacs (1932), a strong proponent of the 'child-centred methods' which came to dominate primary discourse in the 1970s, wrote that, 'Of all the differences between one child and another, inborn intelligence turns out to be the most stable and permanent . . . we cannot cater properly for the brightest and the stupidest children together in one class.' The old ideas of fixed innate intelligence pervaded the pedagogies post-Plowden.

A shift in thinking had taken place with the gradual discrediting of methods of psychometric testing and with public disenchantment with the unfairnesses of the selective system. The Piagetian concept of a fixed progression in children's learning which cannot be hurried, and whose order cannot be changed, became the dominant explanation of learning. Throughout the Plowden Report (1967), the uniqueness of each individual was stressed, the 'enormously wide variability' in maturity, with different mental and physical abilities maturing at different rates within each child, so requiring the individualisation of teaching programmes.

Given this heterogeneity, streaming was no longer thought either possible or desirable, since it merely masked variety. Plowden recommended 'de-streaming' and opposed any fixed forms of grouping by 'ability' within the classroom.

'De-streaming' appears to have taken place very rapidly across the country in the wake of Plowden and, perhaps more importantly, with the demise of the 11-plus examination. However, as we saw above, not all schools accompanied the organisational change with changes in teaching strategies (HMI 1978; Galton *et al.* 1980). Meanwhile, the underlying expectation of different 'abilities' leading to differential achievement remained: 'There will be big and growing differences in children's ability and attainment but they will follow no tidy pattern because interest and motive can make havoc of prediction' (Plowden 1967: para. 824). Let us now see some of the effects on later practice.

Mortimore and his colleagues (1988) carried out a study of 2,000 pupils from 50 junior schools across four years. They found that most teachers prepared different levels of work in mathematics and language according to their perception of pupils' abilities. In a quarter of the classes children were also seated according to 'ability' for at least some of the time. These grouping arrangements seemed often to have been influenced by the judgements of previous teachers. The result appeared to be a widening achievement gap as certain groups developed a wider range of skills.

Critics of post-Plowden pedagogy such as Valerie Walkerdine (1984) have drawn attention to the way in which learning was separated conceptually from teaching, as an innate process carried out by the child alone. The role of the teacher was limited to the provision of the learning environment and the monitoring of each child's 'readiness' to progress. The *social* context of learning was made invisible, with little space for intervention or collaboration in learning.

Ethnographic studies by Sharp and Green (1975) and Ronald King (1978, see Chapter 19 in this book) gave illustrative examples of this process at work. Sharp and Green suggested that a new process of stratification began to take place; for example, a variety of activities was offered in the reception class, but children assessed as more mature if they showed themselves 'ready' for more academic-type work by choosing to take part in valorised activities. As the teachers themselves worked alongside those who 'chose' to read and write, for example, the gap in attainment between those who chose to work with them and the others widened. Similarly, those children whose home experiences had led them to make certain sorts of responses to books which were taken as signs of 'maturity' by educationists, could be seen as 'brighter' and more advanced by the teachers (Brice Heath 1983). Thus, although streaming was abandoned, and in many schools setting was also in little use, a 'masked' form of social selection was seen to be taking place. Those pupils whose experience and responses were most like the teachers' own came to be assessed as 'brighter' and received differential teaching, feedback and a wider range of experiences. In this way, a residual belief in fixed abilities enabled a too easy acceptance of differential attainment in many classrooms. Ultimately, it may be this rather than problematic teaching strategies which will be the main criticism of post-Plowden practice.

'ABILITY' AND TEACHER EXPECTATIONS

For some years, researchers have produced evidence showing that teachers' expectations are to some extent self-fulfilling. For example, if one thinks that particular children are 'dull' one might treat them differently from 'late developers', perhaps giving them more or less time and attention, feedback or praise. Lower expectations might be had of individual children, for more or less explicit reasons, or might be applied to most children from certain social groups.

Mortimore and his colleagues looked at classroom interactions in detail and over time. They found that lower-attaining children tended to have more individual contacts with their class teacher and to receive more feedback on their work than more 'successful' children. However, the interactions with lower attainers were found to be less often work-related, and more often about behaviour. Teachers gave more feedback on the work of higher attainers, giving them ideas on what they could do to improve it. They simply praised the work of lower attainers. The researchers concluded that it seemed that teachers were less prepared to accept poor work from pupils they believed were capable of producing a high standard. However, they wondered if in that context all the pupils did not see through the praise that was given: 'The real meaning of such praise (to lower attainers) may be that the performance is poor, or the expectations are lower' (1988: 170–1).

They concluded that the school made a far larger contribution to the explanation of progress than was made by pupils' background characteristics, sex and age. They identified 12 key factors which appeared to make schools more effective in improving the attainment of pupils, including a positive climate, leadership and staff and parent involvement, clear structures and consistency, intellectually challenging teaching, a focus on work, good record-keeping and maximum communication. High in importance was the issue of teacher expectations. Their study showed, however, that low expectations are transmitted in very subtle ways.

RECENT MOVES

In recent years, there has been increased interest from educationists in social approaches to learning, based on the work of Vygotsky. In contrast to Piaget's concept of the isolated individual learner, Vygotsky has offered a way of conceptualising the learning process which sees it as essentially arising out of social interaction and dependent on social experience. 'Ability' has come to be redefined in terms of differences in background experiences and in preferred styles of learning. The focus has shifted from the monitoring of development to the monitoring of attainment. Through observation of the learning process, it is believed that instead of waiting for 'readiness', teachers can build on what children know and can do, challenging their existing knowledge and skills and extending them by working together, co-operatively, before expecting them to achieve new skills on their own.

Of course, this is what many teachers have believed in and tried to do all along. However, as it becomes legitimate 'common-sense' practice, it is important to be aware of how new moves may be subverted where there is still a deep and ingrained belief in one general, underlying and fixed 'ability' widely accepted in our society.

The teaching profession in the United Kingdom is entering into an unprecedented period of public testing, with compulsory national testing in the state school system at 7, 11, 14 and 16. It seems vital to look closely at what those tests mean for expectations of pupil potential.

The Task Group on Assessment and Testing (TGAT) Report (1988) remains the only clear statement of the testing strategy underpinning the National Curriculum. I shall start with some of its positive aspects. Its starting point is the assessment of attainment, not of potential: 'The assessment programme depends on a clear view of what children should be being taught and should learn: the curriculum' (para. 140). It warns that 'care should be taken at all reporting ages, but especially at [age 7], to avoid giving the impression that the assessment is a prediction of future performance' (para. 148). It therefore recognises the potency of expectations upon performance. It also recognises differences in 'the pattern of attainment at intake' (para. 18). It argues that 'poor performance against a target should not be seen as a prediction of personal inadequacy; it should usually be regarded as an indication of needs. Such needs must be met' (para. 14).

However, critics of TGAT consider that there are a number of aspects of the TGAT model which are cause for concern. First, learning seems to be presented as taking place in a fixed, hierarchical sequence; thus 10 levels of progression are established in each subject area. Goldstein and Noss (1990) point out that it is not at all clear that one particular sequence of learning is either a necessary sequence or the best for everyone.

Secondly, whereas TGAT argued that 'to tie the criteria to particular ages only would risk either limiting the very able, or giving the least able no reward, or both' (para. 99), it then suggested that, on average, 'a pupil could reasonably be expected to progress by one level in two years of work' (para. 101). An attainment model of testing has been turned into an age-related normative model. We should also note the in-built acceptance of 'the able'. Goldstein and Noss argue that such 'average' expectations can in practice easily become statements of minimum levels of attainment. However, a child may attain a number of requirements across a range of levels, while at the same time not enough to be deemed to have fully achieved any one of the levels: 'The danger is that such a student will be forced to concentrate on achieving the lowest level not yet attained . . . before being allowed to move on' (Goldstein and Noss 1990).

Finally, although TGAT claims to be about assessing progress rather than ranking children, the way each child is given a level clearly invites comparison. The edifice of SATs testing begins to carry its own form of validity, a new selection device replacing the old mystique of psychometric testing. It legitimates and even encourages the streaming of children, for emphasis on differences *between* individuals may lead to the overlooking of differences *within* individuals, and thus bring us back to the old notion of ability as common across subjects, a fixed and underlying general intelligence.

At this point one needs to turn to a range of official statements on primary teaching from government-appointed bodies, to see how the issues of streaming and 'setting' have once more become an issue for the primary classroom, for in 1992 'beyond grouping by ability in mixed ability classes, there is little evidence of any widespread move towards other forms of ability grouping such as "streaming" or "setting"' (OFSTED 1993: 19).

The Alexander, Rose and Woodhead Report (1992) rejected streaming as 'a crude device which cannot do justice to the different abilities a pupil may show in different subjects and contexts'. Like Plowden, it suggested flexible grouping according to ability 'for a particular purpose' and warned teachers of 'the pitfall of assuming that pupils' ability is fixed' (para. 85).

Soon afterwards, HMI (OFSTED 1993) recommended 'carefully planned and appropriate groupings of pupils for tasks' and 'teaching specifically targeted to specific individuals or groups' (p. 22), statements which again suggest flexible and changing groupings for particular tasks.

The re-formed National Curriculum Council (NCC 1993) called for attention to be given to 'the setting of pupils according to ability' in different subjects. This statement still clearly recognises that a pupil may have a range of different levels of attainment in different subject areas, but does seem to suggest rather more fixed and less fluid groupings. No explicit indication is given in any of the above reports of how 'ability' in the different subjects is to be assessed. Are they referring to ongoing teacher assessment of achievement against NC levels of attainment, or to longer-term groupings according to SAT results? What will teachers make of these suggestions?

A DFE circular responding to the reports was soon afterwards sent to all schools, asking them to consider 'How to achieve a better match of work to children's needs – including the introduction of setting where possible, and of grouping by ability if setting is not possible, taking into account the problems of smaller, rural schools' (DFE News Circular 16/93, 18 Jan. 1993). The HMI and NCC recommendations seem slightly reworked here to introduce into the debate the need to establish more fixed 'sets'. There is no mention of different groupings for different subject areas.

The issue of grouping children according to 'ability' has thus come back into focus once again, but based on a different system of testing and assessment. Can this system overcome the problems identified in the past? They seem equally applicable and equally formidable today: lowered expectations through labelling, a widening achievement gap between sets, lowered morale, the production of hierarchies which reproduce themselves, and the possibility of unfair discrimination against certain groups through the assessment norms set and assessment procedures adopted.

For example, there are pressing issues relating to the placement in any set of pupils at an early stage of learning English. In which group would they be placed? If placed in a more slow-moving group (and why should they be?), what monitoring of transfer would there be to ensure that as their English improved they moved into groups of 'higher attainers'? Would it really be possible to move groups as the content covered by the 'higher attainers'' group increased and the attainment gap widened inexorably? Similar issues arise for many groups of pupils, even those with summer birthdays! Would, for example, a low level of attainment on reading and writing at age 7 influence 'setting' across a range of other subject areas, such as history, geography and science? How could such a system meet the demands of equal opportunity policies?

Although there is a danger that fixed forms of 'ability' grouping could lead back towards the hierarchically structured system of schooling of earlier times, it is clear that the informal limitation of the potential of certain children by theories and practices based on individual 'readiness' cannot provide the alternative. One must distinguish two different strands in the development of assessment: on the one hand, a stronger focus on the process of interaction between teacher, pupil and task in learning and its outcomes; on the other, a search for some legitimising technology in order to rank children for the differential distribution of resources and access to different kinds of knowledge.

Ensuring equality of opportunity in the classroom will continue to require imaginative solutions, where the best developments of the past years in co-operative teaching and learning strategies, effective communication, and a principled mix of whole class, flexible groupings, pair and individual work, are supported and improved. But central to the improvement of primary practice must be the recognition that no child's potential is fixed.

I shall end this chapter with a quotation from Mortimore and his colleagues (1988) challenging 'common views of intelligence':

> What our data illustrate is that children's performance changes over time. Given an effective school, children make greater progress. Greater progress leads to greater capability and, if handled sensitively, to greater confidence. . . . The responsibility of teachers is to ensure that their pupils do not adopt fixed views of their own abilities but, rather, come to realise that they have considerable potential which, given motivation and good teaching in an effective school, can be realised . . . many parents still regard their children's ability as fixed. We hope our data will persuade both teacher and parents that this is not so and that change is possible. We believe that, in the right circumstances, children can become more intelligent.
>
> (p. 264)

REFERENCES

Alexander, R., Rose, J. and Woodhead, C. (1992) *Curriculum Organisation and Classroom Practice in Primary Schools: a Discussion Paper* ('The Three Wise Men's report'), London: DES.

Barker-Lunn, J. (1970) *Streaming in the Primary School*, Slough: NFER.

Birchenough, C. (1914) *History of Elementary Education in England and Wales*, London: University Tutorial Press.

Brice Heath, S. (1983) *Ways with Words*, Cambridge: Cambridge University Press.

DFE (1993) DFE News 16/93, 'Improving primary education – Patten', London: DFE.

Galton, M., Simon, B. and Croll, P. (1980) *Inside the Primary Classroom*, London: Routledge & Kegan Paul.

Gardner, H. (1983) *Frames of Mind: the Theory of Multiple Intelligence*, New York: Basic Books.

Goldstein, H. and Noss, R. (1990) 'Against the stream', in *Forum*, 33(1).

Hadow Report (1926) *Report of the Consultative Committee on the Education of the Adolescent*, London: HMSO.

—— (1931) *Report of the Consultative Committee on Primary Education*, London: HMSO.

HMI (1978) *Primary Education in England: a Survey by HMI*, London: DES.

Howe, M. (1990) 'Children's gifts, talents and natural abilities: an explanatory mythology?', in *Education and Child Psychology*, 7(1).

Isaacs, S. (1932) *The Children We Teach: Seven to Eleven Years*, London: University of London Press.

Jackson, B. (1964) *Streaming: an Education System in Miniature*, London: Routledge & Kegan Paul.

King, R. (1978) *All Things Bright and Beautiful*, New York: Wiley & Sons.

Mortimore, P., Sammons, P., Stoll, L., Lewis, D. and Ecob, R. (1988) *School Matters: the Junior Years*, Wells: Open Books.

NCC (1993) *The National Curriculum at Key Stages 1 and 2: Advice to the Secretary of State for Education*, York: NCC.

OFSTED (1993) *Curriculum Organisation and Classroom Practice in Primary Schools: a Follow-up Report*, London: OFSTED.

Plowden Report (1967) *Children and their Primary Schools*, London: HMSO.

Rose, J. (1984) *The Case of 'Peter Pan' or the Impossibility of Children's Fiction*, London: Macmillan.

Salmon, P. and Bannister, D. (1974) 'Education in the light of personal construct theory', *Education for Teaching*, 94: 25–38.

Sharp, R. and Green, A. (1975) *Education and Social Control*, London: Routledge & Kegan Paul.

Simon, B. (1971) *Intelligence, Psychology, Education*, London: Lawrence & Wishart.

Sternberg, R. (1984) 'A contextualist view of the nature of intelligence', *International Journal of Psychology*, 19: 307–34.

TGAT (1988) *National Curriculum Task Group on Assessment and Testing: a Report*, London: DES/Welsh Office.

Tomlinson, S. (1992) 'Back to the future: streaming and selection', *ACE Bulletin*, 45.

Walkerdine, V. (1984) 'Developmental psychology and the child centred pedagogy', in J. Henriques *et al.* (eds) *Changing the Subject*, London: Methuen.

Part V

Classroom studies

Chapter 19

Creativity and conventional reality

Ronald King

This chapter follows on from the last, and illustrates the way post-Piagetian theories of 'readiness' became part of 'professional' understanding of children's learning. In this extract from a classic study of infant classrooms, Ronald King shows how theories of child development influence the way teachers understand children, and their achievements and interests. Although it was published in 1978, many readers still find the book has resonance with their experience of primary classrooms.

Drawing, painting, sewing, collage and model-making were all common activities in the classrooms, in that all children did some of these things during the course of the day. Sometimes they were organised around a theme or class project based upon the children's imputed interests, and at certain times of the year they were directed towards special public occasions, such as the Harvest Festival or Christmas Concert. Although apparently free and expressive, these creative efforts were constrained by the actions of the teachers, who defined them in terms of the presumed developmental capacities of the children, and the consequences of this definition were shown in the products of the children's activities. Creative work was also partly organised to reproduce conventional or orthodox reality, a process given greater priority, for different reasons, when the products were to be publicly presented.

PAINTING AND DRAWING – REPRODUCING CONVENTIONAL REALITY

Every day every child probably did a drawing or drawings. These were sometimes parts of mathematical or number activities, the prelude or accompaniment to a story. The drawing of pictures was also used by teachers as a way of sustaining busyness, to be done in spare moments on pieces of paper or in busy books. This kind of drawing activity was common among the younger children, who, to begin with, were allowed to make their own definition of a drawing.

> Teacher looking at girl's drawing: 'I like it, what is it?'

Paintings, too, could be defined by the younger children.

> Teacher introduces the new boy (his second day in school) to painting. He is shown the easel, the paints, the brushes, and the apron he must wear, but he is not told how or what to paint. He uses one colour to cover most of the paper. Another boy says to him, 'What are you painting?' He replies, 'A colour.' The other boy, 'A colour, just blue!' He changes brushes and completes the painting in green.

The boy had defined painting as covering a surface with paint.

In the absence of the teacher defining a drawing or painting, young children learned from one another; a whole table frequently did the same basic drawing by copying. The familiar images were those of houses, trees and flowers. These were seen by some teachers as expressions of the children's needs for security, a therapeutic introduction to school, and a few of the younger ones drew on the authority of 'what they told us at college' to support this. The college orthodoxy also forbade asking what a picture was of.

The representations of houses, trees, flowers and people were versions of cultural images of these things. Although not directly presented to children by the teachers these were displayed in the classroom, other than in other children's paintings and drawings. Lollipop trees and houses based on a rectangle and a triangle were found on Leggo cards, teacher-prepared and commercial word and number cards, mathematics workbooks, and in some storybooks.

Left to define paintings for themselves, the children drew on the limited resources around them, but to the teacher their limited images were an indication of the limited resources within them: their relative immaturity. I tried a simple, ethically acceptable, experiment one day. A boy was about to paint. I asked him what he was going to do. 'I don't know.' I suggested, 'Why don't you paint a boat?' The teacher was quite excited when she asked him her usual question, 'Tell me about your picture', and he replied, 'It's a boat.' 'He's never done anything like that before,' she said to me later. At least three other children, following his example, 'progressed' to painting boats that day.

These early drawings and paintings were defined by the teachers as expressions of childish innocence.

> Teacher, looking at boy's painting: 'Cubist. I suppose he'll lose all that soon.'

Children were emancipated from their innocence by the actions of their teachers. After a period in which they could paint or draw what they wished, older children's images were monitored by the teacher's comments so as to introduce more elements of conventional reality.

> Teacher: 'Where's the door on your house?' Girl: 'Hasn't got one.'
> Teacher: 'How do you get in?'

> 'Poor daddy! He hasn't got any arms.'

These comments sometimes denied the children the ability to express perspective.

> The girl's picture has a house and a girl of the same height. Teacher: 'I like the girl and the house, but could she get in the door?'

The conventional reality that the children were required to represent was often more a conventional picture reality.

> A group are making collage trees from squares of sticky paper. Teacher: 'Have you ever seen a black tree trunk?' 'You're not doing a green tree trunk are you?' No trees outside the window have the chocolate brown trunks that she requires. Some are shades of green, others almost black, and even white.

This conventional picture reality was used in the learning of colours.

> There is a 'blue' display of pictures prepared by the teacher, including ones labelled 'The sea is blue', 'The sky is blue'. Outside the sky is grey. It can be red, purple, orange, yellow, or white.

Children learned to reproduce these picture realities.

> Girl, of another's painting: 'Sky don't go that colour.' (Green)

Some children presented token representations of picture reality. It was common to observe a child to first paint a blue line along the top of the paper to represent the sky, and then a green one at the bottom for grass. Teachers did not find this acceptable in the paintings of older children, and asked for a 'proper' sky that stretched down to the horizon.

Teachers also constrained children into the reproduction of conventional reality by their provision of materials.

> Children are making collage fruits and vegetables from sticky paper. 'Cabbage people, here are yours' (two shades of green). 'Tomato people, these are yours' (red).

Teachers used children's painting and drawings as an index of their developmental state or maturity – an internal state inferred from an external product mediated by the teacher.

> We are looking at the afternoon's picture work on the 'sea' project. The teacher makes judgements of the children's maturity: 'They haven't got the concepts to draw properly yet.' The drawings of the less mature

children are less detailed, the heads are large, there is no perspective. She is delighted with a boy's picture of a diver. 'He has come on.' She is nonplussed when I tell her I saw him copy it minutely from a Ladybird book.

PUBLIC DISPLAY – THE EFFORT/PRODUCT DILEMMA

Teachers defined children's creative work as being an expression of their development, and acted in such a way as to make the nature of their creative products correspond to the presumed stages of development. In this the teacher judged the children, but when their products were on public display the teachers felt that they too were being judged. This was tacit acknowledgement of the teacher's part in the creative process, and one which, when I had gained their confidence, they were prepared to admit.

The classrooms were public places to the extent that they were visited by other teachers, the head teacher, and parents delivering and collecting their young children. Children's paintings and drawings were displayed on the walls, often mounted on coloured paper with a teacher-provided caption. 'This is Darren's daddy.' The three schools held Open Days for parents and on these occasions the classrooms were more than usually decked with creative work. Some of the captions were clearly for the benefit of the parents: 'Some collage pictures', 'Splatter painting', 'Wax-resist paintings'. On these occasions it was possible to see how the teacher had sometimes strengthened the outline on a child's picture or even added some detail.

At Seaton Park and Burnley Road every teacher had a turn at taking prayers. This was a performance put on by one class in front of the rest of the school, and typically involved the display of children's creative work. At Seaton Park this was put into a public area of the school for a period after the prayers. Taking prayers was a minor ordeal for the younger teachers. 'This is where the butterflies start,' said one as we walked to the hall for her first performance. Afterwards she was sympathetically congratulated by her colleagues (even though she forgot to do the closing prayer).

Each performance was arranged around a theme or story such as 'growing up' or 'things we like to do'. Rehearsals and the production of material often started weeks before the performance. The latter presented the teachers with a dilemma. Left to create their own efforts the children would produce elephants and giraffes that did not look much like elephants and giraffes. To use these would be to evaluate the effort over the product. Most teachers intervened to make the product correspond better to conventional reality; the product was evaluated over the children's efforts. Many argued that the children enjoyed contributing to making a recognisable product. For others this was a compromise with their professional ideologies and a source of conflict.

Mrs Pink's class project for prayers is 'Ourselves'. For this each child is doing a self-portrait on the reverse side of a continuous roll of wallpaper to make a 'mural'. She is concerned on two accounts. Firstly, the children are clearly copying the previous portrait in doing their own. She feels they should really be drawing themselves, so she covers over the previous portraits (with great difficulty because some are still wet). She is then, secondly, concerned to find that some children are drawing bodiless figures with the arms and legs attached to the head. She compromises 'as it's for assembly', and unrolls the paper so that the previous acceptable figures can be copied. She feels guilty about this as 'they should find out about people having bodies for themselves'. Later she even mediates verbally. 'He's something missing.' Other children chorus, 'Arms.'

In the production of work for public display the teacher was the designer and the children routine workers. One teacher said quite explicitly, 'They are the manual labourers.' Their labour included their (happily) filling in outlines prepared by the teacher; for example, an elephant of paper clips and an owl of different kinds of seeds, the mass production of leaves and fish from templates prepared by the teacher, and the assembly of parts to make angels or Easter cards. In these efforts it was the teacher who was being creative, and as a later section shows, the quality of her class's work was one way in which she was evaluated by her colleagues and the headmistress.

There were, however, observable incidents of genuine creativity by children.

A boy finds an old record in the junk box. He makes a record-player from a cornflakes packet, a cotton reel, and rolled-up corrugated paper. He moves the record around by hand on the cornflakes packet and sings, 'I'm a long-haired lover from Liverpool'.

PROJECTS AND IMPUTED INTERESTS

Many of the activities that the teachers arranged for children to do were based upon their imputations of children's interests.

We must start from the natural interests of the children.

(Notes for teachers, Seaton Park)

Teachers made assumptions about children's interest in providing books, reading stories, and in starting off projects which stimulated the children's interest, so proving the original assumptions to be 'real'. They were assumed to be interested in animals, flowers, people's jobs, cars and trains, singing, poetry, and royalty. 'They are all royalists,' said one teacher to me at the end of a day when she had used Princess Anne's wedding as a topic at news time, having previously asked them to bring in newspaper cuttings of the event, displayed a portrait of the wedding couple from a women's magazine framed in flattened milk-bottle tops, got every child to do a picture of the event, and set the older ones to write about it.

> Boy: 'Can I do [a painting of] Princess Anne?' Teacher: 'If you want to.' Boy to another, excitedly: 'I'm going to do Princess Anne.' Later he does his writing. 'I like Princess Anne. I like Captain Mark Phillips.' The names are written on the board. I look back in his writing book. Yesterday he wrote, 'I like swets and is lolly.' The day before, 'I like dogs.'

This is not to suggest that children's interests were totally teacher-stimulated.

> Girls chatting as they work: 'My mum says Princess Anne's veil was the Queen's.'

However, some manifest interests of children were not given educational status by their teachers.

> It is singing time. The teacher asks the children to choose the songs. After 'Mary Mary quite contrary' and 'Little bird' a boy suggests 'I'll be your long-haired lover from Liverpool'. The teacher says, 'No, we're not having that, we don't all know the words.' She ignores the many children who call out, 'I do, I do.' 'No, we'll have Humpty Dumpty.'

The only pop songs that children sang were at least 20 years old, such as 'How much is that doggy in the window?'. Other interests of the children that were ignored included most television programmes, a frequent topic of conversation among children in the classroom, comics, and anything to do with fighting, death or wars, unless these were safely set in a historical context (the Vikings comprise the major part of infant history), or, in a story world setting, particularly pirates. The following overheard snatches illustrate children's non-approved interests.

> Boy: 'Who likes Scooby-Doo?' 'Me!' chorus the children around him. They sing a snatch of the Scooby-Doo song.

> Children are swapping horror stories in the Wendy house. 'My dad has a bit cut off the end of his finger.' 'My friend's dad had half his tongue cut off.'

Non-approved interests also appeared in the children's writing, despite teachers' oblique disapproval. ('Not another war story.')

> One day there was a man half monster and they called him Francken Stein and one day when superman looked and a saw people coming upstairs so he got in to decgiese clark kent and he and he saw Francken Stien and killed him.

One day there was a boy called Dennis the mennis and when he was eating his dinner he said it was horribel and he chucked his dinner in his mums face so she got daddy and daddy smaked his head and told him.

Disapproved and unutilised interests were those which contradicted the teacher's definition of the pupils as being innocent and those that related to orders of reality, including television programmes, which were outside her control.

Chapter 20

Coping strategies and the multiplication of differentiation in infant classrooms

Andrew Pollard

While the last chapter looked at the effects of theories of learning on teachers' responses to children, this chapter illustrates the way children themselves, in interaction with the teacher, are actively involved in the production of different levels of 'ability' as they develop different ways of 'coping' with classroom demands. The extract contains the summary of an ethnographic study of an infant school classroom. Because of the way that I have edited the chapter, you will need some background information. The school was located on the edge of a council estate in the inner suburb of a northern town. The children in the class were 6 or 7 years old. In a second section of the paper, not included here for reasons of space, Andrew Pollard goes on to describe and analyse a second classroom situation. Although differently worked out in practice, Pollard concludes that in both situations the particular 'coping strategies' adopted by teacher and pupils were reflected in the way pupils came to be assessed as 'clever', or not.

This chapter is concerned with processes of social differentiation in school classrooms and with the influence of teacher and pupil coping strategies on such processes. It thus relates directly to a core concern of the sociology of education in that it offers an opportunity for analysis at a micro-level to make an unequivocal contribution to the macro-structural debate on schooling and social reproduction.

Of course, the issue of differentiation within classrooms is a well-researched area in which many different approaches have been taken. For instance, the classic study by Rosenthal and Jacobson (1968) claimed to have identified the effects of a 'self-fulfilling prophecy' and argued that pupil performance was dramatically influenced by teacher expectations. Rist (1970) suggested that the kindergarten teacher whom he studied used a 'roughly constructed ideal-type' based on social class criteria with which to classify children into a three-table/group 'caste-system' within her classroom. Consequent variation in teacher behaviour resulted in differences in child performance and the caste system began to be institutionalised. From a Marxist perspective, Sharp and Green's (1976) analysis of teacher ideologies and social control in a 'progressive' infant school concerned itself with the formation of child identities through the teacher structured processes of the classroom – in particular, as an implication of the teachers' 'busyness' ideology.

The present chapter has implications for these arguments, but it retains its primary focus on processes rather than outcomes. More specifically I argue that, in classrooms where a 'working consensus' exists, teachers and children interact to reinforce *mutually* classroom differentiation, as a by-product of the mesh of their coping strategies. The analysis thus particularly utilises the concepts of 'coping strategy' and of 'working consensus', and it is important to clarify my use of them.

The concept of coping strategy has been most formally developed by Andy Hargreaves (1978), who analysed the context of teaching and argued that the constraints and dilemmas impinging on teacher action have macro-structural origins and thus represent 'societal demands' to which teachers have to respond. In my own work (Pollard 1982), building on Woods' (1977) analysis as well as that of Hargreaves, I sought to develop the concept by emphasising the importance of biography in influencing the particular perception of 'coping' necessities with reference to which teachers *or* children will act. The concept of coping strategy thus has linkages to the macro-concerns of history and social structure *and* to the micro-concerns of biography and the unique social contexts which exist in classrooms.

The concept of 'working consensus' describes a type of negotiated 'truce' between the teacher and the children, by which each recognises the coping necessities of the other. It is a socially constructed set of understandings which reduces threat and enables the participants mutually to accomplish the social situation in their classroom. As David Hargreaves (1975) has put it:

> The absolute imposition of the teacher's definition of the situation is really impossible and the side effects of attempts to do so make such a course inadvisable. . . . He aims instead at a negotiated settlement whereby teacher and pupil each go half-way with respect to some demands and whereby in other areas the teacher withdraws or moderates his demands on the pupils in return for conformity to other teacher demands. This negotiated settlement may fall short of the teacher's ideal definition of the situation but it is realistic in that it averts discord and ensures that a fair number of his demands are met and that teacher–pupil relationships are generally good. The pupils, realising that their position is not a strong one from which to bargain, are usually content with the concessions made by the teacher.

(p. 133)

Of course, in the classroom context, the teacher normally has greater power than the children. This gives him or her the advantage of initiation, and it is clear that the working consensus will reflect the power differential between the teacher and the children. The children in a sense take up a tactical position, accepting teacher power to a great extent. However, this teacher power *is* circumscribed, because if it is used 'unfairly' or 'unreasonably', from the subjective perspective of the children, then they will change from their tactical compliance to more offensive strategies leading to a breakdown of the working consensus. They will defend themselves, often through forms of 'disorder', thus increasing the 'survival threat' experience by that teacher (Pollard 1980).

When a working consensus is established it thus represents a mutual accommodation for coping. Of course, such a truce cannot be taken for granted. The particular strategies which children develop when faced with their coping problem will vary depending on their biographies and on the particular nature of the cultural, institutional and classroom contexts which exist. Some may try to 'take on' the teacher and to challenge their authority, but I would suggest (Pollard 1979, 1981) that it is far more common, among primary school children at least, to find a type of acceptance of 'how things are' which supports the idea of a working consensus having been negotiated. This may reflect the predominantly class-based organisation of primary schools and the emphasis placed by teachers on 'establishing a good relationship'. Certainly the continuity provided by the class-based primary school system is far more conducive to the establishment of understandings between a class of children and 'their' teacher than is the more time-structured and subject-centred system found in most secondary schools (Bird 1980).

Even in the primary school there is a range of child response. My own research in a middle school (Pollard 1984) suggests that the nature of this response ranges from a grudging 'doing of time' with a watchful eye out for opportunities for 'messing about', to an active engagement within the teacher's frame of reference and an endorsement of 'pleasing teacher' strategies. One way of placing these alternatives conceptually is to see them as responses to the basic ambiguity of the child's structural position. The 'resistance' strategies generally articulate from peers and child culture, whilst the more 'accepting' actions orientate more towards adult expectations. Between these alternatives a third type of response represents attempts to be seen favourably in both spheres. In my view the majority of children attempt this third form of adaptation, and they do so by negotiating the 'working consensus' with the teacher. Since it is normally in the teacher's interests to support this development the working consensus routinely becomes established as 'what-everyone-takes-for-granted' (Ball 1980). As I clarified above, it is not, in fact, quite what *everyone* takes for granted for 'the children' cannot be regarded as a homogeneous group. However, if it is initially primarily the work of the dominant group of children, I think it can still be argued that in most circumstances in a primary school context it eventually becomes established as the fundamental basis of the 'moral order' of the classroom and hence as a source of legitimation for teacher and child actions which is applied to the class as a whole.

In this chapter I wish to attempt to identify what, in terms of sociological consequences, might be called the 'multiplier effect' of some forms of coping and of the 'working consensus'. The working consensus is seen as a product of both teacher and child coping strategies having achieved some sort of balance *vis-à-vis* each other. In each case the particular coping strategies of the other represent a major factor to which their own strategies must have adapted. It follows that over time the strategies of both the teacher and children tend to become 'meshed' together, with those of the children being the more adapted because of the teacher's greater power. Indeed child strategies have sometimes been seen as 'counter-strategies' (Denscombe 1980) and as primarily reactive. One result of this is that, whatever the sociological significance of the teacher strategies may be, the children's reactive coping strategies within the parameters of the working consensus may reinforce and amplify this consequence. Such amplification may re-inforce teachers' strategic decisions by leading to their favourable evaluation, their continued usage and their continued 'multiplication' of effect.

In the context of the work on classroom differentiation reviewed earlier, this analysis is suggesting that, in addition to the self-fulfilling prophecy and the consequences of labelling or teacher control ideologies, there are *socially* fulfilling processes at work in classrooms which can powerfully reinforce more individualised factors.

MRS ROTHWELL AND HER CLASS

Mrs Rothwell had a teaching certificate and was in her late thirties. She had taught for 12 years. She was married to a civil engineer, had two children and lived in a pleasant rural village outside the town. She had been brought up as, and was, a practising Christian.

A core aspect of Mrs Rothwell's perspective could be decribed as 'famil-ial'. As she explained to me: 'A school should be like a good family, with discipline, love, and room to explore.'

Mrs Rothwell felt a sincere caring duty towards the children in her class whom she believed came from generally poor and unstable home backgrounds. She felt that these homes failed to provide a discipline, standards of behaviour or support for the children and, to compensate for this background, she emphasised 'developing an awareness of right and wrong'.

Mrs Rothwell frequently used personality constructs. Children were often described as 'extrovert' and 'lively' or as 'introverted'. Mrs Rothwell also identified those children who were 'immature' and those who were 'growing up'. From her experience with her own children she believed that she 'knew the stages that children go through'. Mrs Rothwell had a complex array of descriptions to describe the intelligence of the children. These ranged from 'exceptionally bright', 'very bright', 'reasonably bright', 'intelligent', 'capable', 'great ability', 'very able', 'thoughtful' – to 'poor', 'not very clever', 'needs help', 'backward'.

Mrs Rothwell had a clear image of her ideal pupil (Becker 1952) but felt a type of resigned concern towards many of those who could not match up to this image. As she put it:

> It really is rewarding when you get a child who is bright, one who you can really talk to and rely on, but we don't get many of those . . . most of them here really do need a lot of help. We do what we can for them but some of them are very hard to help even when you want to do your best for them.

Regarding pedagogy Mrs Rothwell felt that learning took place best when she transmitted the knowledge, usually in a discussion → blackboard → book-work sequence, and when the children had had 'enough practice'. Thus there was frequent recitation of maths tables, practice of sums, reading and writing. In Mrs Rothwell's view, the children worked best when they had an 'incentive', and she provided this with a star reward system. Competition was encouraged so that children would 'get on quickly and carefully'. However, some children 'didn't try' and were 'careless', whilst others 'lacked concentration'. These children were regarded as 'unsettled', in contrast to those 'well adjusted' to school.

Mrs Rothwell's perspective seemed internally consistent. She believed that the skills and the body of knowledge, which it was her duty to teach, were linear by nature and she believed that learning occurs through practice and reinforcement. She therefore introduced work in a careful order and took her planning and preparation very seriously. She provided a fixed timetable in which there was plenty of time for work and practice, and awarded stars to stimulate competition and to provide reinforcement. In Mrs Rothwell's view the structured routines and timetables which she maintained provided the security which the children needed. In turn, she felt that security made it possible for the children to be happy – and: 'They should be happy in school, even if they learn only a little, because they come from broken homes.'

Mrs Rothwell's perspective was thus organised around what she saw as her two main duties: the compensation for poor home backgrounds by providing moral standards and security, and the efficient imparting of knowledge and skills.

In Mrs Rothwell's classroom the tables were arranged in two rectangular blocks with the blackboard and the teacher's desk at either ends of the blocks. Seating places were officially allocated by Mrs Rothwell and fixed. The 'brightest' and 'average' children each occupied the majority of a table block (the 'top' and 'middle' groups), with a group of 'less able' children split between the two blocks and clustered at the end of each nearest to the teacher's desk (the 'bottom' group).

Mrs Rothwell used classwork for almost everything – during craft activities everyone made a flower in the way they were shown, in writing practice everyone copied the patterns from the board, in number lessons everyone chanted their 2-times, 3-times, 5-times and 10-times tables; in poetry times children spoke verses chorally, in creative English everyone wrote on the subject suggested using the words written on the blackboard. These examples occurred consistently and regularly.

The consistencies in Mrs Rothwell's image of her ideal pupil, her typifications and dominant constructs, her formal pedagogy, classroom organisation and child-grouping methods, are quite clear. They are all associated with the particular teaching technology (Hammersley 1980) by which she sought to cope in the classroom. They were the means by which she reconciled her image of herself and her role with her daily practical situation.

From their close similarity to those found by Rist (1970), Mrs Rothwell's teaching strategies appeared likely to produce a social hierarchy within the class, and this was investigated by analysing the relationship between the friendship structure of the class and indices of academic achievement.

A sociometric analysis showed that friendship groupings of girls and boys were distinct, and this was confirmed by observations of their play in the playground. The boys tended to be interested in 'Action Man', guns, fighting, chasing, 'Steve Austin', space, and so on, whilst the girls tended to be more involved with skipping, dolls and home games. This distinction was often reinforced by Mrs Rothwell: for instance, boys and girls lined up separately, were dismissed from the classroom separately, were given different types of classroom 'jobs' and were spoken to in qualitatively different ways. It was also found that the friendship groupings corresponded closely with the official academic stratification system used by Mrs Rothwell. There is a pattern of association between informal friendship groups, group seat places and reading-book levels.

It should be remembered that Mrs Rothwell's criteria for allocation of seat places were not designed to reinforce friendships. The seat places were fixed and maintained by Mrs Rothwell for occasional pedagogic convenience, and the internal stratification which resulted was validated by her perspective concerning the nature of children's abilities and by her view of the competitive spur which the possibility of 'moving to a higher table', or 'being on the highest table' might provide. There are thus good reasons for doubting that the friendships had developed independently of the seat place structuring. My conclusion then is that the children's friendship groups did seem to have been influenced by each child's degree of achievement and by their official identities in the classroom. These are fairly unremarkable conclusions and appear to be a consequence of Mrs Rothwell's perspective, classroom organisation and teaching strategies. One way of putting this is to say that she had created the conditions for 'primary differentiation'. She had a clear image of her 'ideal pupil', and a highly developed set of constructs and typifications. This was combined with forms of classroom organisation and pedagogy which derived from, and reinforced, her perspective.

I want now to focus on what could be termed 'secondary differentiation', which lies in a similar relationship to that between primary and secondary deviance as identified by Lemert (1967). The crucial processual influence which I suggested earlier was that of the children and their coping strategies meshing interaction with the teacher and hers. Indeed, I suggested that this could set up a 'multiplier effect' whereby the social consequences of a particular teacher strategy are amplified when children develop their own strategies around those of the teacher. As we have seen, the teacher's use of a particular set of strategies has a primary significance because of the teacher–pupil power differential, but I am suggesting that when a working consensus exists this gains secondary reinforcement from child-coping strategies.

An illustration of child strategies in Mrs Rothwell's class which can briefly be described as 'collaboration to produce' may make this argument clearer. First, it should be said that a type of working consensus did appear to exist. The majority of children appeared to accept the dominant definition of the situation, as initiated primarily by Mrs Rothwell, without demur. Indeed, in almost all their work, the majority tried to 'please teacher' by producing correct results; they wanted to 'win a star' and, above all, they did not want to fail. As I have described, the most common setting requiring accomplishment in the class was the 'seat work setting'. In a typical lesson of this type such as 'number', sums were put on the blackboard for everyone to do. Mrs Rothwell's movement pattern was then regular. After setting the lesson-task and checking that the children had begun, she went to her desk to hear readers. The result of Mrs Rothwell sitting at her desk, in combination with her class work and the children's determination to please her, was that the potential for collaboration to find 'the answers' was enormous and such collaboration was widespread. In fact, the children appeared to have traded a degree of compliance with Mrs Rothwell's goals in exchange for her unwitting non-intervention with their strategies for attaining them. It was this trade-off that appeared to be the underlying basis of the working consensus.

The collaboration system was very interesting. On those occasions when there was general unease among the children about how to accomplish a set task, such as their sums, observations suggested that a few key children on each table actually did the work and that these 'answers' then flowed through friendship groups in a 'ripple effect' for knowledge comparable to Kounin's (1970) for desists.

In other circumstances when the work set was familiar and most of the children felt confident, then they could work alone. Of course, most commonly, situations occurred somewhere between these alternatives and also varied within the class. However, collaboration was far from unusual and was an active process, as the following transcript of a conversation recorded on the top table shows.

MRS ROTHWELL: Today we are going to try to do two sorts of sums at once, we'll try to do the take-away ones and the add-up ones, but I'm going to try and trick you by mixing them up . . . (*writes sums on board*) . . . this is my day for tricking people. (*The children work. A little later . . .*)

JANET: She hasn't caught me out yet.

SANDRA: She hasn't caught me out yet.

NIGEL: She hasn't caught me out yet – has she . . .?

JANET: She has – you're caught – she's caught him out!

NIGEL: Why?

JANET: He's got two 'ten take-aways' . . .

NIGEL: I think she has caught me out.

DUNCAN: Nigel, I think you'd better copy off me, or you'll make a messy job. Ten take away nought makes ten.

SANDRA: Ten take away nought makes ten?

JANET: You've done the second one wrong, you've done the second one wrong.

NIGEL: I haven't.

JANET: You have – oh, there shouldn't be a four there should there?

DUNCAN: There should.

JANET: Should there? (*Janet alters the answer.*)

NIGEL: Yes, oh yes, that's right.

SANDRA: You've done it wrong, there shouldn't be a four there. (*Children change answers.*)

DUNCAN: Mine's right.

NIGEL: So's mine.

JANET: Mine is.

SANDRA: Mine is.

JANET: Everybody knows ten add ten makes twenty.

NIGEL: Ten add ten makes twenty.

NIGEL: What's ten add nothing?

DUNCAN: Nothing.

SANDRA: Ten add nothing is nothing – it's nothing.

NIGEL: Janet's done it wrong, she's done ten.

SANDRA: Mine are right.

DUNCAN: They are tricky – oh Sandra, you've done that one wrong, no, look. (*Shows and Sandra alters.*)

DUNCAN: That's it.

In effect these children were negotiating among themselves for the 'right' answer. As we have seen, academic criteria were important to the children's social system, and observations of 'negotiations for right answers' between children suggested that some children with a reputation for generally 'getting them right' had considerable prestige – for instance, the child who managed to get 'ten add nothing is nothing' accepted was the most chosen child on the sociomatrix.

A related strategy for accomplishing the seat-work lessons which was frequently observed was one of waiting for someone else to have their work marked and then checking and perhaps changing one's own answers. Some children seemed highly dependent on these collaborative strategies, and in these cases, their timing was very important, because if they failed to collect enough answers early in the lesson, they ran a risk that some key children might finish, be marked and put their books away in drawers. In these circumstances the only possible strategy was to attempt to move seats, and some children were repeatedly 'told off' for doing so, as well as subsequently receiving sanctions for 'not having tried'.

Quantitative and non-reactive evidence was available to support observations and cassette-recordings of collaboration, in the form of analysis of 'errors-in-common' made by children in their sum books over half a term. These data indicated high percentages of 'errors-in-common' between neighbouring children sitting at the top and middle tables. The top group tended to complete more sums than the middle group, and also to get more sums correct. The fact that they made relatively few mistakes means that the percentage of 'errors-in-common' was based on fewer items, but this in itself is interesting because observations suggested that they had a more efficient collaboration system than the other tables, in addition to being better able to work alone if necessary. In contrast, the bottom groups were seated apart. They tended to be shunned by other children and thus to have poor access to correct answers via the collaboration system. To make their difficulties worse, they were often given individual work cards when the class work was considered too hard for them; this meant the comparison of answers was impossible and they tended to do only a small percentage of the work set.

The system of star rewards for 'good work' had a first unintended consequence of reinforcing the collaborative system as well as the work itself. Indeed, on several occasions a complete sequence of negotiation was witnessed, from getting answers from friends to receiving star reinforcement from Mrs Rothwell.

A second consequence of this was that it contributed to the self-fulfilling elements in the internal stratification system of the class: Mrs Rothwell evaluated the work which the children produced and presented, and she consequently assessed that some children were not capable of good work, and should be on the bottom table, and perhaps do special work cards, whilst others produced good work and therefore should be on the top or middle table and could do class work. Those judged not capable thus continued to be sealed off from the hidden means of accomplishing the lessons, whilst those judged capable were enabled to produce overt evidence.

Overall, the collaboration system functioned efficiently as a means of producing the explicit responses required, for it enabled the majority of children to cope with the difficulties of a formal class-based lesson. I do not mean to suggest here that the children learned nothing in the lessons or that they necessarily entirely tricked the teacher; indeed, Mrs Rothwell specifically allowed quiet talking so that children could discuss their tasks. A second important point is that from Mrs Rothwell's point of view, she also accomplished these seat-work lessons satisfactorily in terms of her educational perspective and structural position. The children were kept busy on educational tasks which gave them the practice which she felt they needed and during this time there were no discipline problems. Mrs Rothwell was able to hear her readers, and at the end of the lessons their value was tangibly shown in neat rows of sums which in themselves legitimised her work. Thus the collaboration system rewarded the teacher, just as the teacher unwittingly reinforced the collaboration system. It was a stable process, with resources in the perspectives and common-sense knowledge of the participants which provided comprehensive schemes of internal legitimation. The classroom process, with its outcome of social differentiation, was a product of the mesh of the coping strategies of the participants. Although the teacher clearly initiated and continued to structure such process because of her power, the actions of the children significantly reinforced and 'multiplied' the social consequence of differentiation.

REFERENCES

Ball, S. (1980) 'Initial encounters in the classroom and the process of establishment', in P. Woods (ed.) *Pupil Strategies*, London: Croom Helm.

Becker, H.S. (1952) 'Social-class variations in the teacher–pupil relationship', *Journal of Educational Sociology*, 25: 451–65.

Bird, C. (1980) 'Deviant labelling in the school and the pupils' reaction', in P. Woods (ed.) *Pupil Strategies*, London: Croom Helm.

Denscombe, M. (1980) 'Pupil strategies and the open classroom', in P. Woods (ed.) *Pupil Strategies*, London: Croom Helm.

Hammersley, M. (1980) 'Classroom ethnography', *Educational Analysis*, 2(2).

Hargreaves, A. (1978) 'The significance of classroom coping strategies', in L. Barton and R. Meighan (eds) *Sociological Interpretations of Schooling and Classrooms*, Driffield: Nafferton.

Hargreaves, D. (1975) *Interpersonal Relationships and Education*, London: Routledge & Kegan Paul.

Kounin, J.S. (1970) *Discipline and Group Management in Classrooms*, New York: Holt, Rinehart & Winston.

Lemert, E. (1967) 'The concept of secondary deviation', in E. Lemert (ed.) *Human Deviance, Social Problems and Social Control*, New York: Prentice-Hall.

Matza, D. (1964) *Delinquency and Drift*, New York: Wiley.

Pollard, A. (1979) 'Negotiating deviance and "getting done" in primary school

classrooms', in L. Barton and R. Meighan (eds) *Schools, Pupils and Deviance*, Driffield: Nafferton.
—— (1980) 'Teacher interests and changing situations of survival threat in primary school classrooms', in P. Woods (ed.) *Teacher Strategies*, London: Croom Helm.
—— (1981) 'Coping with deviance: school processes and their implications for social reproduction', Unpublished PhD thesis, University of Sheffield.
—— (1982) 'A model of coping strategies', *British Journal of Sociology of Education*, 3: 19–37.
—— (1984) 'Goodies, jokers and gangs', in M. Hammersley and P. Woods (eds) *Life in Schools: the Sociology of Pupil Cultures*, Milton Keynes: Open University Press.
Rist, R.C. (1970) 'Student social class and teacher expectations: the self-fulfilling prophecy in ghetto education', *Harvard Education Review*, 40: 411–51.
Rosenthal, R. and Jacobson, L. (1968) *Pygmalion in the Classroom*, London: Holt, Rinehart & Winston.
Sharp, R. and Green, A.G. (1976) *Education and Social Control*, London: Routledge & Kegan Paul.
Woods, P. (1977) 'Teaching for survival', in P. Woods and M. Hammersley (eds) *School Experience*, London: Croom Helm.

Chapter 21

Making sense of reading

Colin Mills

The last chapters began to draw out the importance of social processes in the classroom. The next extract continues this theme, and also links back to illustrate Neil Mercer's chapter (Chapter 7) on the role of educational practices in moulding what it is children come to know. In this extract, Colin Mills looks at 'learning to read' as 'learning a culture'. He explores the social interactions through which one child is drawn into stories which link his personal life to books. The extract is also useful as a model for beginning teachers of one approach to the observation and analysis of 'reading' in the classroom.

In my work as a trainer of teachers I often take students into classrooms, where they observe and talk to young children learning to read, and to their teachers helping them to do that. I like to think that these observations help them to know and to understand some of the ways in which teachers and children live and work together in classrooms, creating and sustaining the activities, situations, episodes and routines that make up literacy lessons. Back in college they will read books, go to lectures and take part in seminars that will put them in touch with current theories and ideas about the development of literacy. But during the time in school I ask them to tell me about the things they have seen. What they say is often novel and insightful. They ask searching questions about the books in the classroom, and ways in which teachers organise their time, the diverse modes in which different children enter into, and participate in, the social activities that enfold reading and writing.

As their tutor I am often confronted with the fact that, although I have spent my working life in and out of such classrooms, there are things that I do not see, or take for granted, as a result of my over-familiarity. For the students there is enough that is recognisable in the classroom scenes they look at to enable them to make sense of them. It is not so long since they were young children: they often show surprise at seeing the same books with which they think they learned to read. Yet what heightens the novelty of the processes they see is that they are thinking and orientating themselves into a new role, that of a teacher. They seem to read the 'culture' that is an infant school classroom and to begin defining their understandings with an acuteness of purpose. Learning a culture, learning a role, is what the students share with the children.

STORIES

Some stories from my observations in Miss E.'s classroom reveal some of the social practices, the complex real processes, which are *constitutive* of modes of looking, talking and thinking that are central to literacy. They are stories which seek to keep the narrative flow, the sense of what happened. In trying to explore, in a vague and hazy way at first, the connections between social practice and literacy, the ways in which children were becoming readers within the context of a bustling and lively classroom, I looked and listened carefully to all aspects of life in the classroom. Routines, conversations, early number work, PE lessons were observed and participated in, as well as storytelling sessions, times when children were reading with one another, and with their teachers.

One day, quite early on in my time in the classroom, the children were gathered around Miss E., who was getting them ready to go home at the end of the day. I had switched off my tape-recorder and put away my notebook. At that time there were 45 children, aged from 'rising 5' to 7 years, the whole of the school's infant department. Nine of the children had been in school for just three weeks. They had started at the beginning of the spring term, when I had begun my work. I was tending to focus my attention upon them for some part of each day, watching for the ways in which they were being socialised into reading and writing. I had already grown quite accustomed to these routines at the end of the day. It was often the time at which the many activities of the day were discussed, mulled over: stories written, models made, paintings done, books read. I tended to use the time, not as a vigilant observer, but as a chance to read my field notes, wind back my tape-recorder, and go through any ideas I wanted to talk through with Miss E. or Mrs R. after the children and left. This day my attention was brought to the session in a sharp and particular way when Miss E. produced a large brown cardboard box, and held it up in front of the assembled children.

1 MISS E: In this box, there's something we've been waiting for for a long, long time: can anyone guess?

There then followed a series of exchanges in which the children, mostly the older ones in the class, gave the names of animals.

2 ROBERT: A bear, Miss E.
3 MARTIN: No . . . er . . . a giraffe (*laughter from older children*)
4 LUCY: A hamster.

Throughout these exchanges, Miss E. showed mock-surprise and exasperation. At one point, she said:

5 MISS E.:   I think you're thinking of *One Hunter*, aren't you?

This referred to a picture book recently read with the older children, Pat Hutchins' *One Hunter*, where varied animals are hidden in a jungle setting, well camouflaged. Then:

6 DAVID:.   Maybe it's Robert's hamster.

Recently Robert's mother had brought a pet hamster into school. The children had observed it, played with it, drawn it. A class book had then been planned and written together, *Harry the Hamster Goes to School*.

7 MISS E.:   No, good boy for remembering. Harry was in a box like this, wasn't he? But if it was Robert's hamster, I think we'd hear a noise like sssss . . . beginning with ssss. What's a word, beginning with sss?
8 MELANIE: Scratching . . .
9 MISS E.:   Yes, good girl, scratching. (*Miss E. looks in mock-surprise, holding the box up to her ear.*) I don't think I can hear that noise, can I?

I noticed throughout these exchanges that the nine new children in the class sat throughout, looking and listening to the responses and actions of the older children.

One little boy, in particular, caught my eye: Dilwyn (5.1), a small, rather reserved boy whom I had been observing a lot over the weeks since we had both been new to the classroom. In earlier episodes I had seen him looking over at the book corner where the older children read books together, and talked openly and freely about the books there. The morning of the day that the 'box' had arrived had been something of a milestone in that I had watched Dilwyn look over at the corner with interest. One of the other 'new' children, Amy (5.2), had ventured over for the first time (Miss E. later told me) to join her sister, Anna (7.2), one of the older children in the class. Dilwyn slowly followed after Amy, and, after looking at some picture books, sat in between Amy and Anna, who read aloud to both younger children.

In a long episode a few days earlier I had made notes of how Dilwyn had watched carefully and learned to participate in the process of asking one of the teachers, or one of the parent helpers in the classroom, for a word that he wanted to spell. Now this 'box' episode could be providing Dilwyn with a model of the guessing, play with words, linking of reading experience to real-life experiences, that constituted 'being a pupil' in Miss E.'s class (Willes 1983). After another series of exchanges, in which various uses for the box were proposed and talked about, Miss E. opened the box and pulled out some polystyrene blocks that were used as packing:

10 MISS E.:   (*looking at blocks*) Aren't we lucky? But I still can't see what's inside. . . . (*pause*) Oh no. . . .

11 ⌈ROBERT: I can't stand this. . . .
12 ⌊DAVID:

13 MISS E.:   (*laughing*) No, I don't think I can either.

The refrain 'Oh no, I can't stand this' is one that I had often heard during my first days in the classroom, sometimes from Miss E., sometimes from some of the older children. At times, such as in this exchange, it was a joint cry! Finding out where it came from was one of the 'rites of passage' I had to go through to be a member of the class. It was a repeated chant in a story shared by Miss E. with the class many times, Jill Murphy's picture book *Whatever Next!*

Sustaining the air of mystery, secrecy, suspense and surprise, Miss E. pulled out of the box a blue BBC hymn book:

14 LISA: Ah . . . the hymn books.
        (*General movement and jostling to see the book Miss E. holds.*)

15 MISS E.:   Yes, that's right, Lisa, the hymn books. Now, the newcomers won't know about these will they?

16 VARIOUS
   VOICES: No. . . .

17 MISS E.:   Would one of you big children like to explain
        (*Hands raised, jostling*)

18 MISS E.:   Yes, Stephen, yes. . . .

19 STEPHEN: Miss E. . . . er . . . you sent for these, we sent for these before.

20 ALEX: We use them, sing from them on the radio.

21 MISS E.:   Yes, these are the song books that we sometimes sing with, from. Not just on the radio, Kelly, Dilwyn, but in assembly sometimes – when we all go in the hall with Mr J. and the juniors. Now, some of these big children said they'd like to buy one. Who can remember saying they wanted one?

22 SOPHIE: Ordering one. . . .

23 MISS E.:   Yes, Sophie, ordering one. That's a good word, Sophie. Some of you ordered one. Who can remember, I wonder?

Social action was accompanying the words we listened to. At the stage at which we left it, some of the children confidently put up their hands. Some wavered, raising and lowering their hands. Of the group of nine young children, the 'newcomers', nobody raised their hand at this point. Dilwyn looked rather puzzled by the whole business. Amy, the little girl who earlier in the day had followed her elder sister, Anna, over to the book corner, turned round and whispered something to her elder sibling. She then turned round to face Miss E., looking much more confident. Anna was one of the children who held up her hand with certainty. Amy then whispered to the girl who was sitting next to her, who happened to be Mrs R.'s daughter, Katie (5.0). Katie then looked around to the set of lockers at the side of the room, to where her mother tended to sit if Miss E. was talking to the whole class. Her mother wasn't there – I was, with my notebook and tape-recorder. Mrs R. was in an adjoining small resource room, preparing some children's art work for display.

Miss E. then went through a slow process of counting the books out of the box, encouraging the children to join with her. The counting took on the form of a ritual chant. There were 24 books in all, and she again counted the hands of the children who said that they had definitely wanted one. The total number of children who said they wanted one was 18, although there were some waverers and floating voters! Significantly, at this stage Amy put up her hand. Miss E. continued:

24 MISS E.:	I'm afraid I've got some very bad news, children.
25 MICHAEL:	You can't have one! (*shouting*)
26 MISS E.:	Erm . . . Michael. You don't always have to say something silly. (*Lightening tone, smiling*) I wouldn't play a trick like that, would I, Stephen?
27 STEPHEN:	Yes, Miss E.
	(*Laughter from class, and mock indignation from Miss E.*)
28 MISS E.:	No, the news is that I'm afraid they've gone up from 50p to 75p.
	(*Some bustle, and confusion*)
29 MISS E.:	I mean, when we ordered the books, quite a long time ago. . . .
30 DARREN:	A long, *long* time ago.
31 MISS E.:	Yes it was a long, long time ago. Well, I told you they were 50p. Well now they've come, I'm afraid the price has gone up to 75p. Now, who doesn't want one?

At this stage there was considerable confusion and bustle amongst the children, and I focused again upon the younger children, the newcomers, who tended to sit together, near the front of a large arc which formed when all the children sat around the area of the classroom reserved for this kind of communal gathering. Of the nine new children, four put up their hands, with a quiet certainty, when asked, 'Now who doesn't want one?' One, a boy, Kevin (5.4), looked very confused and a little anxious. Four who were grouped together – Mrs R.'s daughter, Kelly, Amy, Anna's younger sister, Catherine (4.8) and Dilwyn – looked at one another, behind them at the older children, at Miss E. Dilwyn, once or twice, looked at me at the side of the room. Katie looked once over to the resource room, where she'd guessed her mother would be. Miss E. continued:

32 MISS E.:	If you want one, and Mummy says you can have one, can you bring in. . . .
33 GARETH:	Seventy-five pennies. . . .
34 MISS E.:	Yes, good boy. Bring in seventy-five *pence*. You don't have to have one, though.

I sensed at this stage that Miss E. was getting rather agitated, unusually so for her. It was getting near to home time (3.15), and I guessed that she thought that many of the children, especially the younger ones, were unsure as to what she wanted to communicate in the message home. Mrs R. entered the main classroom at this stage. Miss E. turned and voiced her concern to her colleague:

35 MISS E.	(to Mrs R.): I don't want them all going and demanding the money.
36 MRS R.:	No. . . .
37 MISS E.:	Now you mustn't go out today and say . . . (*silence*) say . . . what. . . .
38 STEPHEN:	Mummy, mummy, can I have a hymn book. . . .
39 MISS E.:	Well, yes . . . but I don't want you to say. . . . (*short silence*)
40 ROBIN:	Can I have a hymn book?
41 MISS E.:	No, oh dear. When you go out of school, after school today. When you run out of the gate, what doesn't Miss E. want you to say. . . .
42 ELLIE:	Mummy, mummy I *must* have a hymn book.
43 MISS E.:	That's right, you lovely girl. When you go out, Miss E. doesn't want you to say, 'Mummy, Mummy, I *must* have a hymn book.' Do you little ones understand that? (*Miss E. focuses upon young 'newcomers', and there is general nodding and agreement.*)
44 MISS E.:	When you go out, and when you're telling your mummies about the hymn books, Miss E. doesn't want you to say 'I . . . I . . .'
45 KATIE:	I must have a hymn book.
46 MICHAEL:	Her Mummy's here! (*Giggling from children*)
47 MRS R.:	Yes, I'm here, Michael.
48 MISS E.:	Yes, Michael, Katie's Mummy is here. But lots of mummies aren't here – and I just didn't want your mummies to think that you've . . . Dilwyn
49 DILWYN	(*speaking for the first time*): Got to have a hymn book.
50 MISS E.:	Good boy. But if you want one. . . .
51 DILWYN:	I can . . . I can . . . bring some money.

52 AMY: 75p.
53 DILWYN: Tomorrow. . . .

READING THE STORY: SEEKING MEANINGS

On first listening, and upon subsequent examination of field notes made during the early weeks in Miss E.'s classroom, such events meant little to me. I was rather exclusively concentrating on 'literacy-related events': reading, writing and social activities related to them. I was, after all, in this classroom, one I knew of as a place where children learned to read successfully, to explore what I hazily posited as 'the social context of literacy'. The episode of the hymn books only began to make sense and to shape into an idea that became significant to me when read alongside other such episodes, narratives lifted from the daily patterns that all teachers will readily recognise.

For a long time I viewed such an episode as one concerned with control and with the communication of information – and there is a sense in which Miss E.'s talk here is shaping the children's talk into acceptable patterns. She is socialising them into such aspects of classroom life as turn-taking, appropriateness and explicitness. She singles out, gently but in a no-nonsense fashion, the 'clown' in this episode, Michael, an older boy (7.1) who was often singled out for similar comment. But beyond the surface linguistic structure of the episode there are meanings, patterns being developed and sustained, and some of these are central to literacy.

One important feature of the episode is that the text as a whole, the set of exchanges between teacher and children, is in fact a narrative, a slowly unfolded 'story' of the hymn books' arrival in the classroom. It is not linear, but it is constructed by the participants in its telling. Miss E. perhaps plays a major role. But it is *created*, made, in the classroom as they talk together. There is nothing surprising in the fact that Miss E.'s and the children's classroom discourse can be read as a 'story'. The story or narrative form has long been acknowledged as 'a primary act of mind' (Hardy 1968). Providing the scaffolding for children so that experience and social action can be intermeshed through talk is the prime way in which children are helped to become 'meaning makers' (Wells 1987: 195).

The particular status I want to claim for such classroom talk relates to the personal learning I experienced during my early days' observation in the classroom, and the ways in which I came to listen to and value such interaction. What the teachers seemed to be doing for a great deal of the time was shaping the children's experiences into narratives. Out-of-school experiences were patterned, celebrated and evaluated – as stories to be shared. 'News time' and 'sharing time' were useful sites for the analysis of the ways in which teachers and children (and often children and children) collaboratively constructed narratives out of daily experience and social action. These stories enfolded pathos, drama, expectation, climax, and were often woven together by experiences, commentaries upon those experiences, local and tacit knowledge and the relationships, developed and emergent, between Miss E., Mrs R., and children and their parents.

This episode shows that through such classroom discourse, private meanings and personal experience are made public and shared. In Miss E.'s acceptance of the children's ideas (2–4; 7–9) there is a publicising of the notion that such speculation, such bridging of real-life and story experience is a normal feature of social practice.

LEARNING TO READ AS A SOCIAL PROCESS

Much of my time in the classroom was spent observing 'story' sessions, and I will now select two different kinds of event to illustrate the modes of looking and interpretation I want to encourage. The first event is a piece of collaborative reading. There was a vast range of books in Miss E.'s classroom: wordless books, picture books, good modern re-tellings of classic stories, 'bridging' books with less reliance upon pictures, more upon texts. Children looked at books whenever they wanted to, meeting in the book area, sharing and talking about their reading.

The episode I want to look at again involves Dilwyn and Amy, whom we met earlier. They were 5.4 and 5.5 respectively, no longer 'newcomers'. The other child involved was Steven, a lively and ebullient boy of 6.10. This episode took place towards the end of a busy Tuesday morning. The notes from my 'field' book were as follows:

11.36   Notice S. in the reading corner alone and note title of book, *Not Now Bernard*, by David McKee, one I have heard both Miss E. and Mrs R. read to the class, though not lately. S. is reading silently, yet 'voicing' the text. Smiling and obviously enjoying the book – sprawled on one of the huge cushions in book area. Children are milling all around him, but he seems oblivious.

11.40   S. is joined by D., who perches on the side of the cushion with him. S. goes back to beginning, and I hear him say in a loud voice, as if now sharing the reading with D. 'Not now Bernard' . . .

11.43   Two boys looking at book, S. reading to D. Go over and put the tape unobtrusively near to them.

11.46   Two boys joined by A., who first stands in front of them, then sits herself on the floor facing the two boys.

11.50   Three still intent on book, taking turns: much switching of roles voices.

This is the bare 'action' of an episode taking 18 minutes and involving three children. The transcript of my *Not Now Bernard* tapes spreads over many pages. The following short extract is from near the beginning, when Steven started reading to Dilwyn and they were joined by Amy:

Printed text		Children's speech
	S.:	I'm gonna read this again.
	D.:	Can I look?
	S.:	Yeah.
Hello Dad, said Bernard.	S.:	Hello Dad, said Bernard. He's the boy (points) in the book. (looking at picture)
	S.:	Eike! He's hit his finger.
	D.:	Who's he? His Daddy?
Not now, Bernard, said his father.	S.:	Not now, said Dad.

The younger child invites himself into the reading. S. begins to read, pausing after the first page, to look at the picture on page 2, where Bernard's father, disturbed by the child, hits his finger. S. explains to D. that Bernard is the boy 'in the book'. He also recounts to D. what is happening, pointing at the picture, and directing the younger child's attention to it. S. accepts, and answers D.'s question: 'Who's he?' by reference to the text, changing 'his father' in the text to 'his Daddy'.

Printed text		Children's speech
	S.:	(banging floor) Ouch, my finger.
	D.:	Ow.
	S.:	(turning page) This is his Mum.
Hello Mum, said Bernard.	S.:	Hello Mum.
	D.:	(points at words) said Bernard.
Not now Bernard, said his Mother.	S.:	Not now Bernard, said his
	D.:	mother. (background noise)
	A.:	said his Mother.

From the tape it seems that Steven bangs the floor or the cushion with his hand and says, 'Ouch, my finger!' Dilwyn's 'Ow' seems to be a play-acting 'Ow', rather than an authentic one – a dramatisation of the story. Steven again explains on turning the page: 'This is his Mum.' Notice how Dilwyn joins in the reading with Steven on 'said Bernard'. They chant, song-like, and much more loudly, the second refrain, 'Not now, Bernard, said his mother.' Towards the end of the extract Amy joins in. She is an extrovert child, more confident than Dilwyn.

Printed text		Children's speech
There's a monster in the garden and it's going to eat me.	S.:	There's a monster and it's going to eat me.
	A.:	In the garden.
	S.:	We know that.
Not now Bernard, said his mother.	A.:	There isn't really

D.: Eh?

A.: It's not really a monster, I've had this with my . . . with my . . . with Mrs R.

S.: Don't spoil it.

D.: (*pointing*) Not now. . . . Not now Bernard.

S.: Said his mother.

D.: Said his mother.

A.: It's not.

S.: It is (*rapidly turning pages*) Look! (*pointing to monster*)

D.: Ouch!

The monster hit Bernard's father.

S.: See! There's the monster. He bites his Dad.

A.: And he broke all his toys and read his comics.

D.: Turn it back.

S.: Where?

D.: 'There's a monster in the garden' page.

Amy begins to take on the reading from the older Steven here. The reader must take it on trust from me that both Amy and Steven tell the story in the same chant-like way, catching the rising and falling, the tune of the text that I had heard from Miss E. and Mrs R. many times. Steven omits 'in the garden' and Amy adds it. 'We know that', says Steven, perhaps indicating that that is an explicit statement of their shared knowledge. Amy says that there is not really a monster, seeming to base that on previous readings. She *may* have a sophisticated reading of the story that she is sharing. The joke at the centre of the book is that Bernard's parents do not recognise the monster as such, even after he has eaten Bernard! Steven rapidly turns the pages of the book to prove that, on a literal level at least, there *is* a monster. Amy projects to a later episode, where the monster will break all Bernard's toys and reads his comics. Dilwyn wants to go back to the stage in the story they were at before the 'monster' discussion. He remembers the point they were at, and seems to want to take control of the reading, to find out what happens next.

What we see here is a piece of collaborative interpretation. Dilwyn, the younger child, has the opportunity to invite himself into a storytelling with an older boy. The older boy is using modes of interpretation and understanding employed by the teachers (the rising and falling of voices and dramatisation). The boys, together, make sense of both text and pictures. Dilwyn, listening to Amy and Steven, learns that there may be multiple readings of the text (is the monster real, or not?). All this happens within a supportive context: the children pace the reading, and take control of the operation.

There are similarities with the way in which the story of the hymn books was unfolded earlier in Dilwyn's school career. There, a text had to be co-created by teacher and children. Sense had to be made of a situation, a story had to be constructed, meanings had to be shared and sometimes argued over. In both situations children draw upon modes of understanding, pragmatic competences and codes of interpretation. When Dilwyn reads *Not Now Bernard* with two more confident and experienced children, he is able to hear the traffic of interpretation that goes on in deriving meaning from a text. The operation is a joint one, learned socially by the older boy in story-reading sessions, and in other such child–child encounters. The discourse that we need to describe and communicate such processes may be different from the traditional ways in which we have talked about reading.

READING AS INTERPRETATIVE PROCESS

Lastly, and briefly, I move on in time to a year or so later. Dilwyn, the younger child in the above two examples, is now 6.6. He has read scores of books, and heard hundreds of stories read aloud in story sessions. I spent a lot of time reading with Dilwyn, one of the 'newcomers', when I was new to the class. During the time at which the next episode was recorded I was tending to spend time each week with Dilwyn and some of his peers reading and talking. He is now inches taller and more confident and worldly-wise. At the time he was very much enjoying the books of Allan and Janet Ahlberg, a husband-and-wife author-artist team. This extract comes from his reading of *Cops and Robbers*, one of the first books he read independently. For clarity I have not included the *actual* text, but Dilwyn's reading of it, which varies slightly here and there. I have transcribed our conversation and my commentary, the format I adopted during these individual sessions.

Reading	*Commentary*	*Speech*
	D. begins by looking at first page of book which shows busy police station in cartoon-type pictures. Bustling activity and humorous-looking characters.	
		D.: Look at this. This looks funny.
		CM.: Yes.
		D.: Look at the dog. I wonder. . . . Cops and

Reading	*Commentary*	*Speech*
		Robbers. Where are the . . .?
		CM.:Shall we read?
Here are the cops of London town, Hard working, brave and true.		
They drink their tea.	Looks at picture.	D.: Who's drinking tea? He's making tea. Let's look.
Stay up till three.		D.: Does that mean three in the night.
		CM.:I expect so
		D.: They work at all night. We saw on a programme about a . . . a police station place. They opened all the night.
		CM.:Wonder why?
		D.: 'Cos robbers work at night . . . people lose things and smash things up. I've got a police car (*noise of car*).
	Goes back to text.	
Stay . . . stay up till three. And take good care of you.		

We go on, taking time. Dilwyn tends to move between pictures, text and comments and questions about the story. We reach the page where all the robbers are introduced. Janet Ahlberg's lovely pictures are framed, like 'mugshots', showing Grabber Dan, Snatcher Jack, and so on.

Reading	*Commentary*	*Speech*
	When we reach this page, D. spends a long time poring over the pictures.	
		D.: Grabber Dan . . . Snatch . . . Snatcher Jack . . . Billy the Boy (*laughter*). What a

Reading	Commentary	Speech
		funny name. Peg Leg House . . . no Ho. . . . What's that name?
		CM.:Horace.
		D.: Peg Leg Horace. I wonder what that means. Do you know?
		CM.:Perhaps it means he's only got one leg.
		D.: Fingers M. . . .
		CM.:Maurice, Fingers Maurice.
		D.: Fingers Maurice. . . . (*pause*) I know why he's called Fingers.
		CM.:Why?
		D.: 'Cos he steals.
		CM.:How do you know?
		D.: Don't know. Grandma Swagg (*laughs*) Grandma Swagg. She doesn't look like a burglar.
		CM.:Doesn't she?
		D.: No, she looks like a lovely old Grannie. (*mock gentility voice*) Doesn't she?
	Goes on to next page.	CM.:Yes, she does.

The extract had lots of pauses and extraneous giggles. Dilwyn looked at the pictures, at the words, and at me to 'gauge' my reading and understanding. He was bringing those same interpretative processes that he was beginning to employ when he read the book with the older children, that he was using when he listened to the story of the hymn books.

Dilwyn uses devices in his interpretation of messages, representations, pictures and symbols. When he perceives that Grandma Swagg is not just a kind old grannie but a robber, he is understanding a joke that is at the centre of the book: things are not what they seem. It is hard to interpret and enjoy that story if you don't comprehend that early on. They look respectable, some of them – but they are robbers. How has he learned to do that? Partly, but not wholly perhaps, from the talk around stories and books that has gone on in Miss E.'s class. Remeber the guessing game about the contents of the box of hymn books – could there really be animals in there? Understanding what is not said is the root of the humour of many popular picture books for young children. As in conversation, secrets are shared, not spoken.

At the beginning of the episode he pores over the pictures, something his teachers have often done when reading a new text. I remember a whole half-hour discussion led by Miss E. looking at the 'map' of the story at the front of another of the Ahlbergs' books, *Each Peach, Pear, Plum*. He asks me for confirmation in his interpretations; he uses his common sense and his cultural knowledge. I do not want to make large claims for this piece of text. I am more concerned to encourage others to look closely at what has been too long overlooked in our collection of 'evidence' about reading. When children read their first independent texts, they not only bring linguistic resources, they bring social and cultural understandings. They bring understandings of other texts, codes of interpretation learned from their 'reading' of popular culture. They bring the 'stances' of wonder, interpretation and evaluation that they have learned from their teachers and from other co-readers ('Isn't that funny?', 'I wonder what?'). They use also those shared processes of sense-making which they have learned socially.

READERS, TEXTS AND CONTEXTS

Many literary critics have recognised the interlocking of literary and every-day forms of understanding. Studies of literacy and literature which have taken social action into account have built up a particularly strong case for literary conventions as related to broader social processes. Indeed, I am borrowing from varied unacknowledged sources in journeying to a tentative proposal. That is, that we account for those interpretative, social processes in our *discourse* about reading. My major debt is to Vygotsky, significantly both a psychologist and a literary critic. In *Mind in Society* (1978) he worked towards a comprehensive account that would make possible rich description of the origins of higher mental processes. He urged, first, 'specification of the context in which the behaviour developed' (p. 6) and 'speculative reflection on cultural forms of behaviour . . . tracing the qualitative changes [in behaviour] occurring in the course of development' (p. 7).

When children are learning to become readers, they are transforming sign-using activity. External activities are being reconstructed and beginning to occur internally. Dilwyn is beginning to do, independently, with the help of a skilled author and artist, the things he has learned to do with his classmates (look at what's shown for clues about what might be) and with his teachers (construct stories from looking and interpreting what he sees). In Vygotsky's terms an interpersonal process is becoming an intrapersonal one. We still need 'a reasoned theory of how the negotiation of meaning as socially arrived at is to be interpreted as a pedagogical axiom' (Bruner 1986:

124). This chapter indicates some of the ways in which reading is 'socially arrived at' through social processes, and social practice, within classroom life.

How can we encourage the next generation of teachers, who started *my* story, to look at these social processes? What kinds of questions could they ask? They could begin by examining the discourse teachers, parents and children use to talk about reading. Where does it come from? Is it describing or constraining what's being seen or done? We could ask students to discern whether or not social relations in the classroom are conducive to the exploration that reading entails. Are children given the time and space to make sense of reading and to make their own interpretations? Reading requires children to make sense, explore possible worlds, invent, sort out what is not said. Real, lively texts connect all that with the polyphonic and diverse social interaction that goes on in lively infant school classrooms ('Oh no, I can't stand it!'). It is the living mix of varied voices that links literacy, literature and talk with social practice. Reading changes for each generation of learners and teachers. Approaches change, aspirations change. Our way of looking at it and talking about it needs to change to take into account new readers, new texts and the contexts in which they will all interact with one another.

REFERENCES

Bruner, J.S. (1986) *Actual Minds, Possible Worlds*, Cambridge, MA: Harvard University Press.

Hardy, B. (1968) 'Towards a poetics of fiction: an approach through narrative', in *Novel: a Forum on Fiction*, Providence, RI: Brown University.

Vygotsky, L.S. (1978) *Mind in Society: the Development of Higher Psychological Processes*, Cambridge, MA: Harvard University Press.

Wells, G. (1987) *The Meaning Makers*, London: Hodder & Stoughton.

Willes, M. (1983) *Children into Pupils*, London: Routledge & Kegan Paul.

Part VI

Pupils' perceptions of primary practice

Chapter 22

How to be a 'good pupil'

Perceptions of boys and girls in primary school science classes

Clayton MacKenzie

This final part of the book focuses on pupil perceptions of primary practice. This chapter examines how children think of themselves as learners. Clayton MacKenzie asked a number of 10-year-olds what they thought made a 'good science pupil', and offered them a range of options as answers in a questionnaire. He found clear differences in the views of boys and girls, and discusses the implications for children's achievement. The chapter, therefore, connects usefully with Patricia Murphy's discussion of assessment and gender in Chapter 16, and with the chapters on the construction of 'ability' and pupil differentiation. The chapter also provides a useful model for beginning teachers of small-scale questionnaire research methods.

In recent years there have been some careful and intriguing studies of teaching styles and their effects on learners (Hacker and Carter 1987; Cullingford 1987; Hazelwood *et al.* 1988). Some such work has accorded particular importance to an exploration of the relation between teaching and learning, and gender issue (Bayliss 1988; Craig and Ayres 1988; Burgess 1989). Notably, Jan Craig and David Ayres have studied what they term 'girl-friendly' and 'boy-friendly' teaching styles, drawing up a checklist of the kinds of qualities that male and female pupils like with regard to their teachers. A number of researchers have looked specifically at gender issues in science lessons (Robertson 1987; Johnson 1987; Kelly 1988; Pickersgill 1989). The work has shed valuable light on the kinds of prejudices and perceptions that operate in our own and other education systems. This is an important area of investigation, particularly as the implementation of the National Curriculum in England and Wales, for a variety of reasons, has brought science in the primary school under closer scrutiny than has been the case in the past.

In many studies of gender and science, the research focuses on determining pupils' perceptions of and responses to differing teaching styles. This, of course, is a perfectly valid research approach and can comment usefully on teaching practices and processes. However, if we are going to ask pupils questions, it seems to me equally valuable to ask them questions about themselves and about their perceptions of other pupils. Several recent studies have accorded particular importance to this approach to gender studies in the science classroom. Alison Kelly (1988) has provided us with an excellent study of varying gender reactions to science lessons. My own work has focused on issues of pupilage. What do pupils consider constitutes 'good pupilage'? What would be their pupil role model? My research approach has been one which has sought to question pupils directly on their experiences and perceptions. The project, instigated during the 1989–90 teaching year, involved a study of science pupils in three primary schools, two in Inner London and the third in Kent.

METHODOLOGY

A total of 60 10-year-old pupils, drawn from three schools, were questioned during the survey. There was an equal number of boys and girls. All the pupils questioned were studying science as part of their school curriculum, and the questions asked related to them as 'science pupils'. A 24-item, self-report inventory was used, and related to a single basic question: 'What do you think makes a good science pupil?' Pupils were asked to complete a sentence beginning, 'I think a good science pupil . . .' by selecting the five completions that they deemed to be most valid to the basic question.

No discussion of issues was permitted prior to the survey, but the nature of the task was explained carefully and consistently to the groups, and the researcher read through the questionnaire with the children who were invited to ask any questions of clarification. The pupils were then allowed a 30-minute period to make their selections. It was made clear to pupils from the outset that they should not put their names on the questionnaires, but that they should indicate (by ticking the appropriate box) whether they were male or female. Pupils were allowed to complete the questionnaire without interference from teachers, the researcher or other pupils. The intention was to secure complete anonymity and privacy of response.

The 24 items in the inventory were placed in random order, and were not identified by numerical or spatial groupings. For the purposes of the present study, the questionnaire indicated in Table 22.1 has been grouped under sub-categorical headings, and selection items have been accorded a number for convenience of reference. The list was not intended to be exhaustive but covered a range of areas and issues of interest to the researcher. The sub-categories identified are: aptitude for science; factors outside school; science classroom learning interaction; and discipline. Six completion item phrases related to each of the four sub-categories.

Table 22.1 Good science pupil questionnaire

Pupils were asked to tick the five sentence completions that they thought were most desirable. The broad sub-titles, shown in italics (below), were not included in the questionnaire, and questions were placed in random order, without any indication of sub-division or spatial gaps. Pupils were told not to write their names on the papers, and were asked only to indicate whether they were male or female.

Basic question: What do you think makes a good science pupil?
  I think a good science pupil . . .

(*Aptitude for science*)
(1)   is clever at science;
(2)   wants to be clever at science;
(3)   tries hard in science;
(4)   wants to find out about things;
(5)   is usually a boy;
(6)   is usually a girl.

(*Factors outside school*)
(7)   has extra lessons in science;
(8)   has parents who help him/her;
(9)   reads science books at home;
(10) watches science programmes on television;
(11) does science experiments at home;
(12) gets help from an older brother or sister.

(*Science classroom learning interaction*)
(13) asks the teacher lots of questions;
(14) usually sits at the front of the class;
(15) helps other pupils in science lessons;
(16) finds things out for herself or himself;
(17) doesn't usually ask questions during science lessons;
(18) gets on well with the science teacher.

(*Discipline*)
(19) always does her/his homework;
(20) does not chatter with his/her friends;
(21) pays attention to the teacher;
(22) doesn't like pupils who behave badly in science lessons;
(23) is never late for science lessons;
(24) does not do things behind the teacher's back.

FINDINGS

The questionnaire was issued for completion to 30 boys and 30 girls. This therefore offered a potential of 300 responses, each pupil having been asked to identify five choices. Since anonymity had been guaranteed, questionnaires were not checked while pupils were completing them. Subsequent inspections revealed that five questionnaires (three boys and two girls) were incomplete or invalidated in some way. In order to equalise factors relating

Table 22.2 Responses to the good science pupil questionnaire

Items 1–6 (Aptitude for science)

Item	1	2	3	4	5	6	Totals
Boys	12	9	9	7	2	0	39
Girls	23	4	9	2	6	0	44
Totals	35	13	18	9	8	0	83

Items 7–12 (Factors outside school)

Item	7	8	9	10	11	12	Totals
Boys	3	7	14	6	5	6	41
Girls	5	8	4	0	0	9	26
Totals	8	15	18	6	5	15	67

Items 13–18 (Science classroom interaction)

Item	13	14	15	16	17	18	Totals
Boys	12	0	2	6	0	15	35
Girls	11	4	5	2	0	12	34
Totals	23	4	7	8	0	27	69

Items 19–24 (Discipline)

Item	19	20	21	22	23	24	Totals
Boys	6	3	8	2	0	1	20
Girls	12	9	9	1	0	0	31
Totals	18	12	17	3	0	1	51

to the analysis of findings, one questionnaire completed by a girl was removed at random from the batch of valid questionnaires. This effectively reduced the study groups to 27 boys and 27 girls, offering a total of 270 responses. The results are shown in Table 22.2.

The research suggests that the 10-year-olds interviewed considered aptitude for science as being of greatest importance in determining the nature of the good science pupil. In this respect, Item 1 was the most frequently selected option, chosen by 64.8 per cent of all the pupils surveyed; and the popularity of Items 2 and 3 suggests a concern with the need for a positive attitude towards the study of science. Factors outside school were accorded notable significance by pupils. Interestingly, over 14 per cent of the total number of responses identified the help of a person or persons outside the school (Items 7, 8 and 12) as being a significant factor in the make-up of a good science pupil. Pupils also revealed greater faith in the reading of science books at home than in watching science programmes on television.

Items relating to work interaction in the science classroom revealed considerable selection discrepancies. Helping other pupils (Item 5) was not deemed to be a priority quality of the good science pupil. On the other hand, asking the teacher lots of questions (Item 13) and getting on well with him or her (Item 18) were viewed with much greater enthusiasm – the two options securing the vote of 42.5 per cent and 50 per cent respectively, of all pupils

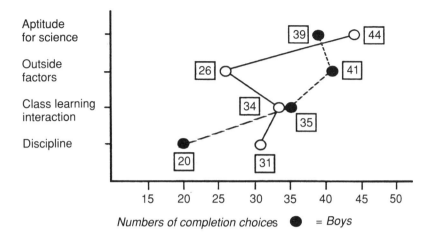

Figure 22.1 What makes a good science pupil? Differences in response between girls and boys

surveyed. The items in the discipline sub-category were, generally speaking, the least favoured group. While paying attention to the teacher and/or always doing homework (Items 19 and 21) drew strong interest from the selectors, chattering with friends (Item 20) or doing things behind the teacher's back (Item 24) were not seen as particularly heinous failings for a good science pupil.

From a gender point of view, a number of significant observations may be drawn from the results indicated in Table 22.2 above. These I shall identify in terms of the sub-category headings.

(1) *Aptitude for science.* One of the most striking features of the questionnaire relates to Item 1. While less than half the boys surveyed identified being 'clever at science' as a quality of the good science pupil, all but four of the girls in the survey sample (or 88.9 per cent) nominated this as one of their top five options. Boys and girls were mutually supportive of this notion of positive attitudes towards the learning of science (Items 2 and 3) but boys were more impressed with 'discovery' science learning (Item 4) than girls. Intriguingly, while anecdotal evidence might have suggested that gender stereotyping would have revealed itself in responses to Items 5 and 6, this was not entirely so. Only two boys regarded male gender as a prominent characteristic of the good science pupil; but almost one girl in four considered this to be the case. Overall, less than 15 per cent of all pupils regarded gender as a priority factor in determining a good science pupil.

(2) *Factors outside school.* As Figure 22.1 indicates, it was on the issue of outside factors that boys and girls had their widest sub-categorical differences. Individual item responses indicate substantial discrepancies in the

significance accorded to the reading of science books at home; the watching of the science programmes on television; and science experimentation at home. Only 14.8 per cent of girls thought that the reading of science books at home (Item 9) was the hallmark of a good science pupil, while 42.4 per cent of boys considered this a priority quality. The low number of pupils opting for television science programmes (Item 10) is perhaps surprising, and it is notable that not a single girl in the sample considered this to be a top five quality of the good science pupil. Boys and girls in the survey were generally similar in the rating of outside help (Items 7, 8 and 12).

(3) *Science classroom learning interaction*. Both boys and girls in the survey sample supported the idea of positive learning interaction with the teacher (Items 13 and 18) – selections of these items accounting for 18.5 per cent of the total number of responses in the survey. Over 55.5 per cent of boys and 44.4 per cent of girls felt that a good science pupil must get on well with the science teacher (Item 18). Almost one in five girls considered that assisting other pupils in class (Item 15) was a top five quality of a good science pupil. Only two of the 27 boys in the survey sample held a similar view. Some 22.2 per cent of boys but only 7.4 per cent of the girls considered that finding out things for yourself (Item 16) was a crucial quality of the good science pupil. All were agreed that a good science pupil was not particularly noted for being reticent when it comes to asking questions (Item 17), though 14.8 per cent of girls felt that such a pupil would sit at the front of the class (Item 14). It was in their perception of science classroom learning interaction that the genders were in closest agreement overall.

(4) *Discipline*. On the whole, discipline qualities did not feature particularly prominently in pupils' perceptions of good science pupilage, and selections of questions pertaining to this sub-category lagged significantly behind selections made in other categories. For example, while only 18.9 per cent of total selections came from the discipline sub-category, some 30.7 per cent came from the aptitude for science sub-category. This said, some interesting results did emerge. Girls were more strongly concerned that a good science pupil would always do his or her homework (Item 19), with 44.4 per cent judging this to be a dominant quality. Boys, by contrast, appeared to consider that paying attention to the teacher (Item 21) was more important than doing homework – though girls expressed stronger preferences in both items. A third of the girls sampled felt that a top five quality of a good science pupil was that he or she did not chatter in class, but only one boy in nine offered an equivalent rating. Peer disapproval (Item 22), punctuality (Item 23) and misbehaviour behind the teacher's back (Item 24) received little interest from pupils.

CONCLUSIONS

Pupils were consistent on a range of issues pertaining to the 'good science pupil', but the research revealed a number of differences in the perceptions of boys and girls. Clearly, the girls in the sample saw the 'good science pupil' as someone with a naturally 'clever' aptitude for the discipline, while the boys were less inclined to take this view. Overall, the boys tended to regard the good science pupil as one combining perseverance, discovery and adventure, while the girls tended to perceive her/him more narrowly as a given talent, enhanced by the school process. In line with this, girls were much less persuaded by the efficacy of factors outside school in the determination of the good science pupil than were boys.

It is difficult and perhaps dangerous to attempt to deduce why this should be so, but one possibility is that gender attitudes in the home may covertly militate against the concept of a girl who watches science programmes or reads science books or conducts scientific experiments. Perhaps significantly, girls tended to see the good science pupil largely in terms of aptitude, classroom learning interaction and discipline – qualities which exercise themselves essentially in the school rather than outside it. By contrast, boys favoured the 'Factors outside school' sub-category more than any other, with twice as many selections for this as for 'Discipline'.

The fact that only two boys believed that male gender was a key determinant of the good science pupil is heartening. Less comforting is the knowledge that six girls believed that gender was this significant. One need not go into the now familiar, but no less valid, explanations of this. Suffice to say that all of us in education need to persevere with our efforts to break down damaging stereotypes. Where the questionnaire may give us some help in this respect is in its identification of boys' and girls' differing perceptions of what constitutes the good science pupil. Naturally, if one accepts the doubtful premise that a good science pupil is simply 'born clever' at science, then it becomes that much easier to accept the fallacious equation 'I am a girl; girls are not clever at science; therefore I cannot be clever at science.' If we can bring our pupils to understand more fully that ability in any domain is significantly dependent on endeavour and interest and curiosity, as much as it is on aptitude, then it may become that much easier to persuade them to have faith in their capabilities.

REFERENCES

Bayliss, T. (1988) 'Girls and boys come out to play', *Bulletin of Physical Education*, 24 (3): 4–6.

Burgess, R.G. (1989) 'Something you learn to live with? . . .', *Gender and Education*, 1 (2): 155–64.

Craig, J. and Ayres, D. (1988) 'Girl-friendly or boy-friendly teaching styles', *Primary Science Review*, 6: 25–6.

Cullingford, C. (1987) 'Children's attitude to teaching styles', *Oxford Review of Education*, 13 (3): 331–9.

Hacker, R. and Carter, D. (1987) 'Teaching processes in social studies classrooms and prescriptive instructional theories', *British Educational Research Journal*, 13 (2): 261–9.

Hazelwood, R.D. *et al.* (1988) 'Student perceptions of teaching and learning styles in TVEI', *Evaluation and Research in Education*, 2 (2): 61–8.

Johnson, S. (1987) 'Gender differences in science: parallels in interest, experience and performance', *International Journal of Science Education*, 9 (4): 467–81.

Kelly, A. (1988) 'The customer is always right . . . girls' and boys' reactions to science lessons', *School Science Review*, 69 (249): 662–76.

Pickersgill, D. (1989) 'Girls and science: the latest blow to equality', *Education in Science*, 132: 25.

Robertson, I. (1987) 'Girls and boys and practical science', *International Journal of Science Education*, 9 (5): 505–18.

Chapter 23

Pupils' views of management

E.C. Wragg

This is a highly edited version of a longer chapter by Ted Wragg on the findings of the Leverhulme Primary Project. In it, he argues that teachers ought to know what pupils think about their teaching, so that they can be aware of the effects of what they do on the classroom. Many beginning teachers have begun to welcome some form of pupil appraisal of their early teaching experiences, and this chapter may help to provide an initial research base for such investigations. The extracts I have chosen look at pupil views of classroom rules and of what makes a 'good teacher'.

Relatively little research into teaching has solicited pupils' views. Yet they will spend several thousand hours sitting in primary school classes, and the German social psychologist Kurt Lewin (1943) claimed that children as young as 3 or 4 could be even more sensitive than adults to certain situations. [. . .] The reluctance to use pupil perceptions is understandable. Most primary pupils have only experienced one school in one particular social setting, and they have a restricted view of teaching and of what adult life or the secondary phase of schooling may hold for them, so they will often favour the familiar. Were one to base a school or classroom system entirely on pupil opinion it would probably be ultra-conservative. On the other hand, even with limited experience from their interactions with and perceptions of others, from their reading, conversations, viewing of television, children are capable of asking questions or making observations about classroom practice. Whilst few would advocate basing teaching entirely on pupil opinion, it is difficult to justify ignoring it completely, especially when such research as exists reports certain consistent findings.

It has commonly been found that pupils, when given a list of teacher behaviour or characteristics, will rate competence in key professional skills most highly. In one of the earliest studies Hollis (1935) gave more than 8,000 pupils seven statements about teacher behaviour. Highest ranking was given to the teacher's ability to explain difficulties patiently, though the format of this particular study does not allow one to infer whether it was the explanation or the patience that was most valued. Nearly 50 years later Wragg and Wood (1984) analysed the responses of 200 pupils aged 11 to 16 on a checklist of 32 items using a five-point Likert scale on their concept of 'the best teacher in the world'. The most highly rated statement was, 'This teacher would explain things clearly.'

Research into pupils' perceptions has been summarised by several writers. Evans (1962) concluded that pupils seemed to prefer personal characteristics such as kindness, friendliness, patience, fairness and a sense of humour. They disliked sarcasm, favouritism, domineering and excessive punishment. Nash (1976) used a repertory-grid technique to elicit constructs from young secondary pupils and found almost exactly the same characteristics, good discipline, explaining skills, interest in pupils, fairness and friendliness. Summaries by Meighan (1977), Cohen and Manion (1981) and Wragg and Wood (1984) reported a similar picture. The empirical study by Wragg and Wood also found that teachers were expected to be firm but fair. Teachers who were bossy or punitive were not esteemed, but neither were those who were too permissive. 'This teacher would let you mark your own tests' and 'This teacher would do something else if that's what the class wants' were both statements which received very low ratings on the 'best teacher' schedule.

Despite the paucity of research into the pupil perspective on classroom life, there is, none the less, a tenable view that teachers ought to know what pupils think about teaching, not so that they can abdicate their own responsibility for setting and maintaining an agenda, but so that pupils' concepts of teaching can be a legitimate part of classroom teaching and learning. Weinstein (1983) argued the case strongly: 'Being aware of students as active interpreters of classroom events forces teachers to examine more closely the effects of their own behaviour on the recipients of these interventions.' It was decided, therefore, that we would interview pupils as part of the Leverhulme Primary Project.

We decided to interview children across the whole primary age range, from 5 up to 12. A sample of 430 pupils aged 5 to 12 in 20 classes in eight different schools was selected. The schools were in the North-west and the South-west of England and in London. They represented a mix between inner-city and rural schools, were all in schools where we were studying teachers, and were almost equally divided between boys and girls, with 52 per cent and 48 per cent respectively. The interview questions asked after an explanation of the purposes and nature of the interview were: 'Can you tell me what things you are allowed to do in the classroom?', 'Can you tell me what things you are not allowed to do?', 'Do you think children should be allowed to talk to each other during lessons?' (Why?/Why not?), 'Imagine the best teacher in the whole world, someone who is absolutely brilliant at teaching. What do you think this very good teacher would be like?' (followed by 'Imagine the worst teacher in the whole world', and so on), 'What sort of things do children do in class when they are naughty?', 'What happens when children do that?' (Whatever the child replied), 'Are you ever naughty?', 'What do you do?' and 'What happens?' These were designed to allow children to give their own perceptions of effective teaching, of inappropriate behaviour, and their own accounts of what they themselves do. A sub-sample of 105 of [their] detailed responses, consisting of one class each of 5–6-, 6–7-, 7–8-, 9–11- and 11–12-year-olds, are reported here. The intention of the first question, asking what pupils are allowed to do, was to generate positive rather than negative responses. The five most common responses were (1) work, (2) talk to each other, (3) play when we've finished our work, (4) choose something we want to do, and (5) walk freely in the classroom (with a reason). This mixture of work and choice came out clearly in several responses, some respecting the freedom, others not:

> We've got to do our work, then, sometimes in the afternoon, if we do all our work we're allowed to play with the Lego and we're allowed to write letters over there [pointing] to people when it's their birthday or something.
>
> (7-year-old)

> We're allowed to get on with our work, sort of on our own. We don't have to do everything, we don't have to do the same things all the time.
>
> (11-year-old)

> You're allowed to talk quietly, but you're not allowed to shout, which is what everyone usually does instead of getting on with their work.
>
> (8-year-old)

> We're allowed to choose. We're allowed to play in the house, we can play in the big sandpit or the little sandpit, which is out there, or we can play outside or do some writing or drawing.
>
> (6-year-old)

Play was principally mentioned by the 5–6- and 6–7-year-olds. It was perceived as play by pupils, but teachers saw it as school work with choice.

When it came to asking children what they were not allowed to do, the list of responses was much longer. In first five places were (1) shout, (2) be silly/mess about, (3) fight, (4) throw things, (5) run. Even younger pupils had a well-shaped sense of what the teacher's rules were:

> We're not allowed to muck about, we're not allowed to fight and we're not allowed to yell at the top of our voices, and a few other things which I can't remember. We've got quite a lot of rules – loads.
>
> (8-year-old)

> We're not allowed to scream, we're not allowed to shout, we're not allowed to throw things around the classrooms, not allowed to be

Table 23.1 Replies to question 'Should children be allowed to talk to one another in lessons?'

| Response | Age group | | | | | |
	5–6	6–7	7–8	9–11	11–12	Total
Yes	4	2	8	19	17	50
No	13	15	12	2	0	42
Sometimes	1	1	1	2	2	7
It depends	0	2	0	3	1	6
Total	18	20	21	26	20	105

naughty, we're not allowed to do mean things to people, like scratch and punch and kick, and that's it really.

(7-year-old)

You're not really allowed to copy, you've got to do your own work. When you [are] working with someone, you're to discuss it with them and not shout at them. If you haven't finished and you've had a long time to do a certain piece of work then you've got to stay in at break and finish it, and if it's like near the end of the day, then you've got to take it home and finish it for homework.

(10-year-old)

The concern with shouting reflects the category of misbehaviour we observed most frequently; namely, noisy chatter. Pupils were clearly divided by age on the matter of whether talking in the classroom should be permitted at all. Table 23.1 shows how they responded, and the older pupils took a more sophisticated view of classroom talk than the younger pupils, who usually assumed it must be wrong.

Of the 36 9- to 12-year-olds who replied 'Yes', 16 qualified it by adding that it was legitimate only if related to work or if done quietly. The reasons for replies were mainly, for those who replied, 'Yes', because it helped you with your work, stopped you getting bored, helped concentration and allowed you to check your answers. Those who saw it negatively said it interfered with work, you got told off, you wouldn't hear the teacher and it interrupted others. Some of the more aware pupils in the 'it depends' category, gave a balanced view of the pros and cons:

If it's about work, then yes, and they're not making too much noise, but if they're mucking about or talking about what they did at the weekend, then no, because they're not getting on with their work properly and they'll probably get told off and get extra work.

(10-year-old)

The question about the best and worst teacher in the world produced responses not unlike those reported in other studies described earlier in this chapter. The best teacher in the world would, according to this sample, do interesting activities and also let you choose, be 'nice', kind and 'good at teaching', which was variously interpreted as a combination of subject knowledge ('brainy', 'understands a lot') and professional skill ('explains', 'good at teaching you about computers' (seven pupils, all in the same class)). The best teacher in the world would be quite strict, 'not let you get away with things', but not too bossy, and would have a sense of humour. This general picture of pupils' perceptions obtained from these interviews is almost exactly what other studies have found, confirming that the pupil perception literature is astonishingly consistent across time and age groups.

The questions about what naughty children do in class and how the teacher responds reflected and reinforced answers we had received to earlier questions. There were clear views on what constitutes naughty behaviour, and as previously, these reflected violence to another person and noise. Kicking, pushing, fighting, shouting, screaming, throwing or flicking things, messing about and damage to property were all mentioned frequently, closely followed by illicit talking, swearing, not working, fidgeting and running. The most reported responses from the teacher were a telling-off, being sent to the head or sent outside, told to get on with your work, punishing with extra work, shouting, getting cross and warning about future conduct. In classes where teachers actually dealt with misbehaviour in a positive manner, this was greatly appreciated by children, who often spoke spontaneously in approving terms, like this 7-year-old:

What naughty pupils do: '. . . punishing other people. Like Miss Brown [class teacher] says, if they swear at people they're getting bitchy. That's what Miss Brown says.'

What happens: 'We have a circle time [when the pupils and teacher sit around in a circle] and ask people what they do to people. Then Miss Brown tries to sort it out and mostly she gets it all sorted out and she's really good at it. She's good at sorting it out.'

About half (52 out of 105) children admitted to being naughty in class, with older pupils showing few inhibitions about admitting it and younger pupils responding more warily. Only three out of the 18 5–6-year-olds in the sample replied 'Yes', whereas 17 of the oldest 20 children replied in the affirmative. The contrast is revealed by these two responses from a younger and older pupil:

'Are you ever naughty?'
'No. I get on with my work and I don't talk.'

(5-year-old)

'Are you ever naughty?'
'Sometimes.'
'What do you do?'

'Throw rubbers and paper.'
'What happens?'
'I don't know, I've never been caught.'

(12-year-old)

Most pupils were well aware of the consequences of misbehaviour and could describe them in great detail, appreciating such matters as confidentiality or the significance of status, even when the teacher or the school had intricate rituals, often involving the school hierarchy in an elaborate chain of events:

'I got a yellow card. It's just a warning. You get one when you get told off. The first card you get is normal, and then if you do it again you go into a corner or another class, and then you go to the headmistress and then you get a letter home to the parents.'

(8-year-old)

'Well, Miss Gibbon normally takes them [naughty pupils] outside and talks to them so no one else can hear, and they have to sit outside and then the headteacher comes along and gives them some hard work.'

(10-year-old)

Even very young children had a clear understanding of the borderline between what the teacher would regard as acceptable and what would be regarded as deviant. Fighting was the third most frequently mentioned 'naughty' behaviour, but there was a clear distinction between the real thing and rough-and-tumble role-played versions:

'I just plays on my own with my cousin and some of my friends. We plays a little fight, it's not a real fight, it's a play fight. You just pretend to punch like that [demonstrates mock blow], and that's pretending. You won't get told off. . . . You stand near the wall when you're naughty. I don't stand near the wall. I don't be naughty outside.'

(6-year-old)

This part of our inquiry showed that children have a perspective on misbehaviour that is often different from that of the teacher, though they can repeat the school's official policies on discipline with clarity and apparent consent. Spending up to 35 hours a week in school ensures that they experience their teachers' management rituals and routines numerous times. There is little ambiguity in the minds of even the youngest pupils about what is expected, and what will ensue if they transgress. Yet their vantage point is different from that of teachers. They see shouting and telling off as a normal part of classroom life, to be expected even, whereas teachers tend to be more embarrassed at mentioning these, from their point of view, cruder responses.

Not surprisingly, aggression features high on their list of concerns, as they are well aware that a fellow belligerent pupil can easily knock them over in a rush, hit them, or cause them some other mischief, and they appreciate teachers who, without themselves being over-domineering, are clearly in charge when it comes to dealing with over-aggressive behaviour. It confirms the popular child stereotype of successful teaching reported in other inquiries – in charge, firm but fair, knowing their craft, able to explain clearly, pleasant to be with, good-humoured and -natured – and loath to shout.

REFERENCES

Cohen, L. and Manion, L. (1981) *Perspectives on Classrooms and Schools*, London: Holt, Rinehart & Winston.

Evans, K.M. (1962) *Sociometry and Education*, London: Routledge & Kegan Paul.

Hollis, A.W. (1935) 'The personal relationship in teaching', MA thesis, Birmingham University.

Lewin, K. (1943) 'Psychology and the process of group living', *Journal of Social Psychology*, 17: 113–31.

Meighan, R. (1977) 'The pupil as client: the learner's experience of schooling', *Educational Review*, 29: 123–35.

Nash, R. (1976) *Teacher Expectations and Pupil Learning*, London: Routledge & Kegan Paul.

Weinstein, R.S (1983) 'Student perceptions of elementary schooling', *Elementary Schools Journal*, 83: 288–312.

Wragg, E.C. and Wood, E.K. (1984) 'Teachers' first encounters with their classes', in E.C. Wragg (ed.) *Classroom Teaching Skills*, London: Croom Helm.

Chapter 24

Managing the primary teacher's role

Peter Woods

In the last chapter of this book, Peter Woods takes up one of the fundamental issues in primary practice: relationships between teachers and pupils. He looks at the way teachers manage to balance the different professional roles they need to play while meeting the needs of their pupils for warmth and security. In contrast to much other research, this chapter takes the teachers' own perspectives on board and brings out what it is that they themselves seem to be trying to achieve, within the context of the whole school. Researched in this manner, teaching is seen to be not only about developing discrete competences, but also about learning to balance with confidence a variety of different roles and relationships.

MANAGING THE ROLE

Friendship

> What did the policeman say to his tummy?
> You're under a vest!

(Pupil joke)

Relationships between pupils and teachers seem to meet several of the criteria of friendship. In these pupils' own terms, friends spend time together, help and care about each other, give each other things, find each other attractive, and play and have fun together (Woods 1987). Teachers can meet all these requirements with pupils to some degree, while not fulfilling them in their entirety since the other aspects of their role pull against them. In an exercise on friends, for example, Kamlesh, an isolate in the form, claimed the teacher for her friend:

> My friend's name is Mrs Brown. She is very kind. She looks nice as well. She helps me with words all the time. I cannot play with her because she is an adult. Well, she is a teacher as well. She can make me laugh all the time. She taught me about tadpoles as well.

This meets several of the criteria, and although she cannot play with her, she 'makes her laugh', which is perhaps the next best thing for an adult. Further, in being her friend, the teacher does not forsake her formal role – she teaches as well. Friendship, in fact, makes an excellent basis for learning (see Woods 1986).

The teacher befriended many of the children. Farida, for example, a Bengali Muslim, was ostracised by the rest of the class, and clung to the teacher in the playground. She was so serious, never smiled, had considerable domestic difficulties as well (the oldest of five children so was often 'mum'). By November the teacher felt she 'was getting through to her . . . was getting a smile out of her – and thought that Farida now trusted her'.

The teacher also, for her part, can see pupils as her friends. Seema, for example, a very mature girl, was regarded as an equal and as an ally in the classroom. If the teacher was struggling with another pupil who couldn't understand, she would look up and Seema would catch her eye and smile, and make a knowing shake of the head in sympathy. Kamlesh and Seema might be special cases, but they do illustrate the possibilities and terms of which most of the pupils in class 1 availed themselves to some degree at some time or other. This is not to say that the teacher could fulfil all the same services as contemporaries. But the teacher can perform some important functions for pupils, while pupils provide the teacher with moral and emotional support. A great deal of the pleasure of these relationships is manifested in laughter:

> Two older girls came into the staffroom to ask Mr Morris for the computer. 'Don't forget to kneel,' says one to the other. They kneel and bow down: 'Oh Lord and Master, may we have the computer please sir, oh great one.' (Teacher laughs. When they are gone he tells me, 'They're a great bunch, this lot. You never know what to expect next!')

Teachers are bombarded with jokes and riddles:

> Why don't you play cards in the jungle? Because there are too many cheetahs there.

> What do you get if you cross an elephant with a fish? Swimming trunks!

Teachers are quite good at jokes too:

> Wash it in the toilet. Well, not in the toilet, in the basin in the toilet.

Teachers play tricks on pupils: in a 'senses' lesson, two of the 'tastes' (which they sampled blind) are lemon curd and mustard. There was much running out to the sink after the mustard! There were similar booby traps in the bag they had to dip into to 'feel'.

Pupils play tricks on teachers:

> Robert plays a trick on Mrs Coe. He puts the practice clock at 10 and tells her it's 10 o'clock. She says 'Oh dear!' then looks at the real clock. 'That's

tricked you,' says Robert in triumph. 'Gosh, Robert,' she says.

Dipak plays a joke on Mrs Brown. 'Hold out your hands.' She does so. He then chants something, slaps her hands, and then her face with both hands. She blinks and staggers back. 'More gently next time!' she said in astonishment. She told me later, 'I didn't know what to say! It hurt!'

Pupils share intimate confidences with teachers: Richard was ecstatically excited one day to find a china doll in the oddments box. It had no clothes on, and he showed me its rear aspect with great relish. With a glint in his eye, he said, 'This is alive', so heightening the rudery.

Teachers show a certain vulnerability:

Angela teases Mrs Brown with a joke spider. She jumps and shudders 'Ugh!' Angela squeals with delight.

Teachers play tricks on each other:

Mr Morris comes into the room with one of his boys, 'Go and stand next to Tracey,' (a student teacher), he says. Tracey is talking to some of her pupils at her desk, but the boy stands beside her so that they are touching. 'Yes? what do you want?' He says nothing, just looks ahead non-committally. She moves slightly, and he moves with her. They begin to realise something funny is happening, and Mrs Brown caps the joke by putting a paper hat with 'Dunce' written on it (a stage prop) on the boy's head. Mr Morris said he was experimenting with 'invading people's space'.

Mrs Durrant teased Mrs Brown with a large spider in the hall. She pretended it was in her tissue and brought the whole class in to witness Mrs Brown's reaction. Mrs Brown told this to her own class, to their great amusement.

The affection between teacher and pupil is illustrated in so many ways in the course of a day:

'Mrs Brown, my hands are cold.' (Mrs Brown takes his hands, rubs them and warms them up.)

'That's all you wanted, isn't it?'

Kamlesh tries to step into a leotard, but gets in a muddle. Mrs Brown helps her out of it, with some difficulty, laughs with her, wraps the leotard round her face like a blindfold, and smacks her bottom in friendly fashion to send her on her way. Kamlesh sits pleased, slowly blinking her big eyes and long lashes in her way.

Many of these children the teacher felt did not have a great deal of parental interaction, and she felt like a mother to them. She tends to physical and emotional injury. Even the time-honoured activity of inspecting heads, which used to be done by a nurse, is now done by the teachers.

The primary school teacher has her pupils for a year, and comes to form strong affective relationships with them, marked on the one hand by her own regret at losing them at the end of the year, and their frequent visits back to her room the following year. They come to ask 'if she has any jobs', to tell her things or just to talk to her – or they just come and stand. Those of her present year often gather round her at playtime if she is on duty, and she has a laugh and joke with them.

The question might be raised as to *which* children the teachers related to in this way, and whether this showed any connection with structural factors (such as social class, gender, race), as a number of studies have suggested (see, for example, Camilleri 1986). At Albert Road, the offer and taking of friendship appeared to be open to all. No 'deficit' judgements are made about pupils. The teacher seeks to identify good and strong points to draw them out further, and the weak to improve them. Problem pupils are regarded positively. Even Herol, the 'problem of the infants', was going to be given a 'chance', by his new teacher. 'We'll start from the beginning. Perhaps when he gets in this school he'll be different.' The model is to be one of 'consociates' that will be put on offer in so many ways. 'Naughtiness' thus is not always something to be punished. Mrs Brown felt that with Warish, for example, it was a case of lack of social skills. She was even pleased to see Warish becoming a little naughty at times, as that indicated a developing personality from an originally withdrawn and nervous state.

The Family Spirit

> I belong to a family, the biggest on the earth, 10,000 every day are coming to birth . . .
>
> (Assembly Song)

School ethos contributes towards the sense of community and caring and the notion of the school as a family. Family events themselves reinforced this sense. A birth, for example, was a matter for communal joy and celebration. The way the latter was stage-managed on one occasion well illustrates the spirit involved. Mr Thompson had recently become a father. Towards the end of one assembly, the teacher in charge, Mrs Durrant, who, with her pupils, had been illustrating movement and energy, selected 20 pupils from the audience to dance to some music. Somehow or other Mr Thompson got dragged in to this by some of the senior girls, and ended up dancing with Mrs Durrant, to the delight of the audience. At the end he was asked to 'stay where he was' while the other dancers returned to their places. He was then presented with a gift for which there had been a school collection, for his baby from senior girls. There was a small speech and an enthusiastic clap from the audience. He thanked them, expressed his surprise and pleasure at the event and the gift, and then asked 'Do you want me to open it?' There was a massive 'YE-E-E-S!'. He unravelled the paper to discover a giant panda. Everybody was delighted. Later, as the concluding music was played, Mr Thompson, now seated with the panda on his lap, waved its paw at departing classes.

Babies always aroused special interest. When 'Baby Lucy' came to visit, class 1 were fascinated to hear about activities and development, likes and dislikes. They formed a 'welfare club' when a supply teacher brought her poorly young son in with her one day. A high point of the year was a visit from two lambs. Similar interest, care and concern was shown, however, for other members of society with special needs, notably the aged, and those with disabilities (see Woods 1987).

Major school festivals reinforced the 'caring and sharing' ethos. The most important of these were Diwali and Christmas, which between them occupied much time and attention in the autumn term. At Diwali, the Festival of Lights, 'we shared in everyone's happiness'. Pupils enact the story of Ram and Sita, their struggles with wickedness and hardship, and the eventual triumph of goodness and truth. 'Our good wishes go to everyone in this room, outside and throughout the world. . . . Diwali is also a festival of sharing. Part of that is a gift for everyone here. As you receive your gift, think how you can share what you have to offer.' The sharing went down to individual class level. Gita, for example, brought in some toffee for her class that her mother had made specially. (There were other occasions for sharing – on Angela's birthday, for example, she brought liquorice allsorts in. She stood at the front giving them out as names were called, popping every other one into her own mouth.) How to treat others was a recurring message in assemblies. Friendship and relationships among pupils in general was a popular topic. For the most part, the message was straightforward – the need to think of and care for others, help them, treat them properly, share things with them.

TEACHING

A teacher may be a friend and a parent to a pupil, but she must also teach them something as well. Without this, friendships would not develop – it legitimates the teacher's whole position (Musgrove and Taylor 1974). Ironically, however, much of its requirements run against the affective grain. For, while the ideology of pupil-centredness has a measure of control vested in pupils and instruction taking place on demand, the fact is that most teachers are forced through lack of resources to operate a part pupil- part teacher-centred approach. In this, instruction and teacher control figure as prominently as pupil discovery and creativity and pupil self-control. These are, however, blended into a coherent and consistent pattern through a quality of omniscience, or what some have identified as 'awareness' or 'withitness' (Kounin 1970; Lacey 1977) and through a process of what I will term 'orchestration'. I will consider each in turn.

Omniscience

> Yeah, Mrs Brown knows everything. (*One of Mrs Brown's pupils*)

The skilful teacher's knowledge of, and influence in, her classroom seemed boundless. In a class of some 25 children, some working individually, most in small groups on different topics or subjects and at different stages, she knew what each one of them was doing and when they were not doing what they should be. Even though there was a constant noise as pupils discussed, read or reflected, her finely tuned ear soon detected any variant to a legitimate 'working noise', when a brief signal cutting through the swathe of sound quickly restored the situation. It might be a name, a certain tone of voice in what she was already saying, a noise or utterance, or, if necessary, a reminder of different categories: 'I don't mind you talking but I won't have silliness.'

The skilful teacher can see round corners. The classroom with its cupboard and shelves, nooks and crannies, playhouse and reading corners with carpet provide opportunities for quiet work – or concealment and idleness. Where people are is imprinted on her memory and the linkages are maintained by brief signals without the teacher having always to patrol the room. 'How are you getting on . . .?', 'Are you doing that properly . . .?', 'How far have you got . . .?', 'How many have read so far . . .?', 'Is everything all right on the floor?' (Ye-e-e-es!). On one occasion, Tony was banished from the corner reading group: 'I've been watching you . . . that's the second complaint I've had . . . now get on with some writing.' Later Mrs Brown laid emphasis on the privilege of being in the 'advanced reading group', where they could get on on their own in a comparatively private and select area of the classroom. But 'some children had been silly and lost the opportunity'. Here the teacher is attempting to construct a social structure within the classroom which all will accept and which then will run itself without her constant vigilance and being sustained, perhaps, only with some of those briefest of signals. The teacher, herself, is part of that structure. In a sense, she remains its guardian. The better it runs itself without intervention from her, the fewer and less the signals, the more successful she has been in constructing it. But it still depends on her, or at least some other with similar abilities and powers, as was demonstrated when the structure collapsed sometimes when some other occasionally took over.

However, the skilful teacher's influence lives on in the classroom, for a time at any rate, in her absence. One morning Mrs Brown had to leave to teach another group, leaving the class with a pre-service student. After getting them in good order ('Are you listening?' 'Kaushik, get your bottom down!') she gave them a firm reminder of the rules before she went, to lay the platform. The entry in my field notes reads: 'Her influence lingers on, the "spell" of her warning impressed on memory.'

Once established, the structure can be reaffirmed with signals. The signalling can take many forms. It can become progressively more imperceptible to an outsider, and take the form, almost, of a game:

> (After one assembly): Mr Butcher quietens them down with hand signals (rather like the comedian who cuts off the piped applause – and he has a similar effect). The palm held out, depressed means quiet but at ease; when the palm was turned up, they all sit up briskly like soldiers coming to attention.

The game-like qualities of this tactic were demonstrated when, having got them all quiet and orderly prior to leaving the hall while the closing music played, the Maori music (which was the tape of the day) suddenly began with a loud grunt. Mr Butcher jumped and retreated in some trepidation, to everybody's amusement. My notes record a 'good, relaxed, consociable, orderly start to the day'.

Mr Butcher later told me of the other signals in his repertoire. For example, one finger-snapping click means 'attention', and two means 'relax'. He sometimes moves his lips soundlessly – 'you can hear a pin drop as they try to make out what he is saying'. These signals are blended smoothly into the pattern of events:

> Mr Butcher picks out a choir (all hands go up), orders the verses, snaps his fingers and a boy goes out to the front without a pause in the teacher's approach.

The teacher's omniscience, omni-awareness and fine-tuning may seem to indicate superhuman powers. It is easy to see how a lay observer might develop that impression. However, if this were the case for pupils it would run against the grain of the kinds of relationships we have been talking about. The teacher's mystical expertise needs balancing therefore with more identifiably human properties. A certain fallibility was therefore evident – not too much, just enough to show that the teacher was human. A certain humility in the teacher's approach helps to substantiate this.

In some maths blackboard work, Mrs Brown has to draw dogs, birds, rabbits and cats. The pupils laugh at her pictures, and she joins in with them. 'My rabbits are not very good!' On another occasion commenting on her blackboard art work she admitted 'I can't draw fingers. I always draw sausages.'

Sometimes the fallibility is genuine, sometimes contrived:

> In a maths lesson, Mrs Brown sometimes makes deliberate mistakes on the board:

19
04
—
—

'I add nothing . . .' 'No-o-o! The other side!' '9 add 4 equals 13.' She puts
3 under the line. 'No-o-o!' 'There's no catching you lot, is there?'

Teachers must know many things. She must have an idea of standards and
each pupil's capabilities and personalities, how to develop them, when to
intervene, when not to intervene, when to be cross, when to be nice, to
punish, or reward, and so on. This is illustrated, as so often, by comparison
with some of my own efforts. I had ticked Sheela's work as having reached
what I thought was a reasonable standard. But at a later stage Mrs Brown,
who, of course, knew the pupil's capabilities much better, censured her:
'Sheela, you're making silly silly mistakes, you're not concentrating. Your
maths yesterday was not good, not careful enough work. You know why,
don't you? You're always talking, that's why.'

Orchestration

Hey! Not rude! I don't mind fun, but not rude!

Omniscience in itself is not enough, for the teacher must know how to put it
all together in practice in a harmonious whole. This applies not only to her
knowledge of subjects, of pupils, of the classroom, and so on, but of her
potentially discordant roles. 'Orchestration' is an appropriate term for this,
for she must not only plan and organise her work accordingly (with the
score), but also rehearse and conduct a not always attentive and co-operative
orchestra.

Much is a question of striking a balance – in the week, a day or lesson.
Teachers ring the changes to get the best out of their pupils. On a typical
occasion a spelling test was scheduled to follow a viewing of 'Music Time'
and to be followed by playtime and a story. 'Music Time' involved teacher
and pupils enjoying a game of 'question marks'. It worked on the same
principle as 'Simon says'. If the person at the front asked a question, they all
drew a big question mark in the air with their fingers accompanied by a
'Neaoiow – Ping!'. If the person simply made a statement, they remained
silent. This, then, was an instructive game in which we all participated.

This was followed by a spelling test which required some control. This
was a rare event, following on this occasion a number of carefully planned
lessons on short vowel sounds. The admonitions, motivators, teaching
encouragement and control were subtly interwoven into the main text on the
basis of agreed rules:

No talking now. Clean pages please. Right – yes, I'll have the date . . .

John, come on.

This is the first word. PUT, when you *put* something somewhere. Look up and look at me when you're finished. Have you finished, Samson? Then look at me so I know . . . GOT. GOT. It's easy if you listen hard you can hear all the letters. GOT. HEMANG!

If anybody cheats I shall be so cross. It's not that important. You don't get into trouble if you get them wrong. So there's no point in cheating, you're only cheating yourselves because you've not been bothered to learn them.

JOB. Go do a JOB today. It's only got three letters and you can hear all of them. JOB. JJJOBB. Make sure that nobody's written JO*D*. All written JO*B*, have you?

Right! Next one – there's something special to remember about this one. I shan't tell you next time when there's something special to remember. TOM. The name TOM.

Finished, Pradeep? Look this way if you have. Right. DOG. Woof, woof. DOG. (*some whispering*) Shh!

Right! An even easier word this time – ON. Robert! If I hear your voice again (angrily) woe betide!

Another easy one – TOP, either a spinning top, or the top of something. etc. etc. . . .

Without a sound, swop with the person next to you. Don't use crayon. No talking. Put away your pencils. Tell me first of all which is the odd one out, and why (Sheela says it is 'Put' because it had a 'U' instead of an 'O'). Good girl! You can have a house point for that.

I will write them for you and you can mark them. Can you not talk! (*angrily*) . . .

(She invites a pupil to spell each one, and write them on the blackboard.)

. . . JOB. Not G-O-B! But *J* O *B*. Usually with a J it's a softer sound.

TOM. If you haven't got a capital T, it's wrong. I've given you five weeks to learn that.

(*Angrily*) I'm not going to do any more and I'm going to start taking time off your dinner hour. Nobody, but nobody should be talking except Richard. If anybody else talks I'll put a line through your work and write 'cheated'! Now listen! (There is silence as the next few words are spelt out.)

In this formal activity, which contrasts strongly with some of their independent work, these 7-year-olds are learning as well as spellings the difficult lesson of self-control. There are rewards and punishments, lighter and harsher tones, softer and louder pitch, gradations and inflexions of the voice as the circumstance warrants. Reasons are given. And in spite of the changes it is all part of an integrated and continuous presentation.

John had his spelling test crossed out and awarded nought for disobeying and being consistently naughty. Those who got them all right received a star. Afterwards a general reward in a sense ('put your head on your arms and rest if you want to, and listen') was to have read to them the story of 'The Little Match Girl', a sad story with a Christmas message of love and charity. This reflected the general school 'caring' ethos, and made a neat foil to the earlier disciplined activity.

Another, even more relaxed, foil was to follow, for at the end of the day came the distribution of Christmas cards sent through the school post. John received a card with no name on it, and the teacher made a point of going over to him and sharing his pleasure and thus neutralising her earlier anger and restoring their friendship (another aspect of orchestration). 'It's either a secret admirer or a very forgetful person.' The teacher herself received a card ('To Mrs Brown, you are very good, kiss, kiss and no name'). 'They're too ashamed to tell you – it might be a boy,' opined John. This was a familiar event – expulsion, followed by enfolding. On another occasion a boy who had been very naughty was roundly scolded and told to stand near the door facing the wall (symbolically outside the culture of the room). When he was told to go back, the teacher joined him to explain what to do, her physical proximity, help and kindly voice reaffirming the basic relationship.

Later in the year, with the rules of interaction more firmly established, the emphasis was more consistently on rewards:

> The class are writing up the story of Peter and the Wolf. Winston is congratulated. 'That's the best work you've done since you've been here. You've remembered all your full stops and capitals – they go hand in glove I always say.'
>
> 'Daniel, whereabouts are you in the story, love, because you're going to find this ever so hard to copy up.' He says 'where the duck comes out of the wolf'. 'Oh, that's all right then, love.' 'Ann, are you writing in neat, yet?' 'Yes Mrs Brown.' 'Come on, then.'

Gentle cajolery usually had its effect, but not all the time. After persuasion had failed, bright but lazy Tony's unsatisfactory work was torn up and he had to begin again. 'I'm not having it! Go and do as you are told!' Ann also had been tardy though being given plenty of opportunity to finish, preferring talking to writing: 'I think you'll have to finish your work in playtime this afternoon, outside the headmaster's office – or inside. This work should have taken you half an hour.'

With some individuals and on some occasions it is possible to combine a nudge and a joke:

> 'Hemang, I'm going to wind you up, Eeerk, eerk, eeerk.' (*winds him up*)
> 'You children in the corner are making more noise than the monkeys in the zoo!' (a combined admonition and joke which had both effects)

'Those that are in the line stand like soldiers, not like old flowers that are drooping.' (*laughter*)

There are many ways of bridging divides. In the following, a teaching technique is carried over into the informal area and this demonstrates their command of the role. The pupils' amusement at it derives from the incongruence:

A music lesson from Miss Steele practising rhythm. They clap hands and slap knees after her. Mrs Brown and the student join in. Miss Steele asks them to sing their favourite colour in 'so-me'. 'Pi-ink' 'Re-ed'. When the lesson is finished Mrs Brown sings in 'so-me', like a vicar, 'When you are ready will you stand u-up.' 'Richard's ta-ble' (i.e. being given permission to leave). Mrs Durrant comes in and chants, 'Can I have a word with you, Mrs Brow-own?' And they have a 'so-me' conversation.

In a sense, this helps to put the music lesson in its place – within the realm of ordinary experience – as well as consolidating the pitch of the notes.

A difficult part of the school day to orchestrate is the gaps around the edges of planned activity. There is a folklore among primary teachers about 'keeping pupils busy'. Sharp and Green (1975) argue that in the school of their research, 'busyness' was a rhetoric which disguised the school's structural links with a stratified society and enabled the teacher to spend more time with the more able pupils. At Albert Road, there was inevitably some time-filling of a purely occupational nature (given the inequality between pressures and resources). Time needed to be filled in case holes appeared into which disorder might flow. Here again the perceptive teacher had a keen eye for the distinction between 'constructive disorder' (which worked in part on the principle that pupils needed some space during the day to interrelate, to explore freely some aspect of their work, to release their minds in the interests of creativity and their own control over their learning) and destructive anarchy.

Otherwise, time-fillers were devised that fitted in generally with a learner-centred approach. While a teacher might build up a repertoire of time-fillers, there is a need for freshness and relevance which taxes inventiveness: 'While we're waiting (for assembly), how many saw some fireworks last night?' Tony did not go into assemblies, and when the school celebrated Diwali, faced a very long wait on his own. So he was asked to write an account of a competition he had been in.

At the end of one day when there was a gap, teacher and class struck up (with actions):

One finger one thumb one nod of the head
One stamp of the foot
One flap of the wings
One tap of the nose

Stand up sit down (shouted)
. . . Keep moving, we'll all be merry and bright.

On another occasion (with actions, and missing out a line with each repeat though preserving the actions):

In a cottage in the wood
A little old man at the window stood
Saw a rabbit running by
Knocking at the door
Shouting Help me! Help Me! Help Me! he said
Before the huntsman shoots me dead
Come little rabbit come to me
And forever we shall be.

After missing out a line each time, the last reprise was the whole song 'as loud as you like this time', which finished just on 'going home time'. Sir Thomas Beecham could not have arranged or timed it more perfectly.

The achievement in orchestrating is highlighted by considering some failures. The first is a probationary teacher quoted by Pollard (1985):

If you're easy going, you're easy going, you can't suddenly become very forthright can you . . .? I had a very easy home background, very easy relationships at home . . . no particular struggles through life. . . . I've never been a leader, even all through school with friends. . . . I'd rather follow anybody than lead anybody, and to stand up in front of the children and suddenly become this horrible person who had to be nasty to get control . . . it wasn't me in the first place which is why I found it difficult to do.

(p. 33)

This might have been Mandy, a student teacher in another school of the research, of whom her supervising teacher said, 'She was so wet, she couldn't control five kids, let alone a class. You have to get cross with them sometimes!' I sympathise with Mandy, having myself struggled at times with groups of five pupils, and knowing exactly why she found it so difficult to shout at them – you don't usually shout at your friends.

These are over-friendly teachers. One can generally be over-teacherly, and miss crucial links with the pupils that actually promote learning or some other positive function. One class of children complained of an occasional teacher who 'shouted at them, wouldn't let them out for wees, was horrible, wouldn't help them'. Connell (1985) describes a teacher who, in response to early disciplinary problems, 'came down hard on the kids' with the support of the school hierarchy, and established silence and order. 'But she soon came to see this as the wrong solution. She had control, all right; but the kids were not learning anything.'

These examples concentrate on one side of the role or the other. Equally unsatisfactory, some might argue, is the teacher who alternates between one and the other, now a firm disciplinarian, now a bosom friend. Much will depend upon how it is done, but a stilted presentation with sharp divides typical of inexperienced teachers might bring accusations of two-facedness or of multiple personalities. For the pupils will associate self with role, and will never know for sure which one is coming on stage. Such a teacher is not to be trusted, not one to converse with intimately, not one to count amongst one's friends.

These roles, therefore, can be combined in ways that are mutually damaging. One of the secrets of successful teaching in the primary school, it seems, is combining them in ways that are mutually enhancing. This takes considerable skill that seems to derive from experience in ways that are difficult, in the press of day-to-day events, to characterise and to record. Hence the belief in intuition, and the explanation for a certain action that 'It just felt right to do it that way' (Jackson 1977). Hence, too, the view of teaching as an art, the need to be innovative to cope with the unforeseen, to be creative in process, to orchestrate activities into an aesthetic experience (Eisner 1979).

REFERENCES

Camilleri, C. (1986) *Cultural Anthropology and Education*, Paris: Kogan Page/ Unesco.

Connell, R.W. (1985) *Teachers' Work*, London: Allen & Unwin.

Eisner, E.W. (1979) *The Educational Imagination*, London: Collier-Macmillan.

Jackson, P.W. (1977) 'The way teachers think', in J.C. Glidewell (ed.) *The Social Context of Learning and Development*, New York: Gardner Press.

Kounin, J. (1970) *Discipline and Group Management in Classrooms*, New York: Holt, Rinehart & Winston.

Lacey, C. (1977) *The Socialization of Teachers*, London: Methuen.

Musgrove, F. and Taylor, P. (1974) *Society and the Teacher's Role*, London: Routledge & Kegan Paul.

Pollard, A. (1985) *The Social World of the Primary School*, London: Holt, Rinehart & Winston.

Sharp, R. and Green, A. (1975) *Education and Social Control*, London: Routledge & Kegan Paul.

Woods, P. (1986) 'Learning through friendship: the educational significance of a school exchange', Unpublished paper.

—— (1987) 'Becoming a junior: pupil development following transfer from infants', in A. Pollard (ed.) *Children and their Primary Schools*, Lewes: Falmer Press.

Acknowledgements

Chapter 2 'Analysing practice', by Robin Alexander, edited version from *Policy and Practice in Primary Education* (1992), reproduced by permission of Routledge.

Chapter 3 'What we know about effective primary teaching', by Caroline Gipps, from *The London File* (1992), reproduced by permission of the author.

Chapter 4 'Managing learning in the primary classroom', by Neville Bennett, edited version from *ASPE Paper 1* (1992), reproduced by permission of Trentham Books Ltd.

Chapter 5 'Negotiating learning, negotiating control', by Maurice Galton, edited version from *Teaching in the Primary School* (1989), reproduced by permission of David Fulton Publishers.

Chapter 10 'Issues for curriculum development in primary mathematics', by Hilary Shuard, edited version from *Primary Mathematics Today and Tomorrow* (1986), reproduced by permission of the National Curriculum Council.

Chapter 11 'Teaching the arts', by the Arts in School Project Team, edited version from *The Arts 5–16* (1990), reproduced by permission of Longman and NCC Enterprises Ltd.

Chapter 13 'Learning design and technology in primary schools', by A. Anning, from *Teaching and Learning Technology*, edited by R. McCormick, P. Murphy and M. Harrison (1993), by permission of the Open University.

Chapter 15 'Another way of looking', by Michael Armstrong, from *Forum* 33, 1 (1989), reproduced by permission of the editors of *Forum*. Drawing from *Cox Report* 1, appendix 6 (1989), reproduced by permission of the Controller of Her Majesty's Stationery Office.

Chapter 16 'Assessment and gender', by Patricia Murphy, from *NUT Education Review*, 3/2, reproduced by permission of the National Union of Teachers.

Chapter 17 'Bilingualism and assessment', by Eve Gregory and Clare Kelly, from *Assessment in Early Childhood Education* (1992), edited by G. Blenkin and A. Kelly, reproduced by permission of Paul Chapman Publishing Ltd.

Chapter 19 'Creativity and conventional reality', by Ronald King, from *All*

Things Bright and Beautiful? (1978), reproduced by permission of John Wiley and Sons Ltd.

Chapter 20 'Coping strategies and the multiplication of differentiation in infant classrooms', by Andrew Pollard, edited version from *Case Studies in Classroom Research* (1989), ed. M. Hammersley. This article first appeared in the *British Educational Research Journal* and is reproduced by permission of Carfax Publishing Co.

Chapter 21 'Making sense of reading', by Colin Mills, edited version from *Language and Literacy in the Primary School* (1988), edited by M. Meek and C. Mills, reproduced by permission of Falmer Press.

Chapter 22 'How to be a "good pupil": perceptions of boys and girls in primary school science classes', edited version of 'Determinants of "Good Pupilage": perceptions of boys and girls in primary school science classes', by Clayton MacKenzie, from *Primary Teaching Studies*, vol. 6, no. 2, reproduced by permission of the University of North London.

Chapter 23 'Pupils' views of management', by E.C. Wragg, from *Primary Teaching Skills* (1993), reproduced by permission of Routledge.

Chapter 24 'Managing the primary teacher's role', by Peter Woods, edited version from *The Primary School Teacher* (1987), edited by Sara Delamont, reproduced by permission of Falmer Press.

Notes on sources

Chapter 1 Commissioned for this volume.

Chapter 2 R. Alexander (1992) 'Analysing practice', *Policy and Practice in Primary Education*, London, Routledge, pp. 182–91 (edited).

Chapter 3 C. Gipps (1992) 'What we know about effective primary teaching', *The London File*, London, University of London Institute of Education.

Chapter 4 N. Bennett (1992) 'Managing learning in the primary classroom', *ASPE Paper 1*, APE/Trentham Books, pp. 12–27 (edited).

Chapter 5 M. Galton (1989) 'Negotiating learning, negotiating control', in *Teaching in the Primary School*, D. Fulton Publishers, pp. 124–63 (edited).

Chapter 6 Commissioned for this volume.

Chapter 7 Commissioned for this volume.

Chapter 8 Commissioned for this volume.

Chapter 9 Commissioned for this volume.

Chapter 10 H. Shuard (1986) 'Issues for curriculum development in primary mathematics', *Primary Mathematics Today and Tomorrow*, SCDC Publications (edited).

Chapter 11 The Arts in School Project Team (1990) 'Teaching the arts', in The NCC Arts in Schools Project, *The Arts 5–16*, SCDC Publications/ Oliver & Boyd (edited).

Chapter 12 Commissioned for this volume.

Chapter 13 A. Anning (1993) 'Learning design and technology in primary schools', in R. McCormick, P. Murphy and M. Harrison (eds) *Teaching and Learning Technology*, Open University/Addison Wesley.

Chapter 14 P. Woods (1993) 'Chances of a lifetime: exceptional educational events', unpublished ms. forthcoming, *Topic*, Windsor: NFER-Nelson.

Chapter 15 M. Armstrong (1989) 'Another way of looking', *Forum J*, 33 (1) (drawing from DES (1989) Cox Report 1, appendix 6).

Chapter 16 P. Murphy (1989) 'Assessment and gender', *NUT Educational Review*, 3(2).

Chapter 17   E. Gregory and C. Kelly (1992) 'Bilingualism and assessment', in G. Blenkin and A. Kelly (eds) *Assessment in Early Childhood Education*, Paul Chapman.

Chapter 18   Commissioned for this volume.

Chapter 19   R. King (1978) 'Creativity and conventional reality', *All Things Bright and Beautiful*, John Wiley & Sons, pp. 25–9.

Chapter 20   A. Pollard (1989) 'Coping strategies and the multiplication of differentiation in infant classrooms', in M. Hammersley (ed.) *Case Studies in Classroom Research*, Open University Press, pp. 31–48 (edited).

Chapter 21   C. Mills (1988) 'Making sense of reading', in M. Meek and C. Mills (eds) *Language and Literacy in the Primary School*, Falmer (edited).

Chapter 22   C. MacKenzie (1991) 'How to be a "good pupil": perceptions of boys and girls in primary school science classes', *Primary Teaching Studies*, 6(1), October.

Chapter 23   E.C. Wragg (1993) 'Pupils' views of management', *Primary Teaching Skills*, London, Routledge, pp. 136–54 (edited).

Chapter 24   P. Woods (1987) 'Managing the primary teacher's role', in S. Delamont (ed.) *The Primary School Teacher*, Falmer, pp. 124–43 (edited).

Index

ability 212–22; and assessment 218–21; and friendship 237–8; grouping 48, 219–21 (*see also* streaming); as 'readiness' 216–17; and teacher expectation 217–18

activities: discussion group 90–1; extra-curricular 79 (*see also* events, exceptional); learner-directed 163–5; teacher-directed 165–6

administration: time spent on 71

Alexander, Rose and Woodhead Report 3, 7, 14, 219

ambiguity: in progressive practice 60–4

appraisals: of arts 140–3, 147; of pupils by pupils 261–8; of teachers by pupils 269–75; *see also* assessment

aptitude: importance of 263, 264, 265

art: and conventional reality 225–31; public displays of 228–9

arts 138–47; learning in and through 139–40; making and appraising 140–3, 147; processes 143–5; teachers' roles 145–7

assessment 35; and ability 218–21; in arts 146; bias in 191–6; and bilingualism 197–211, 220; critique of National Curriculum methods 181–90; in teaching cycle 49–50; and time management 77–8

Assessment of Performance Unit (APU) 99–100, 101–2, 116; science project 191–6

assistants, classroom 36–7, 78–9

attitudes: to mathematics 131, 132

attribution theory 25

behaviour, classroom: control of 62–5

bias: in assessment 191–6; *see also* bilingualism

bilingualism 122; 197–211, 220; stages in acquiring second language 208–9; and standardised tests 204–6; strengths and weaknesses 198–203

calculators: impact on mathematics 134–5

capability tasks 162

Children's Learning in Science Project (CLISP) 111–13

class size 36

class, social: and education 213–15

classwork 34–5

cognitive flexibility: of bilingual children 202–3

'collaboration to produce' 238–41

common knowledge 88, 90–1, 96

communications *see* discourse strategies; interactions; questions

comprehensive education 12

computers: impact on mathematics 135–6

conceptual understanding: linked to procedural 115–16; research evidence 111–15; in science 102–3

constructivist models of learning 23–4, 43; for mathematics 133–4; for science 100–1, 112

content: in educational practice 16, 18; in mathematics 131, 132; and processes in science 99–119; selection 44–5

contextual frameworks 89